The Spiritual Virtuoso

The Spiritual Virtuoso

Personal Faith and Social Transformation

Marion Goldman and Steven Pfaff

Bloomsbury Academic
An imprint of Bloomsbury Publishing Plc

B L O O M S B U R Y
LONDON · OXFORD · NEW YORK · NEW DELHI · SYDNEY

Bloomsbury Academic

An imprint of Bloomsbury Publishing Plc

50 Bedford Square	1385 Broadway
London	New York
WC1B 3DP	NY 10018
UK	USA

www.bloomsbury.com

BLOOMSBURY and the Diana logo are trademarks of Bloomsbury Publishing Plc

First published 2018

British Library Cataloguing-in-Publication Data
A catalogue record for this book is available from the British Library.

ISBN: HB: 978-1-4742-9240-5
PB: 978-1-4742-9239-9
ePDF: 978-1-4742-9238-2
ePub: 978-1-4742-9242-9

Library of Congress Cataloging-in-Publication Data
Names: Goldman, Marion S., author.
Title: The spiritual virtuoso : personal faith and social transformation / Marion Goldman and Steven Pfaff.
Description: 1 [edition]. | New York : Bloomsbury Academic, 2017. | Includes bibliographical references and index.
Identifiers: LCCN 2017036885| ISBN 9781474292405 (hardback) | ISBN 9781474292399 (pbk.)
Subjects: LCSH: Spiritual formation. | Excellence–Religious aspects–Christianity. | Social change–Religious aspects–Christianity.
Classification: LCC BV4511 .G65 2017 | DDC 248.09–dc23 LC record available at https://lccn.loc.gov/2017036885

Cover images © Stock Montage (Martin Luther) and Justin Sullivan (Steve Jobs)/Getty

Typeset by Deanta Global Publishing Services, Chennai, India
Printed and bound in Great Britain

To find out more about our authors and books visit www.bloomsbury.com. Here you will find extracts, author interviews, details of forthcoming events and the option to sign up for our newsletters.

February 14, 2019

To Nancy,

always an inspiration!

Love,

Mimi

For Paul and Karen

Table of Contents

Acknowledgments

We would like to thank our colleagues in the Religion Working Group at the University of Washington, who contributed to the inception of this project with insightful comments and conversations: Katie E. Corcoran, James Felak, James K. Wellman, and Jason Wollschleger.

As the project took shape, we received encouragement and constructive criticism from: Jim Beckford, Daniel Chirot, Philip S. Gorski, Neil Gross, Michael J. Halvorson, Paul E. Hoffman, Jennifer McKinney, Mary Jo Neitz, Kate Ristau, Marat Shterin, and Rodney Stark.

Special thanks to the Corita Center and Lenore Navarro Dowling and Kari Marken and to the Sociology Department at the University of Washington.

Throughout this project we have been buoyed by the enthusiastic support of Lalle Pursglove and Lucy Carroll at Bloomsbury Publishing.

Our families provided inspiration and abundant support throughout our shared pilgrimage of collaborative research and writing. Goldmans: Paul, Michael, and Henry; Snedkers and Pfaffs: Karen, Arno, and Jonas.

List of Illustrations

Photos

Tables

1 Introduction: The Spiritual Virtuoso

Different as they were in time and place, two men who searched for personal purification and connection to a Higher Power, Martin Luther and Steve Jobs, helped change the world because of their conviction that everyone could reach toward sacred truths and transcendent moments. Luther and Jobs may appear to be an implausible pair but their personal histories, one of sustained religious virtuosity and the other of its lifelong pursuit, can enhance understandings of spiritual virtuosity and how virtuosi can unleash personal and social transformations.

Spiritual virtuosi are absolutely dedicated to expanding their own religious talents and pursuing complete connection with a Higher Power. Their intense personal commitment to spiritual perfection resembles the perseverance of virtuosi in fields like athletics or the arts.

An enduring image of isolated self-denial and intense commitment to holiness stimulated German sociologist Max Weber to coin the term "religious virtuoso" almost a century ago.[1] Like other types of virtuosi, religious virtuosi's paths tend to be highly individualistic, unless they become convinced that they must share their religious innovations and join together to develop and spread new spiritual possibilities beyond their own circles.

In a handful of asides, Weber noted that virtuosi could occasionally join together to try to change the world in terms of their deeply held religious beliefs. When personal virtuosity unites with collective action to widen everyone's paths to salvation and shared spiritual privilege, there can be dramatic religious and social transformations. Contemporary Western culture reflects five centuries of religious creativity that is associated with spiritual virtuosity. Since the beginning of the modern era, spiritual virtuosi and those who aspire to virtuosity have spearheaded a handful of major cultural transformations. Virtuoso religious movements developed during the Reformation and continue to gather momentum in the twenty-first century.

Throughout much of his life, a profound commitment to personal sanctification shaped Martin Luther's thoughts and actions. He was a spiritual virtuoso who wanted to dedicate himself to intense religious practice, striving for spiritual justification and sanctification through rigorous devotions, prayer, and study. Nevertheless, he reluctantly abandoned his cloistered existence to lead the Reformation. Luther introduced essential spiritual innovations that offered everyone opportunities to find God without relying on priests as intermediaries or adhering to the Roman Catholic Church's rigid procedures.

Almost five centuries after Luther posted his *Ninety-Five Theses* on the door of All Saints' Church in Wittenberg and changed Western spirituality forever, Steve Jobs sought spiritual virtuosity by sampling different approaches to sanctification from the Human Potential Movement, a loose configuration of groups that came together in the mid-twentieth century to try to implement spiritual, psychological, and social transformations.

Jobs pursued his inner divinity and connections to a Higher Power through LSD trips, primal screams, and spiritual tourism in India.[2] He even toyed with entering Eihei-ji Soto Zen Monastery in Japan and becoming a full-time spiritual virtuoso, but his *sensi* (teacher) at the Los Altos Zen Center urged him to remain in Silicon Valley and develop Buddhist approaches in his work and relationships.

The religious innovations that began during the Reformation were essential to Jobs's lifelong quest for sanctification, because Luther irrevocably altered Western civilization by unleashing a direct relationship to God. The virtuoso ethic that everyone could and should cultivate their own spirituality in order to attain sanctification on earth and ultimate salvation in heaven is grounded in deep faith that God wants people to nurture and enact their religious capacities.

Throughout modern history, both those who have attained spiritual virtuosity and constant seekers like Jobs have individually and collectively pursued sanctification, a sense of holiness and purification on earth. However, because they are most committed to their own sanctification, even virtuosi activists who stand at the forefront of consequential movements that enact their religious ideals are seldom politically or socially engaged throughout their lives. Moreover, most social movements led by spiritual virtuosi are temporary, local, and limited. Nevertheless, a few virtuosi-led movements have dramatically transformed the ways that people worship and live.

In this book, we explore three consequential movements and some of their virtuosi leaders, because they allow us to understand how spiritual virtuosity in the West has unfolded over the past six centuries. The Reformation, the Antislavery Movement, and the Human Potential Movement successively increased spiritual equality and merged religion and social activism. These successful movements contributed to the relatively recent decline of formal religious affiliation and the growth of personalized spirituality, because they progressively expanded access to spiritual knowledge and experience in many contexts. In the twenty-first century, what is often misconstrued as isolating and self-indulgent seekership is actually the legacy of generations of activist spiritual virtuosi who reshaped the world and shared new possibilities to come to terms with some Higher Power.

Spiritual virtuosity is by no means limited to Christian faiths, but the Protestant Reformation represents the first significant social movement in modern history that activist spiritual virtuosi led. It paved the way for five centuries of other virtuoso movements that attacked religious corruption, progressively diffused spiritual privilege, and advocated for religious equality. It is important to acknowledge Martin Luther's implicit centrality to both the large and small virtuosi-led movements that have affirmed religious and social equality in different ways.

There are no explicit historical or theological connections between the sixteenth-century German reformers, who risked everything in order to challenge the Catholic Church, and the contemporary "Nones," who describe themselves as spiritual but not religious and sidestep established religious institutions in order to pursue sanctification elsewhere. But the impact of spiritual virtuosity continues to spread and the Western world has by no means moved inexorably away from spiritual concerns to vapid secularization.[3] There is vibrant spiritual engagement throughout contemporary life and possibilities for sanctification continue to multiply.

Although the shape of religious culture has changed dramatically since the Reformation, the pursuit of spiritual virtuosity is unabated. Eckhart Tolle, a twenty-first-century spiritual teacher and best-selling writer, captured the current moment when he observed, "The new spirituality, the transformation of consciousness, is arising to a large extent outside of the structures of existing institutionalized religion."[4]

For Tolle, today's seekers are fortified by their personal autonomy and informed by ancient Eastern wisdom teachings. They "realize that how 'spiritual' you are has nothing to do with what you believe, but everything to do with your state of consciousness."[5] Searches for inner purpose have eclipsed traditional religious organizations that had once been favored paths to spiritually meaningful lives, but the pursuit of spiritual virtuosity is unabated.

As autonomous quests for sanctification and spiritual virtuosity continue to expand, established faiths continue to cede their cultural and political influence. This ongoing erosion of their impact reflects incremental changes that can be traced back to the Protestant reformers' enthusiastic support for personal religious practice outside the boundaries of the Catholic Church. Luther affirmed the importance of individual relationships to God and foreshadowed the ways that both the Antislavery Movement and the Human Potential Movement emphasized the need for developing personal authenticity that was shaped by spiritual ideals.

In spite of contemporary religious authorities' repeated efforts to reign in spiritual originality, virtuosi continue to work for more flexibility within their faiths, and they sometimes step outside of institutionalized religion to become leaders and advocates for expanded equality throughout society. These activist virtuosi implicitly extend the ideals of freedom and critical inquiry that were part of Luther's Reformation, because they focus on direct relationships with a Higher Power and personal spiritual practice. Although some activist virtuosi support conservative movements within their denominations and sometimes within the larger society, when spiritual virtuosi disrupt official boundaries and challenge institutional authority, they *always* work for more access to spiritual possibilities and a greater range of religious choices by democratizing spiritual privilege.

Luther and the virtuoso followers that succeeded him in Central Europe unleashed a vital new spirituality that sparked centuries of dramatic religious and social change grounded in ever-widening spiritual options. In order to allow everyone access to new spiritual ideas and techniques, insurgent virtuosi advanced their religious and social agendas by adopting recent technological innovations, such as the sixteenth-century

Photo 1.1 Martin Luther and the Book.

printing press, nineteenth-century steam-powered locomotives and ships, twentieth-century television, and twenty-first-century digital communications.

When the Protestant reformers envisioned possibilities that everyone might read the redeeming Word at any time, in any place, they opened the door to an explosion of religious choices. Reinterpreting those possibilities, Steve Jobs fueled a digital revolution because he believed that people could discover their authentic selves and their higher purpose through personal technology. New ideas, new technologies, and deep commitments to spiritual equality link the three consequential virtuosi-led movements which we will describe in subsequent chapters.

Spiritual virtuosi stood at the forefront of the transatlantic movements for abolition, temperance, and suffrage because they believed that shared sins of slavery, inebriation, and political inequality corrupted every soul regardless of any direct participation in those sins. During the nineteenth century, some spiritual virtuosi temporarily made political activism their highest religious priority, since they fervently believed that no one could be purified and experience a full connection to God unless everyone were liberated from oppression.[6] The activist virtuosi assumed that their own sanctification required a synthesis of intense private spirituality and urgent public advocacy.[7] Their sweeping moral engagement reflected deep concerns that the rise of industrial capitalism had generated crass, narrow, and materialistic self-interest that dangerously obstructed everyone's paths to earthly holiness and ultimate salvation.

In the mid-twentieth century, the Human Potential Movement's spiritual virtuosi also feared that rising American affluence would stimulate even more materialism, aggression, and emotional alienation.[8] They wanted to extend everyone's access to sanctification by advocating for individualized spiritual practices that embraced varied techniques such as encounter groups, prayer, antiwar activism, yoga, environmentalism, simple living, and meditation. These all came to be publicly identified with the movement, because its loose coalition of virtuoso activists embraced innumerable possibilities for everyone to improve themselves, their relationships with one another, and their connections to the cosmos.

Although the Human Potential Movement was visible for little more than a decade, it sparked Americans' lasting interest in personal expansion and healing of their minds, bodies, psyches, and souls. And it laid the foundation for the thriving contemporary marketplace that offers products and services that promote new options for everyone to reach their full spiritual potentials and embark on individualized virtuoso paths. The movement radically democratized spiritual privilege: the combination of material resources, access to social networks of like-minded seekers, cultural knowledge, religious affinities, and desires to experience a sense of holiness and purification.

Steve Jobs chased virtuosity through varied Human Potential Movement groups, where he learned about ideas and techniques that influenced his technological innovations and his public activities as a charismatic multibillionaire spokesman for products that could transform private and public life. He did not dedicate himself fully to religious study, practice, and action, but without Luther's and his followers' religious insurgency, Jobs might never have experienced the varied approaches that changed his perspectives and fueled his visions of universal, unmediated technological breakthroughs that might expand everyone's spiritual growth.

Religious meanings, rituals, and relationships have changed since the Reformation, but while they were extraordinarily different, the first Reformed Easter Mass in Zurich in 1525 paved the way for the Sunday Assembly's Easter gathering in London in 2015. Common threads of full participation and spiritual equality link the two Easters and other increasingly inclusive religious celebrations and rituals.

Two Easters

Zurich, 1525

The Reformation was by no means limited to Luther's work. His teachings and his rebellion against Rome stirred a generation of virtuoso followers who continued to remake religion in his wake. One of the most dramatic offshoots of the Protestant movement coalesced around the radical Swiss reformer Ulrich Zwingli. In his city, Zurich, Zwingli reshaped citizens' religious loyalties, so after years of bitter disputes between defenders of the Roman Catholic Church and different Protestant factions, they were eager to break with old religious tradition and implement his teachings.

Inspired by the hope of redeeming themselves and executing God's wishes through the Word, Zurich's activist virtuosi had attacked the elaborate system of Catholic sanctification on many different fronts. In 1522, some of Zwingli's associates had openly feasted on sausages during the Lenten fast. Zwingli defended them, claiming that fasting was not Biblically mandated, so it was a matter of individual conscience rather than God's law.

As the reformers gathered popular support in Zurich, they challenged the entire elaborate Catholic system of sanctification. They defaced their city's sacred art and statuary and stripped the altars of elaborate adornments. In 1524, they profaned the tombs of Zurich's patron saints, Felix and Regula, whose relics, according to different accounts, were buried in plain graves, thrown into the river, or rescued by a pious Catholic.

As the town council increasingly turned toward the Protestant movement, the reformers shut down monasteries and enabled priests to marry. However, Zwingli and his followers allowed the grand cathedrals to stand after they had destroyed their adornments. Within the old cathedral, they offered a new, simplified, austere style of worship designed to open the Gospels to everyone—poor and rich, women and men.

In April 1525, a fresh liturgy replaced the elaborate Catholic Mass in Zurich, and on Easter Day the service sealed the local Protestant triumph. Worshippers, inspired by the Protestant ideal of spiritual virtuosity, gathered in a resanctified, simply appointed *Grossmünster* to celebrate Easter according to their new model. Free from the old Church hierarchy and ceremonialism of Rome, the soberly dressed men and women affirmed their relationships with God, celebrating a "pure" mass in German rather than in Latin.

Photo 1.2 Grossmünster Cathedral in Zurich.

They worshipped in a sanctuary bathed in light and naked of its former ornaments, reliquaries, and opulently bound holy books.[9] Zwingli, no longer a Catholic priest but instead a pastor, dressed simply in black in order to communicate his role as the congregation's "servant." The service conveyed an implicit message of unpretentious holiness. Descriptions of that first great Reformed Easter celebration emphasize its new modesty and restraint.[10]

Underscoring the equality of all believers before God and emphasizing the authority of the sacred Word over all, Zwingli faced the congregation, not the altar. He appealed to worshippers to reject hypocrisy and falsehood. He prayed that everyone in the congregation should live innocently before God and man. Reading and preaching from Corinthians I (26–31), the pastor spoke of the spiritual obligations and possibilities that were open to everyone who sought sanctification, and he appealed for unity in Christ as he led the Lord's Prayer.

After he described Jesus as the "Bread of Life" (Jn 6:47-63), Zwingli prepared the congregation for a Reformed Lord's Supper that replaced the Catholic celebration of the Eucharist. In a radical reinterpretation of the Catholic Mass, partaking in the Supper became an act of communion with God, not a miracle of transubstantiation (the priestly transformation of bread and wine into the body and blood of Christ). The pastor distributed bread and worshippers broke off pieces themselves.[11] Then they sipped wine from a common cup, in contrast to the Catholic Mass, in which only the priest drank the sacred wine. After communion and a hymn of praise, Zwingli closed the service with a benediction.

That simplified Easter liturgy captured the essence of the Reformation's renewed conception of God's spiritual community and equality for all in His eyes. For many, the event symbolized restoration of the true Gospel and the true church. What must have been dramatic for the worshippers was that in this service, laymen and women were participants—not mere spectators—in the act of spiritual communion with Christ. Their voices blended together in prayers, although women and men sung alternate lines of hymns of praise. Women could not preach, but they were active throughout the service, confirming the worst fear of Catholic traditionalists.

The entire Easter service reflected Protestantism's sweeping innovation: everyone could stand directly before the Word, responsible through faith and by grace for personal salvation. They approached the liturgy as spiritual equals, united in an ethic that required them to strive for sanctification and spiritual virtuosity throughout their lives. Ultimate salvation was God's freely given gift to everyone if they demonstrated unwavering faith in Jesus the Redeemer.

London 2015

Almost five centuries later, hundreds of people crowded into the Sunday Assembly's oddly named "Atheist Easter" at Conway Hall in Central London. Secular humanism had never been more spiritual or more challenging to rigid definitions of religion. Throughout the lively service, everyone affirmed the Assembly's major tenets: "Live

Better, Help Often, Wonder More." A small, energetic band played well-known pop songs and almost everyone in the auditorium belted out the choruses of the Proclaimers' 1988 hit, "I'm Gonna Be (500 Miles)":

> But I would walk five hundred miles
> And I would walk five hundred more
> Just to be the man who walked a thousand miles
> To fall down at your door[12]

Some enthusiastic singers raised their hands to catch the awesome, intangible power that touched them during the song, but their upstretched arms were not surprising, because the assembly is "radically inclusive" and welcomes both believers and atheists. On that Easter, however, the believers far outnumbered the skeptics. The Assemblers' songs, discourses, and spontaneous shout-outs praised a life force that transcends isolated individualism. Both the master of ceremonies and the featured speaker described unlimited spiritual possibilities within everything from "mindful" environmentalism to meditative sexuality, but they never mentioned heaven, hell, God, or any all-powerful, interfering deities.

Assemblers came together to connect with an amorphous mystical force and build a supportive community for ethical guidance and material help during hard times. An elaborately carved phrase over the auditorium's original proscenium arch, "To Thine Own Self Be True," captured their personalized approach to spirituality.

A few hearty elders at the Easter Assembly might have gazed at the arch on the day that the South Place Ethical Society opened Conway Hall in 1929 or they might have listened to the famous philosopher Bertrand Russell lecture to the society in the 1930s and 1940s. Elders smiled indulgently at two-dozen children seated in a corner near the stage, where adults encouraged them to jump up and down during songs and quietly color when someone was speaking. Three girls wore ruffled pastel pinafores that would be welcomed at a High Anglican Easter Mass, while the others wore jeans and bright tops, just like the hundreds of twenty- and thirty-year-olds who packed the service. There was no communion, but generous souls brought foil-wrapped chocolate eggs, marshmallow treats, and granola bars that they quietly passed out during the service.

A rich smell wafted up from the main floor into the thronged gallery, but it was not incense or something else that was connected to a ritual. Scents from damp wool and down jackets, wet hair, and oils of oud and patchouli had blended together in the air, pleasantly engulfing the crowd and adding to the feeling of being part of an embracing community. The collective perfume was another sign that the Sunday Assembly was much younger and hipper than the usual Anglican congregation.[13] The hundreds of enthusiastic, ethnically and sexually diverse young adults that eagerly gathered at Conway Hall implicitly negated forecasts about the inevitable decline and disappearance of religion in the West.[14] And their joyous voices drowned out centuries of lamentations about secularization as a precursor to the absolute disappearance

Photo 1.3 Sunday Assembly at Conway Hall.

of spiritual engagement—predictions that began when the Reformation challenged the Church's religious monopoly.[15]

It is no accident that the Sunday Assembly first emerged in London in 2013 and spread throughout England, since the substantial majority of English people, close to 80 percent, believe in some supernatural force. However, less than half of them belong to established faiths.[16] Some scholars argue that the decline of organized religion in Britain has left behind a nation of unattached believers, prone to personalized spirituality and religious seekership. Others dispute that claim, arguing that Britons have grown increasingly indifferent to religion of all kinds.

We see spirituality as remarkably persistent, even in societies like the United Kingdom, and the trajectory of virtuoso social movements suggests that contemporary desires for personal virtuosity are deeply informed by religious strivings. In the United States, a more religious country where the Assembly has grown and spread, 75 percent of Americans report a religious affiliation and less than 3 percent of the people are certain that there is no Higher Power.[17] They are believers and seekers, but not necessarily permanent belongers.

Millions of believers on both sides of the Atlantic no longer affiliate with mainstream faiths, but they nonetheless acknowledge some Higher Power or divine force, and they want to explore and understand their relationship to something beyond themselves. Although their religious activities may ebb and flow, they still search for a sense of purpose, purification, and holiness as they create their own mosaics of personal practices and public actions. As they seek sanctification, the Sunday Assembly's collective rituals and shared language of faith draw them together in temporary intimacy.

The Assembly requires neither formal membership nor rites of passage like baptism or confirmation, but dedicated Assemblers attend its large gatherings twice a month and join group activities that they promote on Facebook and on local Assemblies' websites. They come together to staff food banks, volunteer for humanitarian causes such as aid to Syrian refugees, and form affinity groups to share insights about new books, offer mutual support, or enjoy outdoor activities—all of which underscore the importance of appreciating life on earth and actualizing one's full human potential.

The Assembly's emphasis on creating ethical and purposeful lives, helping others, and marveling at the awesome beauty and unknown power of the universe is the religion without God that philosopher Ronald Dworkin described.[18] The great scientist Albert Einstein inspired Dworkin, because Einstein saw himself as a religious person, standing in awe before natural forces and the deep mysteries of life that no human could fully comprehend.[19]

Sanderson Jones and Pippa Evans, who founded the Sunday Assembly together, share Einstein's sense of spiritual awe, although they do not describe themselves as religious. They are comedians and minor British TV personalities, not dedicated full-time virtuosi or extraordinary charismatic leaders. Like almost all Assemblers, they have not sacrificed worldly pleasures or abandoned careers in order to focus on their own sanctification. However, they have made some costly trade-offs in order to embark on their personal quests for authenticity, purposeful lives, and a sense of holiness.

The Sunday Assembly opens up virtuoso paths that people can travel with energy and commitment or suddenly abandon without much difficulty. Assemblers often mix practices from traditional faiths and alternate groups in order to pursue spiritual virtuosity and discover a sense of purity and meaning in a rapacious world. Even those who are ambivalent toward established religion develop a spiritual language to frame their experiences and try to incorporate something sacred into their lives. The Sunday Assembly's flexible, inclusive spirituality reflects the early Lutheran legacy that made individuals' ultimately responsible for connection to something sacred through their unwavering faith.

While spiritual virtuosi can be found everywhere in the world and are active in faiths that the Reformation's religious and political legacies barely touched, our emphasis on Protestantism's legacies allows us to explore some specific ways that spiritual virtuosity has changed over time and how activist virtuosi's innovations have contributed to seismic cultural shifts. Possibilities for direct access to sanctification and meaningful lives on earth drew people to the Easter Mass in Zurich and also to Central London's Easter Sunday Assembly. Religious institutions, spiritual meanings, and personal practices are dynamic over time, so in large and small ways, virtuosi continue to influence contemporary religious and social change.

Religion, Spirituality, and the Virtuoso

When it began in 2013, the Sunday Assembly called itself an Atheist Church, although its founders acknowledged the possibility of some awesome unknowable Higher Power and an immanent goodness in humankind. During the group's first year, however, a small coalition of orthodox atheist Assemblers viewed any talk of Higher Powers as heresy and they attacked the two founders' apparent hostility toward speakers and songs that completely denied the existence of some Higher Power.[20]

The conflict over atheism produced a breakaway sect, a common process in first-generation religions.[21] A handful of dissatisfied atheist Assemblers left to establish the unequivocally antispiritual Godless Revival in 2014 in New York City, so that they could spread their hard-line doctrine that absolutely nothing exists beyond nature and human endeavor. However, many other self-defined atheists continue to participate in the Assembly, because they believe that sacred forces somehow touch their lives, although they reject the idea of God as a single divine, responsive being.[22]

The Sunday Assembly's struggle with atheists is an example of the contested meanings that ignite arguments about religion and spirituality. Contrasting definitions and interpretations fuel everyday arguments and academic debates, so questions about their meanings and distinctions between the two concepts necessarily inform our approach to spiritual virtuosity.[23]

We use the two terms interchangeably, because there are simply no clear, fixed distinctions between spirituality and religion and they are by no means opposites.[24] Some people employ both words to refer to the same things and others see religion as something that develops within formally recognized denomination, while spirituality is highly personal and idiosyncratic.[25]

It is fairly common to classify congregational faiths as religions and refer to dedicated personal practices as spirituality.[26] In fact, some sociologists argue that a Western religion without a traditional formal organization and a deity is "an apparently incoherent collection of ideas and practices."[27] This rigid approach ignores the ways that people bring parts of traditional faiths to collectives like the Sunday Gathering and how they may take away something new to integrate into their personalized beliefs and practices.

Moreover, someone may simultaneously belong to a number of traditional denominations or innovative religions if they require no exclusive commitment from their members. Thousands of contemporary Americans laughingly call themselves "Bujews," for example, because they participate in both liberal Jewish synagogues and inclusive Buddhist groups.[28] Someone who belongs to an established faith may have intense spiritual experiences within formal services and also at home during very personal rituals.[29] Because formal and informal spiritualties come together in different ways, someone who seeks a sense of holiness through the Church of England is no more or less spiritual or religious than a devout member of the Church of Elvis. Committed participants in both C of Es are spiritually engaged, and they might simultaneously claim membership in both religious bodies.

Our conceptualization of religion/spirituality incorporates the central features that Sir James Frazer discussed in his landmark work on comparative spirituality, *The Golden Bough*.[30] According to Frazer, all religions share belief in some Higher Power (s) and collective attempts to comprehend, come to terms with, and please the power(s). A set of coherent ideas about the cosmos link beliefs and practices.

Frazer's definition is sometimes criticized as too general, because it includes religions that worship many deities or honor an amorphous supernatural force, as well as those that are devoted to a single God. Sociologist Rodney Stark, for example, argues that lasting religious traditions inevitably have only one transcendent God, a deity that offers individuals sanctification and ultimate salvation in exchange for their obedience to His revealed wishes.[31] In the sixteenth century, Martin Luther's God was just such an authoritative figure who called on everyone to discover the Word and establish a relationship with Him through study and action.

The Protestants shifted the focus of religious life from structured experiences of the sacred through rituals, shrines, and holy objects toward a focus on personal spiritual encounters with a transcendent God. Soon after the first Lutheran triumphs in Central Europe, however, there were heated debates about whether this remote but authoritative God truly desired everyone to attain salvation and enter Heaven. Calvinists and other denominations split from the original movement, but incorporated much of Luther's vision. His God was not accessed by material means and did not intervene in quotidian affairs, but he was critical and judgmental. The faithful were rewarded and sinners were punished after they died.[32]

In 1525, Luther published a pamphlet, *On the Bondage of the Will*, which underscored the belief that everyone that wholeheartedly sought God could enter Heaven, with or without intercession through the Church. He based his arguments on Ephesian's 2:8-9:

> For by grace you have been saved through faith, and not that of yourselves; it is the gift of God, not of works, lest anyone should boast.

A number of theologians challenged Luther's conception of God, and by the nineteenth century, an emerging image of an engaged, benevolent God who demanded social justice inspired spiritual virtuosi at the forefront of the Antislavery Movement.[33] The Methodists', Presbyterians', and Baptists' evangelical God offered everyone possibilities for inclusion in Heaven, and He was no longer distant. Instead, God was both actively concerned with everyone's daily life and more generous and forgiving than the Lutherans' deity. In this view, Jesus Christ died for all of humanity, not just for a limited group, and everyone was worthy of God's grace and protection. Activist virtuosi spearheaded the Antislavery Movement because they fervently believed that they needed to do God's work and ensure that no one remained enslaved or guilty of denying anyone access to God and holiness on earth.

The moral activists of antebellum America assailed the Protestant religious establishment's moderation and conservatism, and they brought down God's judgment on the public evils of alcohol, slavery, business on the Sabbath, and other secular activities. Decades before the Civil War began in 1861, their radical vision of a more holy and just nation divided American Protestants into warring camps.[34]

The revived evangelism of virtuosi antislavery activists like Theodore Weld posited that a personal relationship with Christ, not simply the mastery of Scripture or adherence to orthodoxy, represented the true path to salvation. Presbyterians, Methodists, and Baptists believed that lay preachers could lead everyone to God and rescue them from sin as effectively as ordained ministers. Faith in the power of personal testimony allowed activist spiritual virtuosi to accomplish His work in outdoor meetings or town halls as well as churches. The new activists described a just God who affirmed each person's human dignity and also demanded that they wholeheartedly repudiate their complicity with sins of exploitation and oppression.[35]

Pleading with other Christians to join the fight against slavery, the feminist and activist virtuoso Angelina Grimké wrote:

> God designs to confer this holy privilege upon man; it is through his instrumentality that the great and glorious work of reforming the world is to be done.[36]

After the American Civil War, a number of established Protestant faiths such as Congregationalists and Episcopalians placed more emphasis on a benevolent but very distant God and that image of God began to contend with the Abolitionists' more personal, engaged divinity.[37] A century after the American Civil War, in the late 1960s, the image of a distant, benign Higher Power drew a wide range of spiritual virtuosi into the Human Potential Movement.

A benevolent distant deity or an amorphous cosmic force surfaced in parts of Christian, Jewish, and alternate faiths in the mid-twentieth century. The Human Potential Movement welcomed any virtuoso who embraced one or more of many inclusive, flexible spiritual traditions: liberal Roman Catholicism, Reform Judaism, progressive Protestant thought, Tibetan and Zen Buddhism, and various guru-based alternate religious movements.

Some religious groups associated with the Human Potential Movement trusted in a distant, kindly God, but other faiths that were part of the Movement, such as Americanized Soto Zen, defined their Higher Power in terms of sympathetic cosmic energy. Spiritual virtuosi in the movement came together in critical communities that supported every vision of divinity. They all shared the faith that a distant God or some supernatural force made it possible for everyone on earth to discover and cultivate a divine spark within themselves through beliefs and techniques for self-actualization.[38]

Religious, academic, and artistic virtuosi joined one another under Human Potential's banner to integrate their spirituality with political activism and eliminate every kind of violence and oppression. They defined themselves as messengers of sacred truths, whereas the Protestant reformers or Abolitionists believed that they were God's instruments. And their Higher Power no longer judged people or offered them personal guidance. Divinity was now a distant deity or force that could be both transcendent, above everything, and also located at the core of every human being.

Sixteenth-century Protestants and nineteenth-century antislavery activists focused their spirituality squarely on Christ and would have been shocked and perhaps appalled by notions that a Higher Power could be discovered within everyone. This is hardly a new idea, however, even within Christian traditions. That immanent God can be traced back to the *Gnostic Gospels* and the paganism that influenced the early Church.[39] In the 1960s, as the Human Potential Movement began, this very old conception of an immanent God or Higher Power once again captured the attention of both clergy and laity through a Roman Catholic virtuoso's book: Thomas Merton's *New Man*.[40]

The possibility of an immanent Higher Power within each person expanded the pursuit of spiritual virtuosity to an ever-growing population of part-time seekers, not just the most spiritually privileged individuals who could dedicate themselves to religious study, practice, and principled activism. A well-lived life became aspiring virtuosi's central spiritual focus, because the Human Potential Movement emphasized earthly purification and holiness rather than the afterlife or specific ethical obligations. The movement's emphasis on transformative spiritual ideas and techniques turned the pursuit of sanctification into a hobby rather than a necessarily consuming vocation or a moral measure of every action.

The meanings of spiritual virtuosity and the opportunities to strive for it expanded over the centuries because spiritual virtuosi at the forefront of influential Western faiths redefined not only the meaning of God but also the location. The Lutheran reformers looked *up* to the Heavens, as they returned to a direct relationship with a judgmental distant God that had given them the opportunity to understand and enact His Word. The nineteenth-century antislavery virtuosi looked *outward* to change society. They fought for equality because their benevolent personal God affirmed everyone's dignity and possibilities for sanctification and ultimate salvation. And Human Potential Movement virtuosi looked *inward* to discover the spark of divinity that connected them with a distant, benevolent supernatural being or cosmic force.

Some supernatural force, whether God, gods, or cosmic influence, is essential to all religions and to the pursuit of spiritual virtuosity. Both individual and collective quests for holiness and purification are grounded in the enduring question: "How am I called to implement my faith?" And the options to answer that fundamental problem continue to multiply.

The sixteenth-century Protestants' painstakingly detailed path to sanctification required the Bible to function as their explicit map, but in the mid-twentieth century, for many people, the Bible and other sacred texts merely served as compasses pointing them in a general direction. However, despite many historical differences, virtuosi activists and also isolated ascetics have consistently demonstrated their faith in sustained study and contemplation as means to discover God's wishes and reveal spiritual truths that they could examine together and share with everyone. Over the last five centuries, as literacy has spread and different kinds of media multiplied, virtuosi have increasingly been able to engage one another from great distances and develop new insights and plans for action. Across times and space, virtuosi have used media of many kinds to share their discoveries and convince people of the crucial need to redefine *all* spiritual priorities in terms of new verities.

In the sixteenth century, literacy was a transcendent bridge that stretched upward toward Heaven through the medium of the vernacular Gospels. In the nineteenth century, growing literacy created audiences for morally engaged journalism and emotionally charged memoirs that allowed activist virtuosi to move beyond religious spaces into the sinful society that God had called for them to reconstruct. And the

Human Potential Movement's virtuosi leaders used religious and philosophical books, articles, recordings, television, and films to look inward and enable them to access the sparks of divinity within themselves, learn from one another, and mobilize their new energy to create a better world.

The Central European virtuosi, who spread Martin Luther's vision of spiritual equality, emerged from universities where intensive reading and debate led them to "rediscover" essential Biblical truths. One of the first tasks that they set for themselves was translating the Word from Latin into lay languages so that everyone could learn to read in order to uncover and understand God's true Word by themselves.[41] It is no accident that the first books published in more than one Western language were the Gospels and Protestant catechisms.

Activists in the Antislavery Movement also valued literacy and worked to extend it to everyone. They encouraged discussions of the Bible in small groups and brought their spiritual priorities to large political meetings, where they drew attention to the national sin of slavery. The latest media enabled them to shape a new public sphere that was illuminated by conscience and charged with spiritual unrest.

Human Potential Movement virtuosi revealed new spiritual possibilities to educated audiences in inexpensive popular books and magazines. Movement leaders used the relatively new invention of television to reach still wider audiences and define self-actualization as a universal right. Now, the internet offers virtuosi even more opportunities to communicate about paths to purification and holiness.

Although activist virtuosi and dedicated seekers can be found throughout contemporary society, when most people think of a religious virtuoso they still picture a monk praying and meditating in a remote spot high in the Himalayas or in an Alpine monastery. However, when Luther and his reformers released possibilities for everyone to work toward a sense of holiness on earth, ordinary people could reach toward sanctification without focusing their lives on cloistered spiritual perfection. Virtuosity was no longer an all-or-nothing proposition, limited to a handful of individuals with the personal and social resources to set themselves apart from conventional life. After the Reformation, a religious virtuoso might become a priest unto herself, withdraw into contemplation and private spiritual practice, pursue sanctification while attending to family life and full-time work, or turn into an activist mobilizing for social change. Seekers who did not build their lives around the explicit pursuit of holiness might still strive for personal connection with a Higher Power and aspire to spiritual virtuosity.

The lives of some of the virtuosi who worked to change their surrounding societies can illuminate the historical genesis and dynamics of spiritual virtuosity. We devote three chapters to individuals who were moving forces in the consequential religious/social movements noted earlier: The Central European Reformation, the Antislavery Movement, and the Human Potential Movement. Each of the three movements which we consider in detail added more possibilities for sanctification, so that many millions of ordinary people could reach toward holiness without becoming full-time spiritual virtuosi.

Seeking Virtuosity

Before looking more closely at the history and dynamics of religious virtuosity and its impact over the centuries, it is worth considering its contemporary expressions in terms of one of the extraordinary spiritual seekers mentioned earlier in this chapter— Steve Jobs. He attempted to integrate his search for spiritual virtuosity with commerce and only succeeded occasionally. Jobs's lifelong search for holiness and connection with a Higher Power informed his extraordinary technological innovations, but the quest for spiritual virtuosity was rarely the center of his life. Like most contemporary Americans and Western Europeans, he was an incomplete virtuoso, caught between yearnings for the self-enhancement that is part of secular culture and the self-denial that reflects an encompassing spiritual purpose.

Jobs acknowledged that tension, but he usually chose worldly rewards over spiritual ones. He recognized, however, that his attempts to reach toward spiritual virtuosity could be intrinsically meaningful and fulfilling, and he was confident that his company, Apple, had a noble purpose that reached far beyond its staggering profits. Jobs inspired his company's key engineers and designers with his favorite Zen-like maxim: "The journey is the reward."[42] It reflected the intrinsic importance that Jobs attached to wholehearted commitment, and it also framed his key employees' daily grind as something more meaningful than just doing a good job and possibly becoming rich.

He managed to infuse work with a vaguely religious quality that made it possible for his subordinates to accept the quixotic managerial style that was a mix of Jobs's ambition, perfectionism, and competitiveness. His well-known quest for holiness and personal purification through both spiritual seeking and technological innovation also made it easier for his intimates to forgive his obsessive diets, frequent temper tantrums, and lack of empathy.

In the early 1980s, Jobs drew on his experience as a spiritual seeker to imagine his Apple team as an elect group of virtuosi that was on a mission to transform ordinary people's lives and give them tools to reach toward personal authenticity and spiritual knowledge. This sense of spiritual mission allowed Jobs to present himself as a dedicated spiritual virtuoso whose commitment necessitated engagement in the marketplace.[43] Jobs once told a group of his key employees:

> As every day passes, the work fifty people are doing here is going to send a giant ripple through the universe.[44]

Jobs believed that he possessed unique abilities and insights that could make the world a better place for everyone. He saw his potential for spiritual virtuosity as another aspect of his greatness. Throughout his life, Jobs relentlessly pursued sanctification through alternate faiths, attempting to cultivate the divine spark that lay deep within him so that he could enhance his creativity and insight. He selected, revised, and combined beliefs and practices from a variety of Human Potential

Movement groups that included Primal Scream Therapy, Zen, Tibetan Buddhism, and Hinduism.[45] However, he rarely organized his life in terms of spiritual priorities.

When he was a high school senior, Jobs first experienced an overwhelming sense of connection with some amorphous Higher Power because of LSD. Throughout his life, he credited his early experiences with acid for turning him into a more enlightened human being with unlimited potential for spiritual growth:

> It [LSD] reinforced my sense of what was important–creating things instead of making money, putting things back into the stream of history and of human consciousness as much as I could.[46]

After his 1972 high school graduation, Jobs enrolled at Portland Oregon's Reed College, a high-powered academic milieu that was notoriously tolerant of personal experimentation. Jobs immediately fell in with a small group of other brilliant rebels who investigated powerful psychedelics and explored varied paths to enlightenment.

The young men read books about Asian spirituality as avidly as Luther and his students had poured over the Bible. A few books that were popular in the 1970s became Jobs's lifelong resources; Ram Dass's *Remember, Be Here Now* presented a potpourri of different Buddhist and Hindu philosophies so that readers could dive into spiritual techniques from many faiths. Another important book for Jobs, Paramahansa Yoganananda's *Autobiography of a Yogi*, described a single spiritual path with explicit instructions for study and applications. Jobs tried out meditations, yoga poses, and modified diets that Ram Dass and Yogananda discussed, but it was a third book that became his lifelong touchstone. Shunryu Suzuki's *Zen Mind, Beginner's Mind* was the single greatest influence on how Jobs saw the world, what he created, and the ways that he hoped to live and die.[47]

Jobs dropped out of college after his first semester, but he stayed around the Reed neighborhood and audited classes for more than a year after he officially left college. He continued to explore alternate spirituality, reading voraciously, discussing different books and religious practices, and regularly visiting the local Hare Krishna collective for dinners, chanting, dancing, and discussions about religion. The next year, 1974, Jobs moved back to his parents' house in Los Altos and worked as a tester for the first generation of Atari computer games, saving most of his salary for a personal spiritual tour of India that he could begin in less than a year.

During his seven-month Indian sojourn, Jobs searched for a guru to lead him to spiritual redemption and purification. He met hundreds of other seekers and dozens of virtuosi during a festival at Haridwar, near the mouth of the Ganges, and he journeyed to the foot of the Himalayas to visit a luxurious estate that was owned by an enlightened master and his devotees. Despite his frantic searching, Jobs could not discover the perfect spiritual teacher, and after several months, he met up with an old Reed friend to explore the countryside and learn how ordinary Indians lived. Although he was only sightseeing during his later months in India, Jobs never gave up his desire to find a personal virtuoso path. He returned home with a shaved head, Indian robes, and the determination to meditate and live simply and spiritually.[48]

He went back to work at Atari and continued to sample different possibilities for personal and spiritual growth that came together in the Human Potential Movement, although he was always drawn back to Zen. At that historical moment, the San Francisco Zen Center was one of the most visible groups in the movement, and it was at the top of almost every local seeker's must-try list because of its charismatic American abbot, Richard Baker. Soon after Baker-roshi became the Center's leader in 1971, he changed its direction in order to promote Zen for ordinary people and bring principles of simplicity, goodness, and awareness into the larger society. For almost a decade, the Zen Center reached out to San Franciscans through its bakeries, bookstores, small clothing companies, and restaurants.[49]

Over the next few years, Jobs embarked on the rigorous practice of sitting Zazen meditation in order to focus his mind and reach toward unity with all things, while envisioning how the Zen aesthetic might change the computer industry. He discovered a virtuoso *sensi* (mentor), Kobun Chino Otogawa, who founded a small zendo in Los

Photo 1.4 Steve Jobs.

Altos near the Jobs's home, after having been a major influence at the San Francisco Zen Center and its affiliated Tassajara Zen Mountain Monastery.

Most evenings during the mid-1970s, Jobs sat Zazen with Kobun Chino and hung out in his teacher's kitchen until midnight, in order to explore the meanings and purposes of life.[50] In 1978, Kobun left Los Altos to help found another Zen Center down the Pacific Coast in Santa Cruz, and a year later, with Job's financial help, he built the small Jikoji Retreat and Zen Center in the mountains above Silicon Valley. Kobun officiated at Jobs's 1991 wedding at the Lodge in Yosemite. Jobs continued to sit Zazen with Kobun until his teacher died eleven years later.

Jobs was well known before 1980, the year when Apple's IPO was valued at $1.79 billion, and he abruptly came into $256 million along with torrents of media attention. Even after he earned sudden wealth and international fame, however, Jobs continued to sit at Jikoji and Tassajara without interference. Other meditators barely noticed Jobs's presence because everyone sat on individual cushions, silently facing a wall with their eyes half open. Devotees also respected Jobs's anonymity because of his relationship with Kobun.

Jobs quietly supported Jykoji, and he donated money to other spiritual organizations like Ram Dass's Seva Foundation.[51] However, he concealed much of his philanthropy, because supplicants annoyed him almost as much as high-profile humanitarians like his rival Bill Gates.

After Kobun drowned in 2002, Jobs continued to sit Zazen at Jykoji. He also studied the other two spiritual masters who had first intrigued him at Reed, Yogananda and Ram Dass. His search for holiness and purification took on a new urgency a little more than a year afterward, in October of 2003, when he was diagnosed with pancreatic cancer and had to consider the possibility that he might die in the near future.

After his diagnosis, Jobs called an old friend, Larry Brilliant, who was both a devotee of Ram Dass's guru Neem Karoli Baba and a successful philanthropic advisor to other Silicon Valley moguls. They talked for hours about earthly paths to sanctification and roads to healing.[52] Jobs tried alternate treatments that included meditation and harsh diets, but he sought conventional medical intervention before the end of 2004. After a series of partial remissions, recurrences, and metastases, he died in 2011. At the close of the small memorial service that Jobs had carefully orchestrated for his family and intimate friends, everyone received brown boxes that housed copies of *Autobiography of a Yogi*, so that they too could find guidance to pursue their own paths to spiritual virtuosity.

Becoming a virtuoso without centering everything on religious ideals is a lifelong and almost impossible challenge, even for a multibillionaire yearning for spiritual wholeness and purification. Jobs's recurring frustrations and occasional exhilaration demonstrate how complete spiritual virtuosity is illusive and usually impossible to attain. But in Jobs's and many others' lives, the simple pursuit of virtuosity can become intrinsically fulfilling and religiously meaningful.

Jobs chased sanctification for three decades, but he never renounced his other passions: music, visual art, esoteric diets, and, most of all, his intense determination to create and market groundbreaking technological innovations. He claimed what some Buddhists call a "right livelihood," pouring himself into his work in order to repair the world.

Long before Apple's incredible success, Kobun recognized that Jobs's pursuit of virtuosity necessarily lay outside of religious institutions like monasteries or Zen temples. His vocation could become his central spiritual path. Soon after Jobs's death, the San Francisco Zen Center affirmed the spiritual dimensions of his materialism in this brief remembrance:

> Many of us at Zen Center today are mourning the loss of Steve Jobs. His work at Apple and NeXT transformed the realm of digital technology and made our interactions with it infinitely (loopy?) . . .
>
> Thank you, Steve Jobs. Deep bows and safe crossing over.[53]

The ideal of right livelihood resembles Martin Luther's belief that people could fulfill their duties to God by means of wholehearted commitment to their earthly labors. According to Luther, almost every kind of work might be transformed into a vocation, so long as it was undertaken without vanity or obsession with material rewards and so long as it always reflected a religious purpose. If people studied and observed the Word, their work might express their obedience and love of God.[54] However, while work might lead to an occasional sense of sanctification, it seldom produces the complete unity with a Higher Power that defines a spiritual virtuoso. For Luther, salvation was always a greater good than any worldly endeavor, and no work, no matter how materially productive it was, could in itself justify someone before God.

Extreme Cases and New Insights

Jobs was not universally admired. Critics condemned him for selfishness, narcissism, exploitation of others, and inattention to the consequences of his business practices. Historian Richard Wolin, who knew him at Reed College, asserted:

> Jobs had no interest in social justice. Public-spiritedness was not part of his makeup. Even then, for Jobs it was all about the Self. . . . Jobs' attraction to Eastern spirituality seemed to be motivated less by a search for cosmic oneness that a desire for self-aggrandizement—that is, for a more powerful self.[55]

It might seem like a paradox that Jobs channeled his quest for spiritual virtuosity into the business world. However, his attraction to spiritual ideals and practices was sincere, although he was unwilling and possibly unable to sacrifice his worldly interests in order to make religious study and action his most important priority. Jobs had the virtuoso's deep desire to purify himself and achieve a sense of connection with a Higher Power, but he was reluctant to forgo public recognition or forswear power and material rewards.

Nevertheless, his long search for personal sacralization illustrates how paths to virtuosity have multiplied in the West and how many people, like dedicated Sunday Assemblers, pursue spiritual virtuosity by creating their own combinations of beliefs and practices from different religious traditions. Jobs's seekership illuminates how spiritual virtuosity has spilled over from the religious sphere into almost every aspect of contemporary culture, commerce, and image management.

We have described a famous entrepreneur's search for sanctification in detail in order to explore the ways that everyday seekers currently try out different paths that may lead them toward a sense of holiness and higher purpose. Steve Jobs's fame and the stories of his quests dramatically illustrate how access to virtuoso practices has expanded over the centuries. Spiritual virtuosity is no longer contained within established religious denominations, and it has been diffused across the domains of what social critics sometimes describe as "secularized modernity."

Just as Jobs's personal story adds to deeper understandings of contemporary spirituality, descriptions of a small number of virtuosi can illuminate both the fluidity of virtuosity itself and the ways that spiritual virtuosi can fuel social change. We hope to explore their life histories to better understand how spiritual virtuosity and social activism come together. Each of the three consequential movements that we consider illustrates both different expressions of religious virtuosity and the social conditions that support spiritual activism outside the boundaries of established faiths.

We ask why, when, and how spiritual virtuosi put aside their dedication to personal salvation and come together in order to successfully spearhead social change. The next two chapters will investigate what it means to be a spiritual virtuoso and what social contexts encourage virtuosi to become activists for greater religious and social equality.

Subsequent chapters consider some key virtuosi activists who were central to three of the few extraordinarily successful social movements that generated more spiritual equality and contributed to dramatic social change. Our emphasis on transformative virtuosi-led movements makes it possible to create a framework for understanding the social conditions that allow other, less visible virtuosi movements to succeed or fail.

Virtuosi in the Reformation, the Antislavery Movement, and the Human Potential Movement received a great deal of public attention, and their stories are interesting in themselves. However, they also serve as extreme cases that can reveal the subtleties of religious virtuosity and its historical genealogy. Extreme cases illuminate social processes in ways that typical cases cannot, because they stand out from more normative processes.[56] Close examination of the three movements and some of the key virtuosi activists in them makes it possible to frame and partially answer central questions about spirituality and social transformation. History and biography come together in the three case studies that illustrate the often-overlooked impact of spiritual virtuosity on the West.

2 Virtuosity and Spiritual Privilege

Virtuosity

Spiritual virtuosi can be identified across religions, cultures, and historical epochs. In every setting, they possess affinities and lasting desires that compel them to strive to transcend the mundane world and reach toward unity with someone or something holy. Despite doubts, they sustain their faith in their ability to discover new paths to sanctification and experience religious transcendence of the mundane world.[1]

Steve Jobs never attained lifelong spiritual virtuosity because he did not possess the combination of religious talents, otherworldly commitments, and capacities to make personal sacrifices that could allow him to devote his life to spiritual study and practice. Yet, drawing on the virtuoso ethic and recasting spirituality as visual style, he became a virtuoso in the technological marketplace and trusted that his work could become his spiritual signature. In a sense, his focus on developing his worldly vocation as a path to sanctification cemented Jobs's role as one of Martin Luther's heirs.

In the sixteenth century, Luther countered claims that monasticism represented the highest spiritual calling with arguments that life in the world could be spiritually enriching and no less pleasing to God than secluded asceticism. Luther was acknowledged as a religious virtuoso after he abandoned his legal studies at age twenty-one to enter a rigorous monastic order and adopt a harsh regime of fasting, meditation, prayer, penance, and fervent confession. Luther, the monk *par excellence*, came to realize that institutionalized devotions and acts of contrition diverted seekers from the true internal transformation that alone allows individuals to be sanctified in God's eyes.[2] His pastoral experiences as a friar and later as a professor at Wittenberg shaped his passion for a simpler, more popularly accessible form of spirituality.[3] Nevertheless, it was only with great reluctance that he abandoned monasticism and theological studies in order to enact his commitment to God through religious and political struggles.

The contrast between Luther's and Jobs's levels of virtuosity illustrates how paths to purity and holiness are compelling to individuals with greater or lesser religious talents. The intense inner experiences and emotional moments that can mark virtuosity provide extraordinary intrinsic rewards. The external responses to virtuosi's spiritual brilliance validate their social identities. In every field—music, athletics, the visual arts, or spirituality—virtuosity is at once uniquely personal process and also a social enterprise. The virtuoso ethic is marked by self-scrutiny and a restless desire for excellence that signifies transcendence of the mundane world.

Because great virtuosity requires essential interactions of talent, training, and disciplined practice, even extraordinary virtuosi rarely excel in more than a single field, although an acclaimed virtuoso in one area may occasionally have the confidence to attempt to master something else. The results of this secondary virtuosity, however, usually prove less than spectacular. Michael Jordan, the supreme athlete, for example, failed to become a Major League Baseball virtuoso after earning acclaim as the greatest professional basketball player in history. Jordan's failure to bring his virtuosity to another game illustrates the ways that a virtuoso's talents may be limited to one area.

Martin Luther would have understood this. He adored music and took up composition and hymn writing with gusto and talent, but he nevertheless readily acknowledged his secondary mastery in the musical domain. Exceptions to this pattern usually involve virtuosi who cultivate their artistic talents in service of their spiritual ideals.

Discovering Spiritual Virtuosity

Max Weber, the brilliant early-twentieth-century sociologist, was an academic polymath who excelled in fields as diverse as law and commercial development, politics and state administration, the philosophy of science, and the history of civilizations. Despite his superb academic career, however, he was especially fascinated by activities that he could never master through intellectual virtuosity alone. Personally intrigued by both religion and music, Weber transferred the concept of musical mastery as self-transcendence to spirituality, introducing and exploring the concept of religious virtuosity.[4] In a number of essays, he used his formidable intellectual powers to try to understand religion and music, despite feeling that he had no talent in either field.

Although he had an enduring interest in spirituality, Weber could never experience a sense of emotional connection to some Higher Power or allow faith and revelation to overshadow his methodically rational approach to life. While he believed that there might be unknown forces beyond human endeavor, Weber was never sure what or where those were. He wrote:

> It is true that I am absolutely unmusical religiously and have no need or ability to erect any psychic edifices of a religious character within me. But a thorough self-examination has told me that I am neither antireligious nor irreligious.[5]

His affluent Berlin family and their circle of friends routinely discussed classical music, personal philosophies, and religion around their dinner tables and at social gatherings, so Weber appreciated the importance of music and longed to better understand religion. He diligently studied the Bible long after he privately rejected his father's hollow conformity to Lutheran traditions and his mother's pious Christian humanitarianism and interests in séances and other psychic experiences.[6] Although he was already a skeptic, Weber taught himself to read Hebrew in order to truly understand the Old Testament before publicly professing his faith and affirming his lifelong bond to the Christian church at his confirmation.

Photo 2.1 Max Weber.

Weber read both German and Latin before he was ten, but he seemed to take his own intellectual virtuosity for granted and often longed to become more musically and socially adept. When he attended the University of Heidelberg, he tried to be popular by building up his physical strength so that he could drink and carouse with fellow members of his dueling society. In spite of this new interest in social life, however, Weber continued to be an academic star and he easily pursued a doctorate. In 1896, at the age of thirty-two, he was appointed as a full professor of political economy at the University of Heidelberg, the youngest German to ever achieve this rank.

About a year after that extraordinary early success, his father died and Weber plunged into decades of mental anguish, alternating between depression and frenzied research and writing, until his own death in 1920. He studied religions of the world from a comparative and historical perspective in order to outline the evolution of spirituality from its simple, parochial beginnings to increasing complexity and universality. Weber's meticulous research considered spiritual virtuosity in terms of cross-cultural examples that ranged from ancient Buddhist monks to seventeenth-century Quakers.[7]

In the West, the spiritual virtuosity that Weber described is related to, but not synonymous with, Christian salvation, which promises a glorious afterlife in close proximity to God. The virtuoso's search for sanctification is primarily an earthly pursuit of personal purification and connection to a Higher Power. Sanctification can only be understood in relation to others, rather than as an entirely isolated, individualistic pursuit of the afterlife. Ultimate salvation after death is an important but hardly a universal goal of spiritually inspired people, while the ideal of sanctification is relatively common in many spiritual traditions.

There are degrees of spiritual virtuosity, just as there are degrees of virtuosity in any other area, although fortune and fame that are often linked to excellence in other fields are rarely associated with spiritual endeavors. However, religious virtuosity is never inherently or exclusively moral, since self-interest and worldly desires may fuel commitments to excellence in almost anything. In fact, some religions openly urge individual virtuosi to pursue unconventional morality and imagine spiritual power as a way to dominate the world.[8]

Virtuosity and Vice

In the mid-twentieth century, feminists wrote new histories of spiritual virtuosi that acknowledge some extraordinary, long-forgotten figures in Western religion. They described Hildegard von Bingen, known as the "Sybil of the Rhine," as a prime example of the ways that the mists of time and masculine privilege had obscured women virtuosi's accomplishments. Setting the record straight, a feminist scholar took up her cause:

> But for women of the twelfth century, hedged by the constraints of a misogynist world, her achievements baffle thought, marking her as a figure so exceptional that posterity has found it hard to take her measure. For centuries she was ignored or forgotten, like so many accomplished women of the past.[9]

Revisionist histories about the roles that women played as spiritual virtuosi added an important dimension to the history of religion in Europe and Americas, but many feminists fell into the same traps as Weber and other scholars. Virtuoso spirituality, however impressive, is not uniformly admirable!

Von Bingen was a mystic, a prophet, and a remarkable writer, who also excelled as a composer of sacred music, producing over seventy liturgical songs that stretched the style of traditional Gregorian chants.[10] However, she was by no means consistently moral, good, or generous.

She never wanted to share possibilities for sanctification with ordinary people. Instead, von Bingen sought personal power through the Church and recognition from the wider society. She tried to neither overcome the defects of her religious world nor widen access to spiritual knowledge and experience.

Soon after she was elected *magistra* (prioress) of the small women's community attached to a monastery in the Rhineland near Mainz, von Bingen inquired whether

Photo 2.2 Hildegard von Bingen.

she might remove her community from her abbot's authority and she met with unconditional refusal. Because she was from a noble family and had many powerful sponsors, however, von Bingen reached over her abbot's head to the archbishop of Mainz, who granted her permission to establish an independent women's monastery, increasing both her group's autonomy and her own control.

Until she died at the age of eighty-one, in 1179, von Bingen skillfully increased her power and influence year by year. Her aristocratic origins and her elder sponsor's status as a count's daughter helped attract women from wealthy families to her community, and her youthful charges brought her material benefits and political protection from within and outside the Church.

Some critics attacked Hildegard for recruiting only nobles whom she provided with special clothes, personalized rituals, and songs that she wrote especially for them. Hildegard responded to these criticisms by stating that she was merely doing God's work by sustaining His divine blueprint: "Oxen, asses, and sheep are not kept in the same stable."[11] She believed that separation of the social classes was necessary, noting that commoners might try to join her group out of vanity and she wanted to make sure that the girls in her charge would have no reason to "sniff" at their inferiors.[12]

In order to maintain God's order in other ways, Hildegard also encouraged the absolute suppression of the Cathars, a vibrant dissident sect that attacked the

Church's greed and encouraged simplicity and self-denial. She called them heretics in her letters to archbishops, and she used apocalyptic imagery in sermons against the dissidents. Shortly after von Bingen delivered a fiery sermon about the necessity for violent suppression of the sect in 1163, two Cathars were burned alive in Cologne. Less than a century later, but well after Hildegard had died, Pope Innocent III initiated the bloody Albigensian Crusade that killed tens of thousands of Western European Cathars and nearly obliterated the group.

Von Bingen's vehement intolerance and the subsequent Crusades were by no means unique. When there is intense spiritual conflict, virtuosi have been disheartingly willing to persecute groups that they view as dangerous to their spiritual goals or as threats to the religious innovations that they have championed. Martin Luther's calls for the violent suppression of peasant rebellions, Anabaptist sects, and recalcitrant Jews are other notorious examples of the fact that virtue and spiritual virtuosity are not necessarily synonymous.[13] Von Bingen's desire for power and her bloodthirsty outbursts against the Cathars also illustrate how influential virtuosi may use their unique spiritual privilege for narrowly personal ends.

Virtuosity, Monastic Life, and other Possibilities

When he described spiritual virtuosity, Max Weber primarily tried to understand the ways that talented individuals dedicated themselves to personal sanctification in isolated monastic orders. However, he was also aware that they occasionally tried to transform religious institutions from the inside or even change their surrounding societies.

Throughout most of their lives, spiritual virtuosi in isolated monasteries and in the wider society try to live up to high personal ideals, and every new step that they take toward holiness leads them to strive for greater levels of spiritual understanding and experience. In contrast to athletic or artistic virtuosi, most cloistered virtuosi are primarily inspired by ultimate values that spring from their ardent religious beliefs.

Weber focused on the individuals that were models of complete spiritual commitment whose lives reflected daily self-sacrifice, not those whose virtuosity was tainted by venality or excess of any kind. Most of them had withdrawn from the secular world to live in monastic communities or isolated settings where they reached ever closer to salvation and connection to a Higher Power, with little concern for their personal comfort:

> Concentration upon the actual pursuit of salvation may entail a formal withdrawal from the "world": from social and psychological ties with family, from possession of worldly goods, and from political, economic, artistic, and erotic activities—in short from all creaturely interests.[14]

These virtuosi were doubly privileged. Individually, they possessed the spiritual "musicality" that enabled and enhanced their intense religious experiences. Socially, they had access to the financial means or patronage that allowed them to escape the confines of the mundane world and take part in costly, time-consuming ritual, contemplation, and mystical practices.

In both Western and Asian societies, monasticism became a system for seeking holiness that almost inevitably reflected the realities of religious and social stratification. A few individuals were able to devote themselves to seeking holiness and purification through ascetic withdrawal from society, but most people who sought sanctification lacked the means or opportunities to center their lives on their religious priorities. In their discussions of ascetic virtuosi, Weber and other scholars usually described monks and solitaries, the spiritual virtuosi that religious institutions validated and supported. However, Weber also acknowledged that there was a fundamental tension between elite spirituality and popular religion, observing that some dedicated spiritual virtuosi might be ignored or even punished if religious authorities did not endorse their dedication.

In the sixteenth century, monasticism materially supported almost the entire fortunate minority that could become full-time virtuosi, so the Church necessarily restricted entry into monasteries and other religious institutions. The monastic orders' rules, hierarchies, and systems of internal governance controlled their members' possibilities to enact their spiritual virtuosity, and they could rarely reach closer to union with God without formal authorization.

The constant restrictions made paths to sanctification more reliable for everyone who remained within monastic orders, but systematic regulation also constrained the potentially explosive ethical and radical implications of individual's paths to purification and holiness. Within contemporary Western monasteries, collective discipline still protects virtuosi from the problems of extreme individualism, the dangers of excessive enthusiasm, and the attractions of deceptive spiritual pathways, but it also limits their creativity and abilities to interpret, enact, and share spiritual possibilities.[15]

Photo 2.3 A group of contemporary monks.

Monasteries provide no options for partial commitment to spiritual virtuosity, because a cloistered life requires withdrawal from the outside world and recognition that sanctification is a scarce "commodity." When spiritual virtuosity is institutionalized, members of religions like Roman Catholicism or Rienzi Zen Buddhism must support recognized virtuosi through endowments, tithes, or unpaid services. So, monasticism augments the spiritual privilege of a few, at the expense of many people both in terms of material support for individuals who dedicate themselves to purification and holiness and in terms of limiting paths to sanctification. Somehow this sheltered and exclusive spiritual privilege seems to be at odds with the basic logic of possibilities for universal salvation that is at the heart of all of the world's great faiths.[16]

Ordinary people defer to cloistered and wandering virtuosi, because virtuosi's absolute dedication and distance from the world serves as a proxy for their own efforts to reach some measure of sanctification on earth. However, while priests and monks may pray for the world and perform rituals for the laity, they rarely enrich ordinary people's spiritual lives or willingly invite them to learn more about new possibilities for personal devotions.

Monastic orders wield symbolic power that explicitly or implicitly supports elites that provide them with most of their economic support and political authority. In the West, from the early Middle Ages onward, many monasteries were wealthy landowners and exploited the peasants who farmed their land and paid them taxes.[17] Despite the symbolic importance of dedication to everyone's salvation, cloistered virtuosi rarely made public service their priority, although a few orders such as Franciscan friars have committed themselves to ministering to everyone.

For all of his fascination with religious virtuosity and his insightful recognition of the inherent tensions in monasticism, Max Weber never fully understood the ways that virtuosi may initiate religious and cultural change or the range of spiritual virtuosity that can develop outside of cloistered settings. He failed to appreciate how spiritual virtuosi come to oppose the institutionalized constraints that limit their own practice and their desires to create religious equality for everyone. Moreover, he never understood the potential implications of interactions between spirituality and social activism, because he almost always associated virtuosity with institutionalized orthodoxy and cultural conservatism. Because of monastic virtuosi's obvious accomplishments, scholars have followed Weber and usually ignored the many inequalities that shape the pursuit of spiritual virtuosity and the ways that some virtuosi come to battle against their own privilege. Instead of escaping a wicked world in protected cloisters, virtuosi activists in both large and small social movements believe that they must reshape the world in terms of their religious ideals and at least temporarily step outside of their religious communities.

In the nineteenth century, some activists added women's subordination to their lists of societal sins. Nevertheless, Weber, like his academic contemporaries, avoided questions about spiritual virtuosity and gender and he simply noted that almost all world religions marginalized women.[18] Patriarchy represents another element of elite monasticism and its legacies that virtuosi activists have slowly confronted over the centuries, as they have sought to democratize their own spiritual privilege and bring possibilities for unmediated spiritual expansion to everyone.

Ascetic, Ethical, and Activist Virtuosity

Even the most pious virtuosi may have diverse motives for their dedication and complex relationships to religious traditions and institutions. Moreover, they may change their goals and redefine their commitments over time. Fully dedicated virtuosi may begin their practice cloistered in monasteries, go out into the world to minister to the poor, join with others to fight holy wars, or try to remake the world by inspiring new kinds of spiritual commitment.

Although there are different ways that virtuosi consecrate their lives to a Higher Power, the best-known model of religious virtuosity is still world-rejecting asceticism. In the twenty-first century, people think of spiritual virtuosity in terms of individuals who renounce ordinary obligations in order to take refuge in cloisters, the institutions that were expressly created for spiritually privileged individuals to escape the masses, and the pressures of a sinful world. However, throughout religious history, ethical virtuosi have implemented moral doctrines and viewed service to a fallen world as their responsibility.[19]

Well before the Reformation, some ethical virtuosi in mendicant orders or missions dedicated their lives to spiritual service to those in great need. They pursued sanctification by helping ordinary people through teaching, preaching, or pastoral care of their souls and bodies. St. Francis and St. Dominic were famous early examples of this path of selfless service to the needy, and St. Theresa of Calcutta exemplified ethical virtuosity in the twentieth century, because of her wholehearted service to the poorest of the poor.[20]

Table 2.1 Typology of virtuosity

	Ascetic	Ethical	Prophetic	Activist
Primary ways to act on ideals	Conspicuous withdrawal and antimaterialism	Moral influence and outreach	By example, exhortation, or violence	Social mobilization
Relationship to ordinary people	Spiritual elites	Spiritual exemplars and advisors	Separation or dominance	Spiritual path-breakers and brokers
Relation to dominant political order	Indifference	Moral criticism and tension	Indifference or confrontation	Engagement for change
Personal practice	Self-denial/ mortification	Self-discipline and principled individual action	Forceful enactment of spiritual ideals	Service to collective goals

Spiritual virtuosi may also embrace a prophetic voice that demands justice and mobilizes movements in the name of the divine.[21] Max Weber discussed two kinds of prophetic religious virtuosi and their inspirational roles in religious transformation. However, he never considered possibilities that they might also become activist-leaders dedicated to implementing religious and social equality because of their spiritual principles.

Weber described Buddha as an exemplary prophet who never confronted political or religious authorities but instead showed people the way to salvation through his own extraordinary conduct and spiritual virtuosity. The second kind of prophetic virtuoso, like the Old Testament Biblical prophets and Mohammed, is an ethical prophet who is willing to personally challenge powerful institutions and individuals.

Ethical prophets insist that everyone has the moral duty to obey their interpretations of divine will and create an earthly realm that reflects that sacred purpose. This kind of virtuoso prophet risks everything to warn people that they have allowed the world to stray from God's design and everyone will suffer divine punishment unless they make things right. In some contexts, ethical prophets assume that the righteous cannot fail, and they lead others to take up the sword in order to enact holy vengeance and usher in an era of sacred justice. In 1831, Nat Turner, an African American lay preacher and ethical prophet, led an abortive rebellion of slaves and free blacks in Virginia that was swiftly and violently suppressed.[22]

A nonconfrontational ethical prophetic tradition now thrives in African American churches and so does a different kind of virtuosity, the activism that Dr. Martin Luther King Jr. exemplified in the twentieth century. Reverend King was called to pastor the Dexter Avenue Baptist Church in Montgomery, Alabama, when he was twenty-five years old, and a year later he helped lead the 1955 Montgomery Bus Boycott—a defining moment in the American Civil Rights Movement. When King helped found the

Photo 2.4 Reverend Martin Luther King Jr.

Southern Christian Leadership Conference in 1957, he began to gain wide recognition for both his spiritual virtuosity and his extraordinary charismatic leadership. As his influence grew, King continued to be a prophetic voice in the African American church and also in national and international political movements. In his 1963 speech to a quarter of a million people who had marched for civil rights in Washington, DC, King explicitly turned to prophecy, echoing Amos and Isaiah to condemn American racism and reveal his own vision of national redemption.

In the struggle for social justice, King demonstrated personal courage, organizational talents, and strategic genius that disarmed many Southern white Protestants who had opposed racial equality throughout their lives. He developed a moral rhetoric that evoked the symbols and ethics of a shared prophetic religious tradition that inspired African Americans and at the same time convinced many white Protestants that racial equality was a Christian obligation.[23]

King's moral and political leadership exemplifies the missing element in Weber's typology of religious virtuosity: *activist spiritual virtuosity,* which is distinct from ethical prophecy. Unlike prophetic ethical virtuosi, activist virtuosi never present themselves as God's anointed messengers. Instead, they make it clear that they are driven by their personal religious commitments and moral convictions. Virtuoso activists, unlike prophetic virtuosi who seek retribution through violence, optimistically believe that they can work peacefully to transform their society in terms of their spiritual ideals.

Like prophets, activist virtuosi are in tension, if not in outright conflict, with established elite clergy. Critical of institutionalized methods of sanctification that defer to rules and religious authorities, they believe that social action is part of personal spiritual commitment and that a collective will can be mobilized to create spiritual equality and social change. Virtuoso activists share their approaches to salvation with everyone who seeks an unmediated relationship to a Higher Power. They strive to democratize paths to sanctification and they bring diverse groups together in the process. The activist virtuoso's vision of holiness and purification holds the promise that everyone can lead a religious life and honor the sacred because true religious spirit and dedication can accomplish wonders.

From the sixteenth century onward, when they have organized collective movements for religious and social change, activist spiritual virtuosi have emphatically believed that they should not implement their ideals by means of the kinds of external force that prophetic virtuosi might willingly use. They seek external change through their supporters' interior transformations and their adversaries' wholehearted conversions. Unlike prophetic virtuosi, activists believe that it is not enough for them to implement sacred precepts, reform institutions, or level inequalities by external means. Instead, they feel that they must lead everyone to remake himself or herself, because true and lasting change only occurs when people's spirits have taken flight.

Spiritual Rewards and Personal Costs

Activist virtuosi temporarily sacrifice their intensive study and personal devotions for the higher purpose of implementing fundamental religious and social changes that correspond to their new understandings of sacred truths and religious virtue. However, their commitment to religious and social transformation usually entails personal costs that can be immense. Their quests for virtuosity necessarily require them to sacrifice some or all of their past social relationships, luxuries, and other benefits. Their devotion to personal sanctification also compels some virtuosi to abandon their prospects for political power or worldly recognition and substantial material rewards. However, connections with a holy ideal and the embodied experiences that may signify sanctification compensate for earthly prizes. Moreover, paying a price for religious enthusiasm affirms a virtuoso's unwavering commitment to pursue sanctification and validates his or her dedication both privately and publicly.

Cat Stevens, a celebrated British singer-songwriter, sacrificed his flourishing musical career when he converted to Islam at age twenty-nine. He devoted himself to religious study, practice, and ethical virtuosity within England's Islamic community for two decades before returning to the stage under the name of Yusef. In the 1970s, he combined folk music and rock in the songs that he wrote and performed, sold tens of millions of albums, and earned a number of music industry awards. However, after disappointing romances with other rock stars like Carly Simon, a long convalescence from tuberculosis, and an incident when he nearly drowned, Stevens converted to Islam after a period of instruction with imams in England. Soon after his conversion he changed his name to Yusef Islam, stopped writing and performing, married another Muslim, and auctioned off all of his guitars.[24]

Photo 2.5 Cat Stevens in the 1970s.

Over the decades, other performers covered his most popular songs like "Peace Train" and "Moon Shadow," and two generations of children have sung those songs without knowing about Stevens's conversion. In the twenty-first century, his estimated income from royalties is well over a million dollars a year, most of which he regularly donates to Islamic education and victims of war and famine.[25]

Sacrifices of money and fame were relatively easy for Stevens, but he missed writing and performing popular music. For two decades, he did not perform in public, but at the urging of his spiritual teachers, his wife, and his five children, he began to write music, record, and perform as a messenger for moderate Islam. Yusef dropped his last name "Islam" in order to reach more outsiders, and his recent songs have a more secular character. He moved from separating himself from the larger world and asceticism to outreach that combined ethical service with his musical virtuosity.

Cat Stevens's relatively recent fusion of spiritual and musical virtuosity demands sacrifices of his commitment to sanctification through study and prayer. Activism diverts spiritual virtuosi from cultivating their own sacred priorities, and it tests their spiritual integrity by substituting successful worldly outcomes for less tangible spiritual goals. After participating in movements for religious and social change, many exhausted virtuosi return to their cloistered lives, while others selflessly serve people in need or join progressive movements that integrate politics and spirituality.

When activist virtuosi replace much of their intense spiritual study and practice with social action, they experience tensions between the demands of public engagement and the urgent personal call to develop their private spirituality that originally led them to dedicate themselves to achieving union with a Higher Power. For example, the second Secretary-General of the United Nations, Dag Hammerskjöld, had an extraordinarily successful diplomatic and humanitarian career, but he mourned his decision to step away from his lifetime search for sanctification. He tried to find respite from the demands of diplomacy through time-consuming devotional practices, moral reflections, and intensive self-scrutiny. And Hammerskjöld described the reason that he subdued his longings for an ascetic life when he noted, "In our age, the road to holiness necessarily passes through the world of action."[26] It was an individual cry for change grounded in religious priorities of social justice and peace.

Spiritual Privilege

Hammerskjöld was able to become a virtuoso because of his spiritual privilege. This privilege involves an individual's ability to select, combine, and revise religious beliefs and practices over the course of a lifetime. Strong religious affinities and robust external resources come together to generate spiritual privilege that supports sustained searches for connection to some Higher Power. It involves interactions of spiritual sympathies and the economic, social, and cultural resources that support personal commitment to a religiously centered life.

In the West, spiritual privilege, along with opportunities to pursue virtuosity, has slowly become more common since Martin Luther's movement first expanded everyone's access to sanctification. In subsequent centuries, activist virtuosi have spread their own innovations to ever-wider publics because they believed that they share ethical obligations to spread their privilege much farther and make the pursuit of sanctification and possibilities for spiritual virtuosity available to everyone. However, in the West, spiritual privilege still remains differentially distributed in terms of personal capacities, material sustenance, and social and cultural resources.

Searches for sanctification require both economic supports and social anchors. Even isolated hermits and religious wandering mendicants cultivate their virtuosity in terms of ethics and spiritual priorities drawn from their earlier contact with collective religious beliefs and practices.[27]

The interface of economic, social, and cultural resources with religious affinities shapes spiritual privilege, so that it never remains static and it can increase or diminish as over time. But whatever advantages support someone's pursuit of sanctification, personal abilities to cultivate transcendent experiences and hunger for religious guidance are *the* essential elements that fuel spiritual virtuosity. Spiritual virtuosity is always grounded in religious affinities that an individual can identify, attempt to understand, and continue to cultivate through their extraordinary experiences and their sustained searches for religious meaning. Without spiritual affinities, someone's economic, cultural, and social resources will support only worldly goals rather than religious ones.

Spiritual Affinities

Affinities combine abilities to experience transcendent moments, faith in the supernatural, and dedication to belief systems that provide moral guidance and coherent explanations for both routine and remarkable events. Since faiths differ in the ways that they recognize and support connections with a Higher Power, everything from sudden revelations to *satori* (complete self-realization) can add to religious virtuosity and we will not categorize or evaluate the myriad forms of sacred experience that often reward intensive practice and study. Because this book focuses on the human side of religion and how people reach toward holiness, there is also no need to ask whether religious virtuosi actually experience some divine influence.

By accident or intense effort, individuals must develop spiritual affinities in order to enjoy a modicum of success in following virtuoso paths. There are countless tales of seekers like Steve Jobs who wanted to sustain a lifelong relationship with some Higher Power, but were somehow unable to reach beyond their worldly concerns. And the New Testament is filled with stories of people who failed to recognize Jesus's divinity or mistook it for something else.[28] Innate capacities for transcendence sustain searches for connection with Higher Powers, because religious experience offers intrinsic rewards that can motivate ever-greater commitment. Only individuals who have received robust intrinsic rewards from study and practice are likely to dedicate their lives to pursuing spiritual virtuosity.

Abilities to cultivate mystical moments undoubtedly involve some innate physical predispositions that facilitate religious experiences, but social contexts and subsequent interpretations determine their impact.[29] Without religious guidelines to explain and anchor them, spiritual experiences are usually brief and unfathomable.[30] For example, Hildegard von Bingen was frightened and confused by the extraordinary moments that she had experienced when she was very young, but over time she came to view them as messages from God. It was not until she started to reside in her Benedictine women's community that she began to describe those moments publicly and attribute them as proof of God's light. In midlife, von Bingen looked back and asserted that she saw "The Shade of the Living Light" when she was three years old, although it took years before she came to believe that these were truly sacred experiences.[31] Moreover, her parents never predicted that she might receive messages from God when they eased their financial burdens by dedicating Hildegard to the Church soon after she was born.

She demonstrated her astonishing religious virtuosity by composing sacred music, discovering powerful medicinal herbs, and writing poems and tracts to honor God. All of those accomplishments were grounded in Hildegard's slowly acquired certainty that God revealed himself to her when she was a tiny girl. Von Bingen's powerful religious career illustrates the ways that social interpretations can shape and reshape spiritual experiences, as well as reflect the egoism and ambition that sometimes accompany spiritual virtuosity.

Her early childhood experiences of pain, light, and subsequent euphoria may have been signs from the Holy Spirit that von Bingen only comprehended as she grew up in a Benedictine community. But they may also have been migraine symptoms, because Hildegard's accounts of the scintillating points of light that left her exhausted and then elated correspond with the migraine symptoms that neurologist Oliver Sacks has described in great detail.[32]

It is likely that both biology and sacred destiny came together as she grew more familiar with the Bible and the Church. Mystical moments are open to many interpretations, but whatever their origins, they sometimes chart lifelong dedication to spiritual study and practice. Hildegard von Bingen crafted a multifaceted spiritual virtuosity that cannot be explained by neuroscience alone, and her career illustrates the ways that neurological events may nurture religious affinities and serve as rewards for spiritual commitment.

Unlike von Bingen, Steve Jobs was agnostic through his early teens, and he only began to sense extraordinary moments of transcendence and connections with some Higher Power when he experimented with psychedelics during his last year in high school. Subsequent LSD trips in college cemented Jobs's lasting desires to become a spiritual virtuoso.[33] Jobs and von Bingen's experiences are connected by the nature of their earliest feelings of contact with some Higher Power. The first spiritual experiences that drove both of their lifelong quests for sanctification reflected probable changes in their brain chemistry. Scientists have observed such changes in some illnesses and during intensive meditation, prayer, and psychedelic exploration.[34]

In *The Doors of Perception*, Aldous Huxley described how his personal experiments with mescaline facilitated extraordinary sacramental visions.[35] He viewed mescaline, the natural psychedelic that South and Central American Indians have used for centuries, as a stimulus for spiritual growth. Huxley argued that psychedelics alone could never lead to enlightenment, but he believed that they might create a temporary "gratuitous grace" that could generate deeper spiritual understandings and desires to pursue religious virtuosity.[36]

Huxley's critics asserted that mind-altering substances or events like migraines have no religious significance at all, because they are detached from collective pursuits of holiness and merely reinforce isolated private concerns.[37] And some of Huxley's detractors went a step farther when they argued that even intense physical practices or meditation that produce fleeting feelings of purification and transcendence are spiritually meaningless unless they are grounded in ethical systems of compassion and duty to Higher Powers. Robert Charles Zaehner, for example, referred to St. Paul when he criticized Huxley in terms of the crucial differences between activities that offer temporary personal expansion and those dedicated to long-term, carefully charted searches for spiritual union with God.[38]

Consciousness-altering drugs, neurological events, or physical practices alone never produce religious virtuosity, but they may generate an interest in seeking new perspectives on life and exploring connections to some Higher Power. Huston Smith, a widely read theologian and scholar, believed that inexplicable experiences can lead individuals to disciplined spiritual study and practice, in the same ways that Hildegard von Bingen's childhood visions became foundations for her life of spiritual privilege and virtuosity.[39]

Spiritual experience, religious knowledge, and faith in some Higher Power are the three central elements of the religious affinities that are the bedrock of spiritual privilege. Religious explanations and ethical guidelines locate experiential moments within faith traditions and connect them to collective quests for holiness and purification. Belief and knowledge may precede or follow religious experience, but all three must blend together in the affinities that ground spiritual privilege.

Virtuosi ceaselessly work to deepen their religious knowledge and contextualize their spiritual experiences by thoughtfully contemplating spiritual teachings to interpret how to enact their faith. In some traditions, reading and writing about spirituality ushers in religious experiences, as they did for Martin Luther and other virtuoso leaders of the early Protestant movement. Monastic study was a nearly universal experience for the first generation of Protestant Reformers and the humanist approaches to original Scriptures that orders like the Augustinians developed supported activist virtuosi's need to reveal their newly authentic, unmediated spirituality to ordinary people.[40]

Five centuries later, a major figure in the Human Potential Movement, the writer Michael Murphy, was caught up in transformative, mystical experiences when he read and reread Sri Aurobindo's *The Life Divine*.[41] He defined both reading and writing as his central personal practice, describing ways that he transcended the mundane world through the flow of ideas and words. His other regular spiritual practices included golf, yoga, long-distance running, and meditation, and he exemplifies the Human Potential Movement's doctrine that almost every activity can engender sacred moments if they have some larger spiritual purpose.

Murphy, von Bingen, and Jobs fully incorporated spirituality into their worldviews well after they had first experienced extraordinary moments. When they set aside their first confused responses to extraordinary experiences and defined them as religiously meaningful, they augmented their spiritual affinities and the overall spiritual privilege that was part of their lives. Combinations of spiritual experiences, religious meanings, and faith fueled their resolve to reach toward connection with a Higher Power and added to each of their spiritual privilege.

While von Bingen was born into a devout family and a Catholic culture that encouraged her religious affinities, until she became part of a Benedictine community, she never attributed the headaches and visual distortions that marked her earliest years as signs from God. Somewhat later in their lives than von Bingen, both Murphy and Jobs had powerful, ephemeral feelings of contact with something far beyond their comprehension. A sense of transcendence and serenity passed through a teenage Michael Murphy when he practiced alone on the golf course and when he attended Episcopal religious services, but he did not consider their full spiritual implications until he entered Stanford University and learned about Asian religious traditions, meditation, and integral yoga from his professors and from students who were spiritual seekers.[42]

Steve Jobs also had extraordinary experiences when he used psychedelics with his high school friends. However, at first he was unconcerned about the possibility that spiritual explanations could help him comprehend the implications of altered consciousness or enable him to tie ecstatic moments to a coherent ethical framework. While luxuriating in the kind of hedonism that Huxley's critics feared would contaminate psychedelic experimentation, however, he gradually became interested in philosophy and religious ideas, because the San Francisco Bay area was a magnet for innovative spiritual movements. Moreover, many people that he casually encountered in the psychedelic milieu used alternate faiths as anchors for their intoxicating experiences.[43] Coming of age in the Northern California during the 1960s prepared Steve Jobs to explore world religions with other Reed College students and anchor his transcendent LSD experiences in spiritual study and practice.[44]

Religious knowledge and faith in some Higher Power are not simply meaningful frameworks that contextualize exceptional experiences. They are also integral to the growth of spiritual affinities, because they link individuals to collective religious groups and to the virtuosi who attempt to live according to their spiritual beliefs.[45] When access to religious knowledge is limited to elites in a highly stratified society, institutionalized faiths rarely generate widespread religious enthusiasm and commitment to study and practice. However, when there are possibilities for unmediated spiritual practice in a diverse, pluralistic religious context, ordinary people are far more likely to develop religious frameworks to understand their lives and chart their actions in the face of adversity.[46]

Even in a society that is filled with religious opportunities, however, intellectual interest in spirituality will not generate lasting spiritual affinities unless it is connected to both transcendent religious moments and faith in the power of some supernatural force. Max Weber was fascinated by the historical development of religious systems that ranged from small marginal sects to economically and politically powerful institutions, but as he admitted so often, he could neither feel the ethereal power of religious experience nor suspend his disbelief in a Higher Power. Spiritual privilege and potential virtuosity necessarily involve knowledge and experience, and they flower when abundant material and educational advantages are widely available.

Economic Resources, Social Relations, and Cultural Capital

Although they are less central to spiritual privilege than religious affinities, financial means enable virtuosi to dedicate their lives to personal purification and the pursuit of earthly holiness. Even wandering mendicants and isolated hermits need dependable sources of sustenance in order to set their worldly concerns aside. Established faiths and wealthy patrons support monasteries, but some smaller groups and individual ascetics depend on the generosity of strangers, friends, and their own families. It is no accident that throughout modern history, most fully dedicated spiritual virtuosi have been born into the aristocracy or upper classes.[47]

Almost all of the spiritual virtuosi described earlier in this chapter had access to economic resources that facilitated their spiritual quests. During the Middle Ages, most virtuosi were only able to pursue sanctification because of their families' social position and the Church's largess.[48] Martin Luther and his movement shattered the Church's control of spiritual virtuosity when they spread their convictions that everyone could pursue sanctification without fully withdrawing from their work or family relationships. However, opportunities for religious study, debate, and prayer remained most available to members of the urban upper and middle classes, rather than the rural working class or the poor. It was not until the twentieth-century Human Potential Movement created thousands of paths to sanctification that almost everyone could access some degree of spiritual privilege.

During the Middle Ages, von Bingen's noble origins gave her a place in a Benedictine community and supported her later rise to power within the Church. Three centuries later, copper mines and smelters provided Luther's family with the resources that enabled him to enter the university, move from legal studies to a monastic community, and then leave that community to study theology at the University of Wittenberg. Both of these virtuosi enjoyed the privileges of economic support from their families and from the Church. However, von Bingen was a spiritual virtuoso in a feudal society where family position almost always determined someone's life chances, while Luther benefited from his parents' social mobility during the dawn of mercantile capitalism.

Economic growth enlarges possibilities for individuals to accumulate new kinds of spiritual privilege that facilitate the development of virtuosi movements seeking to extend possibilities for sanctification. During expansionary periods individuals like

Luther, who are satisfied with their material welfare, but bewildered by new opportunities and choices, sometimes retreat from an increasingly complex world and find solace in religious vocations. Others study in religious universities or centers, where they are free to focus on spiritually significant questions.

Wide-ranging social networks are a second element of spiritual privilege that make it easier for someone to work toward sanctification outside of a cloistered setting. Rather than rely on their families or local religious advisors for direction, spiritually privileged individuals can reach beyond close relationships to explore innovative beliefs and practices with other seekers and established virtuosi as well. As they make new contacts and break away from small, closed circles, privileged seekers have fresh opportunities and models for religious engagement. They receive intellectual and emotional support and also possible economic and political patronage for their religious innovations.

When they have many social contacts and access to diverse groups, virtuosi are also more likely to reduce the social distance that often isolates the spiritually privileged from ordinary people. Activist virtuosi often sustain relationships with several different spiritually privileged communities and also have ties with people in the secular world.

After Martin Luther became disgusted with legal studies and his hedonistic classmates at the University of Erfurt, he joined the Order of Augustinian Eremites, where he fasted, prayed, and studied. He did not fully retreat from the world, however, because part of his vocation as a friar was to preach, to listen to the anxieties of ordinary people, and to rejoice with them when they felt a sense of God's presence. Later, he went to the University of Wittenberg to study theology and become a professor. Luther made acquaintances and friends in many places, and as the Reformation unfolded, his scattered associates, not just his close friends, helped his followers reach out to new groups and gain support for their movement.

Social capital refers to the accumulated positive social relationships that enable people to enter a variety of groups, start new projects, and share their ideas for innovation.[49] Those interactions involve emotions as well as shared ideas, and even brief contacts can have lasting consequences. The casual friendships that emerge during short periods of direct personal connection may lead to social support in many other contexts. Twentieth-century virtuoso Corita Kent's life history illustrates how personal social resources can sustain activist virtuosi after they leave religious institutions and work for social justice in their societies.

Corita grew up in a devout working-class Catholic family. When she was eighteen, she dedicated herself to Christ and entered the novitiate of the Sisters of the Immaculate Heart of Mary. She later taught classes and chaired the art department in the order's Los Angeles college, and also reached out to the vibrant artistic communities in the rising city. Corita brought her students and other nuns to gallery openings, museums, and parades, and in the late 1960s she collaborated on posters and other projects with civil rights advocates, encounter group leaders, and famous cultural figures like the composer John Cage.

Her vibrant posters inspired liberal nuns and priests to extend the fleeting antiauthoritarian spirit of the Second Vatican Council, despite the Vatican's reinstatement of rigid rules about prayer, dress, and discourse in the mid-1960s. And she helped sow the seeds of a quiet rebellion of three hundred members of her order, who renounced their vows in 1970 and founded a widely influential lay Catholic community in Los Angeles.[50]

Under constant pressure from the conservative archbishop of Los Angeles because of her feminism, liberal politics, and pop art style that included depictions of the Holy Virgin as a juicy tomato, Corita opened a door and other sisters soon followed her lead. She left her order in 1968 and moved to Boston to join Father Daniel Berrigan and his Vietnam War protests before starting her career as independent printmaker.[51] Because of her relationships with many different spiritual, artistic, academic, and political communities, Corita was able to earn her living as an activist-artist and use her colorful silkscreened posters and paintings to spread the message that God can be found everywhere.

Even fifty years earlier, it was hard to imagine that someone like Corita could leave her convent, become a political and social activist within the Human Potential Movement, and ultimately spread access to sanctification through her art. She was both a spiritual and an artistic virtuoso, so her talents made it possible for her to develop diverse networks of social relationships outside the Church and those loose ties sustained her when she left her order.

From the Reformation to the present, widening circles of acquaintances have supported virtuosi's efforts to break away from established religious institutions and share their spiritual innovations with the public. As Western societies grew more democratic in the eighteenth and nineteenth centuries, access to new personal relationships expanded the social dimension of spiritual privilege and made the pursuit of virtuosity possible for more people.

Abilities to develop contacts with different groups, from elite patrons to working-class supporters, blend with other elements of spiritual privilege, particularly cultural resources. Someone's cultural capital includes literacy, education, and other significant markers of personal status and social achievement.[52]

Virtuosi activists are usually well educated and well spoken and these cultural resources allow them to communicate with potential upper-class patrons who can support their causes. However, because of their commitments to spiritual equality, they also accumulate the cultural tools to reach less-privileged people with limited opportunities to move beyond their local contexts. Virtuosi are able to share their spiritual privilege with others because they recognize a variety of different subcultures within their society and they can spread their ideas through the new technologies that have ranged from sixteenth broadsides to the twenty-first-century internet.

Luther and his students spoke and wrote in vernacular German when they reached out to ordinary people and convinced them of the possibilities for unmediated relationships with God. The Antislavery Movement leaders organized huge meetings that they advertised in newspapers and magazines that had not been widely available until the mid-nineteenth century.[53] In the mid-twentieth century, spiritual groups that were part of the Human Movement cultivated newspaper reporters and TV show hosts and also reached out to rock and roll luminaries in order to convince both the middle-aged middle class and their children that everyone had a spark of divinity deep within them that they could develop through spiritual practice and study.[54]

For six centuries, activist virtuosi's familiarity with diverse corners of their cultures has allowed them to reach new constituencies with their interpretations of holiness and spiritual purification. Burning Man began in the 1980s as a small solstice celebration on a beach near San Francisco. In the 1990s, the event moved to the remote Nevada desert, where its promoters used their cultural capital to share spiritual privilege with others by combining religious experience, innovative art, and hedonism of every kind. As the festival gained international recognition and many thousands of people annually flocked to the Nevada desert during the last week in August, the most economically privileged Silicon Valley elites grew into a visible constituency, and grassroots movements began to create small new festivals that reached new, less advantaged constituencies.[55]

Burning Man's twenty-first-century redefinition as an elite retreat illustrates how social and cultural capital meld together and also how it is almost impossible to tease out the separate effects of economic, social, and cultural resources on spiritual virtuosity. However, when considering spiritual virtuosi's lives, it is useful to distinguish among various aspects of privilege in order to better understand the ways that different combinations of spiritual affinities and economic, social, and cultural capital enable virtuosi to devote themselves to their spiritual priorities.

Hildegard von Bingen, for example, had substantial economic and social privilege, but she was almost blind to the rich cultural diversity that surrounded her cloistered

Photo 2.6 Catacomb of Veils built and destroyed at the 2016 Burning Man Festival.

life. In contrast, Corita Kent, who had relatively little economic privilege, developed her social and cultural capital through her art, and she accumulated spiritual privilege because of the artistic virtuosity that enabled her to become part of a wide range of social networks. Neither woman, however, would have become a virtuoso without the religious affinities that are at the heart of spiritual privilege.

The new religious individualism that began to unfold during the sixteenth century made it possible to become a spiritual virtuoso without entering a monastic community or becoming a solitary ascetic. Five centuries of subsequent virtuoso activism within and outside of established faiths have made it possible for almost everyone with spiritual affinities to go about their daily lives and still have access to enough spiritual privilege to enable them to select, combine, and revise their personal paths to sanctification.

The Spiritual Marketplace and Everyday Virtuosity

Some contemporary Americans may have relatively few material resources or education, but nevertheless display personal affinities for religious knowledge and experience as they explore paths to sanctification in places that can range from intimate home-based Christian churches to massive gatherings like Burning Man.

In the twenty-first century, religious pluralism fuels the diffusion of spiritual privilege and the growth of a vibrant global spiritual marketplace that includes congregational religions like Anglicans, who exemplify centuries-old religious traditions; established nondenominational churches like Joel Osteen's 40,000-member Lakewood mega church in Houston, Texas; and recent alternate faiths like Supreme Master Ching Hai's Quan Yin Method, an Asian-based new religious movement that combines environmental activism, vegan dietary principles, and meditation. Individuals seeking to develop their spiritual virtuosity may move from one faith to another or construct personal mosaics of religious practices and beliefs.[56] However, most contemporary seekers, much like the medieval ascetics, view their paths to holiness on earth as inevitably incomplete because each religious experience spurs their desires for greater spiritual understanding and more challenging practices.

Contemporary possibilities for sanctification rest on the privileges and also the burdens of religious choice. In developed societies, there is no single dominant church, but instead there are national and also global religious markets where different faiths compete to attract and hold adherents. Aspiring virtuosi must remain true to their personal spiritual priorities as well as institutionalized rules, and there are challenges of choice from among an overwhelming number of options.[57]

In the mid-twentieth century, the Human Potential Movement opened up new paths to spiritual virtuosity through contemplative and physical disciplines within a burgeoning religious marketplace. The ideal of spiritual virtuosity has become a general feature of contemporary culture in developed nations, although it is largely unmoored from its religious roots in the Reformation. However, that ideal is as real to those who seek sanctification through religious tinkering as it was to the sixteenth-century reformers who broke through the Catholic Church's religious monopoly.

While it wielded enormous religious, political, and economic power throughout Western Europe, the Church's control of access to the sacred was never absolute. After Constantine the Great's conversion to Christianity in the fourth century, ordinary people complied with their rulers' edicts and officially joined the Church *en masse*, but many of them continued their local pagan practices as well.[58] This foreshadowed possibilities of belonging to more than one religion or holding beliefs and engaging in practices from a number of different faith traditions.[59]

The Catholic Church formally monopolized access to sanctification and had the political power to silence and punish its critics. However, well before the Reformation, competing religious groups that ranged from small pagan networks to breakaway sects like the Cathars weakened the Church's authority and slowly and covertly added to an increasingly diverse spiritual marketplace.

This market analogy does not denigrate the importance of the sacred, but instead offers a framework to view the ways that both successful and failed virtuoso-led spiritual movements challenge religious dominance by quietly creating alternate opportunities for sanctification.[60] Those opportunities, however, were hidden and often suppressed until the Reformers rose up to dispute Roman Catholicism's ultimate authority. The Church's suppression of competing options created parallel religious markets that enabled people to pursue personal purification and holiness in different ways.

While the Church absolutely dominated legitimate possibilities for purification and holiness, people also engaged in other religious rituals and practices that were tolerated so long as they did not threaten Roman Catholicism's religious, economic, and political primacy. During the Reformation, activist virtuosi fueled a growing demand for a black market that directly threatened the Church because it attacked the core doctrines that only clergy could intercede between ordinary people and God and that the Church, not God, was responsible for sanctification. Already weakened by corruption, greed, and its lack of resonance with ordinary people, the Church could no longer monopolize the spiritual marketplace.

Since that time, paths to sanctification have become far more numerous. In the twenty-first century, there are possibilities for spiritual growth in almost everything. The material and spiritual now come together in churches, public squares, yoga studios, and cafes. In this context, only a small proportion of spiritual consumers will dedicate themselves to a single established faith or one alternate religious movement throughout their lives.[61] However, many more will strive to achieve some measure of purification and holiness by integrating spirituality into their work lives and personal relationships, often deepening their desires to create a better world for everyone and carrying the activists' mission to improve society in order to transform themselves.

Spiritual virtuosity is not just a set of abstract qualities. Activist virtuosi breathe life into religious movements for greater spiritual equality and wider paths to sanctification. Chapters on the Reformation, the Antislavery Movement, and the Human Potential Movement will explain how spiritual virtuosi have been central to enduring movements for religious and social change.

3 Spiritual Virtuosity and Collective Action

The virtuoso activism that has introduced both great and small social changes in the modern world first surfaced in the sixteenth century when Luther and his evangelical movement sparked the Protestant Reformation and forever altered religion in the West. A handful of significant virtuosi-led movements like the Reformation, as well as many more small ones, have built on Luther's innovations and progressively widened access to spiritual privilege and opportunities for sanctification.

Capable virtuosi with deep commitment to new spiritual possibilities for everyone are at the center of both major and minor activist movements. However, in order to implement their collective innovations, activist virtuosi must also be able to develop and communicate their messages to large numbers of people, forge supportive networks with one another, and come to terms with powerful opposition. Their relationships with each other and with representatives of established religious institutions change over time and so do virtuosi's abilities and desire to reach toward their own sanctification by redeeming religious and social injustices, although they must sacrifice some of their personal study and practice in order to work toward change.

Virtuosi's shifts from individual commitment to collective action reflect the intersections of personal insights, social relationships, and fundamental structural transformations in their societies. Activists often begin their spiritual journeys as ascetics and turn their backs on social and political concerns. Others start out as ethical virtuosi, ministering individually to powerless people's religious and material needs. However, at certain points, some ascetic and ethical virtuosi encounter pervasive religious and social inequities and feel that they must question and ultimately confront them in the larger world.

The virtuoso ethic moves beyond the limits of individual spirituality when activist virtuosi become aware of sins against humanity that they observe firsthand or learn about from trusted sources. When they can no longer reconcile their new awareness with their own private spirituality or charity, virtuosi come to view moral engagement as a personal religious responsibility. With new understandings, virtuosi begin to envision true service to the world as working toward spiritual and social equality, rather than simply praying for everyone or comforting and aiding disadvantaged people.

The full scope of the relationships between faith and altruism is not clearly understood yet, but all major spiritual traditions emphasize the importance of compassion and help to others.[1] Despite widespread assumptions that religious virtuosi want to help others and that they are naturally altruistic or good, however, there are ongoing debates about whether anyone, religious or not, has innate capacities to understand others' situations and offer aid to the materially or spiritually distressed.[2] Nevertheless, activist virtuosi feel that they must come to the aid of ordinary people, after gaining recent insights about widespread spiritual suffering and its causes ignite their altruistic impulses. Feminist Angelina Grimké wrote about her conversion to the Antislavery cause in her diary:

> My soul has measurably stood in the stead of the poor slave and my earnest prayers have been poured out that the Lord would permit me to be an Instrument of good. . . . Truly I often feel as if I were ready to go to prison and death on this cause of mercy, justice and love.[3]

Spiritually privileged people like Grimké have played an outsized role in the formation and transformation of religious institutions throughout modern history, because they can harness their own material advantages and religious affinities to reach beyond the institutions that had originally nurtured their virtuosity. In the wake of the Reformation, virtuosi have directly inspired and participated in six centuries of moral engagement that fused religion with battles for greater equality and social justice.

During the late eighteenth and the nineteenth centuries, activist virtuosi framed new religious understandings and communicated moral imperatives that shaped movements for cultural and political change. Their campaigns against slavery and oppression raised questions about politics and religion and that transformed Anglo-American spirituality.

Nineteenth-century spiritual virtuosi also developed the powerful mixture of spirituality and public engagement that fueled crusades for social justice and equality in the twentieth century. The American Civil Rights Movement, feminist movements, and peace movements all had their roots in the preceding two centuries of spiritual virtuosi's moral activism. In the twenty-first century, diverse personalized and politicized forms of spirituality, such as the Sunday Assembly, are legacies of the twentieth century's Human Potential Movement. They too can be traced back to the claims for authentic personhood and spiritual autonomy that unfolded in the sixteenth century and took flight in the nineteenth century.

Max Weber noted that on some occasions ascetic virtuosi passionately desired to bring their new spiritual insights to ordinary people and carry their commitments "out of monastic cells and into everyday life."[4] During the Reformation, they deserted their cloisters in order to implement their beliefs that possibilities for purification and holiness were available for everyone, not just small circles of other virtuosi with religious vocations.[5] They temporarily sacrificed their intensive study and personal devotions for the higher purpose of implementing fundamental religious and social changes that corresponded to their new understandings of sacred truths and religious virtue.

The European reformers imagined a virtuoso revolution that would replace religious hierarchies and create an empowered laity with an unmediated relationship to God and full access to the salvific Word. More than that, they wanted every Christian to adopt a virtuoso ethic in daily life in order to generate greater spiritual intensity that could move them closer to sanctification. For Protestants, "Every single mind was expected to become the battleground on which the eternal war of grace and sin was fought."[6]

For leaders of the Reformation, the subjective authority of steadfast faith and personal emotional experience replaced formal obedience to religious rules. This subjectivity meant that sixteenth-century virtuosi activists had the freedom to choose their spiritual compatriots and join them in study, debates, and devotions. They could also come together to spread the news about the one true path to sanctification that they had discovered.

In late-eighteenth- and nineteenth-century England and America, virtuosi introduced major religious innovations that reaffirmed and extended universal ethics of equality. Activist virtuosi beseeched established religious authorities to support their struggles to purge society of the collective sins of slavery and oppression. This new virtuoso spirituality rested on the belief that an individual could be transformed after undergoing symbolic death by acknowledging his own personal sins. At that point, there could be rebirth and new beginnings through conversion to sincere Christianity that radically altered her whole being.

During this time period, virtuosi activists' emphasis on sin moved from individualized concerns with purely personal estrangement from God to preoccupation with collective and especially with national sins. Above all, the centrality of slavery to the world economy and its importance in laying the foundations of Anglo-American prosperity became impossible for activist virtuosi to ignore.[7] They also addressed sexism, exploitation, and alcoholism in rapidly developing industrial and commercial cities.[8]

In the twentieth century, a new generation of spiritual virtuosi took the highly personal spirituality of Great Awakening Christianity even further by asserting that everyone could (and should) cultivate their own divinity in order to implement personal and social transformation. From the early 1960s through the early 1970s, spiritual virtuosi introduced myriad approaches to self-actualization, an enhanced capacity to experience transcendent moments or peak experiences that would allow individuals to recognize their connections to all humankind.[9] In contrast to earlier movements, its foundational doctrine did not focus on one true God, but instead imagined a divine spark within everyone that they could cultivate through diverse spiritual paths.

The Human Potential Movement embraced practices for spiritual and personal growth that could enable everyone to access a spark of internal divinity and contribute to the advancement of all humankind. Activist virtuosi in this movement promoted spiritual expansion that often merged several religious traditions with humanistic psychology, so that all Americans and ultimately everyone on earth could create more vital, spiritually meaningful lives.[10]

All three movements unfolded during historical periods when material prosperity supported spiritual innovation. Like other kinds of spiritual virtuosi, activists who join together and try to change the world in terms of their sacred priorities possess not only convictions and innate talents for religious transcendence, but also the spiritual privilege that enables them to devote time and resources to select, combine, and revise their personal religious knowledge and practice. This kind of privilege touches more people when there is economic expansion and cultural change that bring them into contact with one another.

Spiritual Virtuosity and Cultural Transformations

Activist virtuosity first flowered during the Reformation, when there was a profound break with traditional societies' religious priorities and social arrangements. The great world religions that contend with universal salvation and the soul's transcendence—Judaism, Christianity, Islam—originated in agrarian civilizations with segmental social stratification and a conspicuous split between rural and urban life. However, with economic growth and the acquisition of new territories, most of the small literate classes of aristocrats, priests, officials, and merchants began to reside in cities, while the countryside was still dominated by hereditary lords and populated by peasants and serfs.[11]

Most people still worshipped many gods and looked to magicians for their practical needs like fertility, bountiful harvests, or good health.[12] However, affluent individuals who no longer focused on their daily survival began to change their religious priorities. They started to consider if and how their souls would persist into an afterlife or some future existence. Max Weber archly described this transition:

A certain concern for one's own destiny after death generally arises when the most essential earthly needs have been met, and thus this concern is limited primarily to the circles of the elite and the wealthy classes.[13]

Sanctification, the cultivation and purification of the soul, became the growing focus of both the affluent and the religions that they supported. Over time, priestly classes created a ritual order that could sanctify their wealthier adherents and give less important people a modicum of spiritual solace. The institutionalized religions with priestly caste systems were highly stratified and deeply conservative like the societies where they flourished.

Only privileged people took part in a literate religious culture and cultivated their spirituality through devotions and studies. Scriptures and theological texts offered them a pathway to sanctification and prescribed ethical and ascetic practices that would move them along that path.[14] Theologian Paul Tillich observed of elite monasticism:

A double standard of morality grew out of the monastic attitude; there were higher counsels for those who are nearer to God, and then the rules which apply to everybody. The higher counsels for the monks, such as fasting, discipline, humility, celibacy, etc., made the monks ontologically higher than ordinary men.[15]

After the fall of the Western Roman Empire and the rise of Christianity, the rates of economic and cultural change were slow and there was little social mobility in medieval Europe. Aristocrats and bishops held power and the dominant religious doctrines affirmed their supremacy. Some sensitive, spiritually privileged souls found these social arrangements to be too sinful or too worldly, and they were able to join monastic institutions that allowed them to escape into mystic contemplation or ascetic self-denial. For most people, however, there was no retreat from social injustice and religious corruption.

During the Middle Ages, popular unrest challenged both the distribution of wealth and prevailing religious institutions. The two were inextricably linked because the Roman Catholic Church was the largest landholder in Europe, with an annual income that surpassed that of the wealthiest kings.[16] The Church's religious entrepreneurship was the dynamic force in the medieval economy that fostered greater and greater social inequalities.[17]

Between 1336 and 1525 there were at least sixty German peasant revolts that disputed the existing distribution of wealth and power. The aristocracy brutally suppressed them.[18] And while a few prophetic figures stimulated brief revivals that recast religion, almost all of those movements had limited success and, at best, gave rise to new sects and additional Catholic monastic orders. In these highly stratified societies, established religious and political culture proved to be remarkably durable and persistent.[19]

These settled arrangements began to change rather suddenly around 1500 C.E. The rise of capitalism and long-distance commerce profoundly unsettled Western Christendom's relatively stable economic and religious culture. With growing velocity, the social distances between the urban upper and middle classes narrowed, everyone's awareness of events beyond their immediate context expanded, and the surety and permanence of traditional society and its values became matters of contention. The world's moral horizons widened dramatically, and there was emerging recognition of the spiritual importance of every individual.[20]

As people moved to urban centers, it was difficult for them to ignore or submit to clerical, noble, and mercantile elites' monopolies of spiritual privilege. Their indifference toward the masses' material and spiritual welfare was almost impossible to overlook and it underscored the distance between Christian moral ideals and new social realities. Dedicated ascetic and ethical virtuosi, as well as some ordinary people, found it harder and harder to stomach the small circles of educated humanists, endowed priests and canons, and theologians that demarcated their spirituality and paths toward sanctification and ultimate salvation. They could see that the richest monasteries controlled vast land holdings and housed so many hundreds of dependents and servants that they resembled small cities.[21] Many young theologians and students believed that it was spiritually stifling to retreat into the traditional forms of religious virtuosity, and they welcomed new approaches to sanctification.

By the end of the sixteenth century, a distinctively activist religious culture arose, both within Protestantism and the Counter-Reformation's Roman Catholic Church. Over the next two hundred years, political and religious activists continued the reformers' moral advocacy and local social engagement.

Spiritual virtuosi grew more and more aware of capitalism's global reach and the spreading tendrils of empire during the eighteenth century. European movements for religious renewal and change became concerned with distant strangers and complicated social evils. Faith and politics united into a new form of social movement that demanded morally inspired action from ordinary people, not just rulers or clergy. From that time forward, the novel combination of intimate self-scrutiny and long-distance advocacy inspired virtuosi to become activists.[22]

The eighteenth century's new social awareness and call to activism in the nineteenth century can be traced back to the sixteenth-century virtuosi and townspeople, who began to doubt that priests and monks were really a morally superior class of beings. Luther and his followers made them aware that the worldly economics of a venal Church and its ecclesiastical intrusions into their everyday lives obstructed their personal paths to sanctification and spiritual authenticity.

During the ascendance of industrial capitalism and worldwide colonial empires, an American woman like Angelina Grimké might discover with horror that, despite her efforts to live a morally exemplary life, her family's fortune—and also her nation's—had been made by slavery. Three centuries later, in a globalized and multicultural world, someone steeped in a mélange of Eastern and Western spirituality could feel the need to confront hunger and food insecurity in her neighborhood and on the other side of the world as well.

The Power of Ideas

Virtuoso movements can only succeed if they attack stagnation and corruption within established religious institutions and their surrounding society and also provide solutions to those glaring problems. They tap into widespread dissatisfaction with established faiths that demand spiritual and material sacrifices and offer ordinary people few rewards other than distant possibilities for salvation. Moreover, institutionalized faiths usually provide unsatisfying explanations about the social inequalities that limit spiritual comfort to members of the privileged classes. Successful virtuosi-led movements advance new paths for sanctification on earth, possibilities for social equity and justice, and promises for some sort of salvation in an afterlife. Spiritual virtuosi's ideas and their own examples communicate the direct, emotionally appealing message: "When you truly live spiritual Truth, your life on earth will be better!"

Activist virtuosi revise and reinterpret their own religious relationships, widen paths to sanctification, and open up access to the spiritual privilege that they already enjoy. Significant virtuoso movements build on established spiritual traditions so that members do not have to completely reject their old faiths. Their religious innovations explicitly or implicitly represent improvements that are reinterpretations of familiar Western beliefs and practices rather than absolute breaks with the past.[23] The new ideas sustain continuity with both dominant religions and the societies that house them. New followers need not completely set aside their old beliefs and practices when they support a virtuoso movement, because they build on the cultural capital that they accumulated from their earlier religious activities.

Luther's successful movement attacked the corrupt Roman Catholic Church, its sale of indulgences to limit time in purgatory, and its insistence that people had to rely on clergy to mediate between them and God. However, he maintained that his innovations only made the Church more Christian because they called forth a full embrace of everyone who worshipped within it. In his pleas for a simple religion that returned everyone to God's embrace, Luther never denied the existence of God or His son. Even after they completely broke with the Church, Luther and his followers never repudiated its fundamental tenets, and they maintained that they had simply recovered the truth of the apostolic faith.

The Antislavery Movement's message reframed Luther's belief in God's Word and direct communication with Him in terms of emerging political dissent against blatant exploitation. The movement built on Christianity in its message that everyone could redeem their sins by directly confessing to God, being reborn in Christ, and confronting both personal and social sins. That emphasis on direct confession, symbolic rebirth, and the importance of equality also grounded all of the many virtuosi-led groups that came together under the umbrella of the Human Potential Movement. The Human Potential Movement, however, envisioned God as a spark of divinity that lay both within and outside of people. Creating a full connection between the sacred and secular self, the movement's diverse virtuosi embraced the same kinds of study, self-scrutiny, and dedication to personal and social change that Luther's followers had discovered during the sixteenth century and the fusion of the personal and the political that the Antislavery Movement created in the nineteenth century.

The often-overlooked humanist belief that religion and inquiry go together is fundamental to the Western virtuoso ethic that affirms the importance of direct inquiry of all kinds.[24] Luther left a legacy of scriptural approaches that united faith and reason and extended the emerging culture of inquiry into the sacred realm. The Reformation's innovations encouraged religious reflections that considered changing social conditions and charted new spiritual approaches that guided people's responses to them. Since the Reformation, the most successful virtuoso movements have developed new doctrines and practices that support liberating and effective social relations and direct connections with the sacred.[25] These ideas, not individual leaders, attract and sustain support for religious and social transformation.

Economic Expansion, Social Dislocation, and Spiritual Change

Even if spiritually privileged virtuosi share their compelling ideas with relentless dedication and display their own extraordinary religious talents, they can only create consequential religious and social changes during periods when social conditions disrupt old arrangements and at the same time facilitate religious innovation. Virtuosi come together to try to alter institutions at historical moments when they believe that they can and must implement radical change because pervasive social evils smother their personal desires for spiritual integrity and holiness on earth. When spiritual virtuosi engage with the larger world, they demonstrate that everyone can mobilize their own unique resources to work toward personal purity and sanctity and implement lasting changes.

Economic growth expands the range of possibilities for ordinary people to accumulate new kinds of spiritual privilege and also accelerates their support for virtuosi activism.[26] During periods of economic decline or slowdown, concentrated ownership of land and labor and general material deprivation, people rarely question institutionalized religions. Clerical elites' control of spiritual life is far greater because both virtuosi and ordinary people have few social and material resources to challenge them. However, institutionalized religious authority's power diminishes when there is growing access to new information, economic and cultural resources are more widely distributed, and old spiritual explanations no longer allow individuals to make sense of their daily lives.

If they rarely face daily deprivations or lifelong misery, people become interested in exploring diverse spiritual paths and new means for sanctification.[27] As pervasive fears for survival recede, otherworldly concerns and popular interest in spiritual growth and personal sanctification move beyond conventional religious organizations.[28]

Table 3.1 Structural conditions facilitating virtuoso movements

Conditions	Reformation	Antislavery Movement	Human Potential Movement
Economic growth	Long-distance trade, expanding commerce	Global commodity markets, industrialization	Globalizing economy, post-Fordism
Social change	Developing urbanization	Industrialization, middle-class expansion	Widespread economic security, public education, mass consumption
Political opportunity	Self-governing cities, rise of princely states	Democratization, elite divisions on slavery	Baby boomers come of age, social and political unrest
Communications technology	Printing press; pamphlets and books	Print media; newspapers and periodicals	Mass media: television and publishing
Religious change	Ecclesiastical venality, worldliness of Roman Church	Social complacency of established churches, religious conservatism	Mainline denominations decline, Vatican II, Eastern religions
Elite Support	Aristocrats and urban patricians	Wealthy patrons	Opinion leaders

Sustained economic expansion tends to serve as a religious "demand-shifter," an economists' term denoting structural developments that alter collective desires and expectations. Across the centuries, prosperity has repeatedly increased the demand for meaningful spiritual options and fueled religious innovation, particularly within the urban upper and middle classes. When the Reformation began in the early sixteenth century, Central European towns and cities grew dramatically as commerce expanded. Similarly, in the nineteenth century, America's continental expansion, industrialization, and thriving trade with Europe powered dynamic population centers like New York City and New Orleans.

Expanding towns and cities attract the upwardly mobile, but they also house visible concentrations of poor and destitute groups. Impoverished peasants and disfigured beggars crowded into developing German commercial cities, along with newly affluent burghers. In nineteenth-century America, the contrasts between prosperity and poverty were particularly marked because of slavery and its far-reaching consequences. And after the Second World War, when the United States experienced unprecedented affluence and three decades of global economic dominance, migration to the West and East coasts made New York and Los Angeles into global megacities that included both the newly affluent and the very poor.

During each of these three periods of economic growth, the spread of material security generated growing interest in new religious priorities and support for spiritual innovations.[29] People often leave their old religions as they make life-changing transitions because of their social mobility and physical dislocation.[30] In the three cases that we consider, virtuoso-led religious and social movements became rallying points for people swept up by profound cultural shifts. Activist virtuosi developed

Photo 3.1 Bustling trade in London.

frameworks that helped laypeople reorganize their religious priorities, come to terms with dramatic social changes, and raise their voices for change.

In the sixteenth century, both virtuosi and ordinary people began to question the powerful Roman Catholic Church's power over their short lives on earth and their possibilities for eternal salvation. The reformers viewed the Church as a decaying institution that was controlled by venal, worldly clergy who no longer served God and needlessly complicated the path to holiness.

Virtuosi in the Antislavery Movement built on the evangelicals' innovations when they turned away from established churches where clergy were educated at elite seminaries, separated from ordinary people, and purged of their desires to acknowledge and confront social injustices.[31] Nineteenth-century activist virtuosi saw the Protestant establishment as complacent in the face of evil and more concerned with its own organized benevolence than with spiritual rebirth.

In the case of the Human Potential Movement, disdain for postwar materialism and the spiritual impoverishment of "one dimensional man" created a demand for renewal of the human spirit outside of established Western faiths. Moreover, most liberal Protestant denominations appeared to be stagnant and timid in comparison with vital political movements for peace and social equality that began to emerge in the 1960s.[32]

Virtuosi activism thrives when well-established religions are declining or complacent about social ills. At those moments, activist virtuosi and laypeople tend to seek more authentic, meaningful religious explanations and experiences than their current faiths offer them. Virtuosi are almost always the loudest critics of the erosion of selfless spirituality and also the most visible advocates for revitalized religious life.[33] Their pleas for regeneration can attract wide support when economic expansion and urbanization create pervasive desires for new ways of understanding and approaching the sacred in a changing secular world.

Communication, Technology, and the Diffusion of Spiritual Privilege

Since the sixteenth century, large-scale virtuoso activism has never succeeded without broad avenues of communication that generate public awareness and prompt varied audiences to consider new spiritual possibilities. The proliferation of new kinds of media and their expanded accessibility is consistently associated with virtuoso activism and the diffusion of spiritual privilege across the three movements that are central to this book. Greater literacy and familiarity with newly introduced media ranging from printed texts to digital communications have repeatedly spread spiritual advances and new possibilities for sanctification.[34] While literacy and the development of different types of media are by no means sufficient conditions for the success of virtuosi-led social movements, they are nevertheless necessary, because they contribute to wider awareness of spiritual innovations and they facilitate the formation of networks of activist virtuosi.

Martin Luther. Nach einem Holzschnitte von Lukas Cranach.

Photo 3.2 Luther by Lucas Cranach the Elder: A Widely Circulated Image.

The invention of movable type and the printing press made Luther and his move-ment's success possible and also supported nascent print capitalism throughout Europe. Luther's extraordinary output of inexpensive books, broadsides, and short pamphlets that were written in vernacular German reached far beyond Wittenberg.[35] They even interested people who could not read, because their compelling illustra-tions were so easily understood.

In the late eighteenth and nineteenth centuries, access to print expanded more quickly than ever before, because industrialization led to the development of more inexpensive printing presses and cheap newsprint and paper. National newspapers and the new medium of serialized periodicals featuring dramatic and sentimental slave narratives reached almost everyone in the United States because of improved postal and telegraphic communication.[36] Mushrooming news outlets spotlighted moral advocacy movements of all kinds, and abolitionists, in particular, eagerly exploited recently available media to notify people of coming events and to persuade them to help overcome the national sin of slavery through jeremiads and gripping accounts of the horrors of enslavement.

As railroads, canals, and steamboats knit the country's rapidly growing population together, communication of all kinds improved markedly. It became relatively easy for people to learn about national and international news, as well as to read sermons and pamphlets written by clergymen, moralists, and journalists. Concerned with their own salvations, pious Americans grew increasingly troubled with the godlessness of their society and their own enmeshment in a complex tangle of relationships that imperiled their souls.[37]

In the mid-twentieth century, radio, films, and television became as important to the Human Potential Movement as inexpensive print had been to the Reformation and the Antislavery Movement. Nearly universal literacy and widened access to college and university education increased the audience for paperback books, popular magazines, and local and national newspapers. Moreover, the deregulation of religious broadcasting and the elimination of culturally biased immigration quotas diminished some of the historic advantages of liberal Mainline Protestant faiths and created opportunities for religious and spiritual innovators to bring new ideas to new audiences.[38]

In the early 1960s, publishers recognized the growing demand for accessible ideas and general interest magazines and they appealed to millions of new readers with simple stories about complex cultural changes that were accompanied by many photographs.[39] George Leonard, a senior editor of mass circulation *Look Magazine*, used his extensive professional networks to craft a public relations campaign for the Human Potential Movement that engaged every kind of new mass media. Leonard popularized the term "human potential," in a special 1966 *Look* issue that described California as America's future, and he made sure that the movement was featured everywhere from the highbrow *New Yorker Magazine* to television's immensely popular *Tonight Show Starring Johnny Carson*.[40]

The contemporary internet offers even more possibilities for virtuosi to reach one another and generate popular interest in their approaches to sanctification. Like earlier media revolutions that fueled virtuoso movements, digitization further erodes the wall between conventional religions and popular spirituality and provides new ways for virtuoso-led movements to develop and spread. From the printing press onward, technological innovations have allowed spiritual virtuosi to spread their messages, attack stagnant religious and political institutions, and build their movements for religious and social change.

Patrons, Mentors, and Protectors

Successful activist virtuosity also thrives on dynamic social interactions and relationships with potential patrons, mentors, and protectors. Virtuoso activists are creative and strategic actors who reshape situations to their advantage and persuade others of the urgency and necessity of their mission. When committed virtuosi become activists, they can usher in moments of extraordinary religious and social impact that far exceed their original goals.

Activist challenges to incumbent elites are much more likely to succeed in settings that might accept religious challenges rather than quickly suppress them.[41] It is almost axiomatic to say that, unless there is some access to material resources and political opportunities, virtuoso activism will die quickly or have no lasting cultural influence.

To a great extent, the influence and continuing success of activist virtuosi depend on whether they can convince elite actors that their movement's goals are worthy and advantageous to their interests. Elite patronage tends to be particularly consequential for movements for religious change, because patrons impart resources and legitimacy to upstart causes that face substantial hurdles in challenging social traditions and established religious authorities. Patronage need not take the form of direct political and financial assistance. Sometimes it is enough that influential allies shield virtuosi from the most withering attacks, make them aware of new opportunities, or associate the movement with their own social prestige.

In order to cultivate valuable allies who will support their missions to remake institutions and spread new kinds of spirituality to everyone, activist virtuosi must put forth persuasive ideas and also possess social and cultural capital that allow them to communicate with elites. Activist virtuosi during the Reformation deliberately reached out to the princes of a number of small states, including Saxony and Hessia. The princes and the patrician rulers of cities were important patrons and advocates for their cause.

Elite patrons supported the English Antislavery Movement and parliamentary allies like William Wilberforce campaigned for the 1807 law that banned the international slave trade. Lacking mass support in America and facing substantial political hostility, abolitionists relied on the support of wealthy patrons such as Gerrit Smith and the Tappan brothers to fund activist newspapers and antislavery campaigns. Liberal politicians, wealthy donors like Laurance Rockefeller, and influential writers supported the Human Potential Movement through educational grants, massive donations, and coverage in magazines and newspapers.[42]

Even with substantial patronage and wide support, activist virtuosi's personal and political struggles are spiritually trying. Spiritual mentors play vital roles in nurturing virtuoso leadership and sustaining activism. As a young monk and aspiring theologian, Luther relied on his prior, Johann von Staupitz, to overcome his own crippling self-doubts and intermittent spiritual alienation. Theodore Weld was mentored by famed evangelist Charles Grandison Finney and, in turn, mentored the Grimké sisters and a host of other young preachers and antislavery activists. Human Potential leaders relied on a number of mentors like academic psychologist Abraham Maslow to advise them and support their efforts to attain cultural legitimacy.

Virtuoso activists openly commit themselves to heterodox thinking and radical stances. When they endorse equality in established religions and secular institutions, they risk their reputations, their fortunes, and sometimes their lives. Without protectors, many virtuoso-led movements would have faltered or failed entirely. Sometimes, protection involves literal shielding of virtuosi from the hands of those who would silence them. Frederick of Saxony refused to turn Luther over to the papacy, saving him from the flames that had consumed previous religious dissidents. Beyond the attacks on their reputations and characters, American abolitionists frequently faced lynch mobs, bodily injury, and arrest. They were assailed in Congress and censored. Wealthy benefactors offered protection and legal assistance, as did elite sympathizers like former president John Quincy Adams.

During the 1960s and 1970s, the FBI kept a close watch on major figures in the Human Potential Movement who opposed the war in Vietnam or were active in promoting psychedelic drugs as means to self-actualization and sanctification. Daniel Ellsberg, an American activist and former military analyst, was not well known until his ethic of activist virtuosity compelled him to publicly release the Pentagon Papers, a detailed study of government intervention in Vietnam. Famous attorneys who sympathized with the movement successfully defended him against theft and conspiracy charges that could have resulted in a maximum sentence of 115 years.

Intellectual Communities and Virtuoso Movements

Virtuoso-led movements for religious and social change generate new ideas that inspire people to confront injustices and challenge stagnant conventions and corrupt institutions. Innovative frameworks necessarily involve a diagnosis of ills and prescriptions for their remedy. In order for their movements to succeed, spiritual virtuosi must develop fresh conceptions of problems, inspire activists to address them, and put forth their image of a reformed world. Depending on their primary spiritual focus, various kinds of intellectuals—theologians, writers, philosophers, and theoreticians— play significant roles in crafting rationales for change and envisioning new possibilities.

"Intellectuals" can be found everywhere in society, and the term refers to people who enthusiastically engage in rational inquiry, study, debate, and understanding. They are not necessarily highly educated or trained for specific vocations. Because so many different kinds of people are interested in understanding and possibly changing their societies, there are always far more intellectuals that define ills and suggest solutions than there are virtuosi who lead significant social and religious movements that spread new beliefs and implement change.

Over the centuries, many groups of virtuosi have critiqued the status quo and offered up innovations, but very few have inspired movements that resonate across social classes and result in lasting transformations. Successful virtuoso movements rarely develop within formal organizations, but instead, they tend to emerge informally because of virtuosi's strong ties with one another and with their spiritual mentors. Over time, these relationships turn into pivotal communities that develop a sense of collective identity and common purpose that engenders a social movement.

The activist core of movements is usually composed of individuals who share a strong subjective sense of group identity. Bonds with one another and collective ties with their movement reinforce their view of themselves as comrades and catalysts for change. [43] Across the three cases, innovative ideas unfolded within intellectually and spiritually vital communities before virtuosi actually became engaged in bringing their newly hatched ideas to wider audiences.

Spiritual virtuosi become activists after they develop doctrines that redefine their personal religious experiences and understandings as collective resources that they are morally obliged to share with everyone. In order to spark dramatic changes, they believe that they must carry their radical understandings beyond monasteries, seminaries, universities, and institutes. They long to operate temporarily in far broader social arenas, where they can spread their challenges to prevailing ideas and institutions and mobilize popular support for their ideals.[44]

Both formal and informal centers of theological and spiritual innovation are vital to the genesis of movements for social and cultural change, and they can be described as pivotal communities.[45] Pivotal communities are sheltered, often loosely organized spaces where intellectuals congregate, build social ties with one another, and talk (and talk and talk). These special places begin as bastions of privilege that are removed from the pressures of everyday life and free from overt political control. Such relatively protected settings can sometimes become crucibles for ideological innovations that grow into social movements, because they temporarily shelter spiritually privileged virtuosi and provide spaces for them to explore various theological and practical innovations.[46]

Sixteenth-century universities, nineteenth-century seminaries, and twentieth-century spiritual centers all housed seminars, retreats, and scholarly disputations. Most of the time, the conversations and debates remained purely academic or only of esoteric interest to the privileged few that took part in them. But occasionally, a critical mass of heterodox thinkers came to dominate these rarefied settings. When a community of questioning intellectuals begins to gain a reputation for exciting ideas and radical innovations, they attract an expanding circle of interested intellectuals that includes nonconformists and radical political thinkers along with spiritual virtuosi. When most members of the group commit themselves to questioning established institutions and orthodox thought, a pivotal community emerges.

Participants engage in nearly continuous debates and discussions about prevailing ideas and institutions and formulate their visions for change and the ways to achieve it. At their peaks, these communities are exhilarating places, and the rewards of breaking new ground attract even more participants along with long-distance interest. Community members develop bonds with each other through their shared intellectual excitement and also through expanding social ties and the collective emotions that generate intense commitment and a sense of immediacy about their projects. In the throes of a continuous seminar experience, emotional energy builds and spiritual virtuosi push each other to new frontiers of intellectual exploration and creativity. The sense of being present for a conceptual and spiritual revolution that transforms the self and will change the world is an outstanding feature of the experience of students at Luther's Wittenberg in the 1510s and 1520s, of young clergymen at Lane Seminary and Oberlin College in the 1830s, and of the spiritual seekers gathered at the Esalen Institute in the 1960s.

Through their involvement in pivotal communities, activist virtuosi learn about and help develop innovations and build ties to one another and to influential cultural

Photo 3.3 A sixties encounter group at Esalen.

figures. However, being part of a critical community means far more than exposure to the latest ideas or accessing new social networks. The intense collective emotions and relationships that emerge often generate life-altering experiences that equip virtuosi for their coming spiritual battles

Activist virtuosi enter the world beyond their communities because they view themselves as instruments for some Higher Power. They hear the call to abandon their bastions of spiritual privilege and share new paths to salvation with ordinary people. When they occupy crosscutting social locations, activists can close the gaps that isolate the most spiritually privileged individuals from the rest of the world.

Social Networks and Bridging Activism

Virtuoso activists in significant movements play critical roles as bridging actors who facilitate the flow of innovations from their intellectual communities into the larger religious and political arenas where they struggle for change. They are bridging actors that link intellectual hothouses to popular social movements that have wide appeal.[47]

Activist virtuosi's voices are very likely to be heard beyond their privileged circles because of their apparent holiness and purity as well as their personal commitment to spiritual goals and to broad social movements. Requests to share spiritual privilege and extend human rights to everyone are especially appealing when they come from privileged virtuosi who are willing to set aside some of their own advantages.

Their relationships with ordinary supporters allow successful activist virtuosi to communicate with new audiences and mobilize people to support and spread their beliefs. The activists that occupy crosscutting social locations and develop personal networks that include critical communities of intellectuals, elites, and the middle and working classes can often close the structural gaps that isolate individuals with great spiritual privilege from others.

The spiritual privilege that includes social and cultural capital enables some virtuosi to reach out to elite patrons and opinion leaders and also capture the interest of popular audiences. They bridge social divides and help make it possible for knowledge and opportunities to flow across those gaps. Not merely passive conduits of information, successful activist virtuosi model new kinds of religious engagement and personally demonstrate the possibilities that stem from their spiritual innovations. At the beginning of US Civil Rights Movement in the 1960s, for example, bridging activists from black churches worked across social networks and were able to connect African American communities to white political and religious advocates. They drew upon the resources of the historically black colleges, where they benefited from mentorship and instruction and started the national movement against segregation.[48]

Successful brokers never confine their outreach to like-minded individuals. Instead, they cultivate relationships with people that have varied priorities and different beliefs and values. Broad outreach not only provides virtuosi with valuable feedback and insights into the challenges that they may face but also allows them to better understand both their supporters and their opponents.[49] Diverse network ties also allow virtuoso activists to exercise social influence to convert new supporters to their cause and sometimes recruit other activists as well. Antislavery activists brokered alliances between elite moralists and wealthy donors at the helm of national and local benevolent associations and evangelical clergy outside of well-established faiths. They used their social ties to various church organizations and benevolent associations to connect the spiritual breakthroughs that they were making to the popular religiosity of their times.[50]

Religious innovations that are limited to exclusivist sects and closed, densely knit social networks never attract enough adherents to gain political influence or remake their cultural landscape.[51] Rodney Stark's exploration of the rise of Christianity in the Greco-Roman world illuminates how virtuosi in the early church deliberately avoided self-defeating elitism and exclusivity. They reached beyond their immediate circles to provide charitable assistance to outsiders and to marry across religious lines and convert new spouses. The early Christians were able to influence their pagan neighbors and rapidly build their movement because their ideals and their practical strategies opened them to support from many sides.[52]

Despite their diversity and the differences across time and place, intellectual spiritual virtuosi shaped all three of the movements considered in the following chapters. These virtuosi not only developed new beliefs but also exemplified their ideals and deliberately looked past the erudite groups where they had formulated their spiritual innovations. For example, activist virtuosi in the Antislavery Movement stretched far beyond the worlds of established Protestant seminaries, benevolent societies, and local civic associations to encourage new kinds of popular religiosity. They broke through the established churches' exclusion of "unlettered" clergy untrained by seminaries.[53] Activist virtuosi recruited, supported, and sustained personal commitment to their cause through the new spiritual techniques of Great Awakening Christianity: lay preaching, church revivals, camp meetings, and public pledges of abstention from personal and national sins. The result was a movement that could bring the new theology of spiritual equality and social justice to the thriving cities and to the frontier.

Virtuosity and Charisma: Together and Apart

At its best, virtuoso leadership is so powerful that it is tempting to view it as intrinsically charismatic. "Charisma" is a Greek word, which means a divine gift of grace that is bestowed on a few extraordinary individuals. Charismatic leaders are emotionally appealing, vital, and ostensibly superhuman.[54] Common descriptions of charismatic leaders in religious movements generally focus on their extraordinary personal attributes and their appeal to their followers' emotions.[55]

Max Weber believed that charismatic leaders, not activist virtuosi, were the world's great revolutionary forces, because they mobilized people to confront and change established moral and political orders.[56] He saw charisma as the single most revolutionary force in world history and asserted, "Reason works from *without* by altering the situation of life. . . . Charisma, on the other hand, may effect a submissive or *internal* reorientation [of followers]."[57] Charismatic leaders define their movements and sustain their supporters' enthusiasm until they no longer produce apparent miracles, become emotionally stagnant, or are successfully suppressed by internal rivals or external opposition.[58]

Weber's lasting influence on popular perceptions and scholarship about religion and society has made personal charisma central to discussions of leadership in movements for social change. He associated charismatic leaders with collective action and believed that charismatic leaders were essential for truly creative social changes.

Despite some discussions of prophetic and ethical virtuosi struggling to make the world better by example or exhortation, Weber usually confined his interest in spiritual virtuosity to ascetic virtuosi whose mastery of specific techniques of study and practice could lead to sanctification. Because he focused on monastics, Weber understood religious virtuosity as an essentially conservative force that was embedded in established religious traditions. However, as Martin Luther King's leadership illustrates, spiritual virtuosity and charisma can be complementary. King's inner circle included activist virtuosi like Bernard Lee, Wyatt Tee Walker, and CT Vivian, who continued to preach, teach, and work for social justice for many decades after King's assassination.[59]

Antislavery virtuosi and religious activists in other movements could become so deeply engaged in spearheading popular religious and social transformation that they are forced to spend much of their time in organizational development and practical affairs that diminish their emotional energies and limit their time for their spiritual practice. Quotidian obligations can easily submerge the sacred priorities that first drove them to spiritual virtuosity. Moreover, if either their sense of responsibility for the movement's success or their growing personal ambition become their primary motivations, virtuosi may cast aside their principles and manipulate or overpower those who disagree with them or stand in the way of their goals. In order to become charismatic leaders, virtuosi may have to set aside their spiritual practice.

Spiritual virtuosi become charismatic heroes because of their innate qualities, the pressing needs of people seeking their guidance, and their importance to the continued success of their movement. However, they may grow capricious and self-serving if they come to believe in their own divinity and have absolute power over their followers.[60] In rare instances, however, the transition from virtuoso activism to charismatic leadership seems to be inevitable and invaluable, as it was for Martin Luther King.

The activist virtuosity that compelled King to take on the world as his responsibility added to his charismatic appeal. He fused his activism with the Black Church's prophetic traditions in the faith that true social change must and will grow through each person's inevitable inner transformation.[61] However, while spiritual principles grounded King's political priorities, he had to give up his own intensive study and prayer in order to galvanize movements for full social and spiritual equality. At the urging of his mentors and peers, he harnessed his extraordinary abilities and became a towering charismatic leader.

As a charismatic leader and an activist virtuoso, King had both religious and political goals. He inspired people spiritually and also worked ceaselessly to encourage them to act for the social justice that he was certain was God's plan. One member of his inner circle, Congressman John Lewis, a clergyman, lifelong civil rights activist, and an influential legislator, was a high school sophomore in 1955 when he first heard King's voice on the radio. Lewis described the electrifying combination of charisma and virtuosity that touched him:

> I was on fire with the words I was hearing. I felt that this man—his name was Martin Luther King Jr.—was speaking directly to me. This young preacher was giving voice to everything I'd been feeling and fighting to figure out for years.[62]

Yet leaders rarely blend spiritual virtuosity and charisma successfully, because charismatic figures often alter their spiritual priorities or make capricious decisions that irreparably damage their movement's earlier achievements. A number of brilliant and spiritually powerful charismatic leaders with personal agendas and little self-discipline strayed from their religious responsibilities and destroyed their movements with remarkable alacrity because they and their followers had come to identify themselves as essential to true spiritual change.

Among the most destructive and disheartening of these self-serving charismatics was Sabbati Zevi. Zevi, a seventeenth-century Turkish-Jewish virtuoso, mobilized Diaspora Jews in the Mediterranean and Eastern Europe after a widely respected rabbi proclaimed him to be the new messiah in 1665. They were looking for a savior, because hundreds of thousands had endured recent dislocation and persecution and were desperate for restoration of some stability in their lives, supernatural protection, and possibilities for sanctification.[63]

As news of this savior spread from Turkey to Morocco and then into Germany, Ukraine, and Russia, Jews engaged in extreme fasting, lavish alms giving, and constant prayer in preparation for the coming age of full redemption. However, in the middle of 1666, Zvi publicly renounced his religion and abandoned his followers. The Turkish Sultan had captured him and forced him choose between death and conversion to Islam. He chose the turban and a luxurious life as the Sultan's doorkeeper.

Photo 3.4 Sabbatai Zevi.

The collapse of charismatic movements can powerfully reinstate institutions that support spiritual privilege. Soon after Zevi denounced his faith, Jewish leaders and clergy throughout Diaspora communities applied the 613 Jewish laws (*mitzvoth*) more rigidly and further restricted ordinary men's access to clerical training and study. The rabbinical hierarchy and its wealthy supporters separated Jews in Europe and North Africa from access to sanctification. That changed in the mid-eighteenth century because of the explosive growth of the virtuosi-led revitalization movement that was the foundation of contemporary Hasidism.[64] The movement's founder, the Baal Shem Tov (Master of the Good Name), was an itinerant healer and a prophetic virtuoso who believed that every action might hold spiritual significance and that the world could only be redeemed if each person's soul were saved. His movement developed spontaneously as he moved through villages to bless, comfort, and heal ordinary people.[65]

The Bal Shem Tov was a reluctant virtuoso leader, while Sabbatai Sevi deliberately formed his movement around his charismatic personal identity. His messianic movement rose and fell with him, while the Bal Shem Tov cared little for personal glory or power. The Bal Shem Tov and the virtuosi who followed him from one village to another spread a message of personal redemption through new spiritual practices that could free Jews from spiritual oppression, he never directly criticized the Eastern European rabbinical hierarchy or ruthless, pervasive Anti-Semitism.

Successful virtuosi-led movements galvanize people when both the messengers and their messages allow them to make sense of their collective discontent and offer new possibilities for equality and liberation. Even when activist virtuosi believe that they must assume charismatic leadership, they remain determined to widen the circle of spiritual privilege and empower ordinary people.

Faith in Action

Enmeshed in direct and indirect long-distance relationships, contemporary virtuosi often find themselves unable to experience a lasting sense of spiritual repose through traditional religious practices. Unable to retreat from the world, some people regard political engagement as both a moral duty and a spiritual necessity. Organized into communities that support and sustain virtuoso activism, they are at the heart of modern social movements.

In three very different cultural moments that range from the sixteenth to the twentieth centuries, individual commitment and collective action became inseparable because activist virtuosi joined with each other in order to spearhead social movements. Social movements can be defined as collective, sustained, and counter-institutional challenges. They can address specific authorities and power holders as well as dominant cultural views and practices.[66] However, while social movements can grow out of religious organizations and be religiously inspired, they are not identical to groups that only dispute sectarian questions within established religions. Virtuosi-led social movements confront both religious institutions and the world outside their boundaries.

Looking at spiritual virtuosi and their centrality to three significant movements for spiritual and social change that emerged in very different contexts adds another dimension to understanding the personal urgency that leads to social transformation. One of the defining aspects of modern and contemporary social movements is "interlacing of a sense of intimate responsibility and attention to far-flung social problems."[67] The next chapters illustrate how this interdependence originated in the profound spiritual innovations that began in the sixteenth century. They are driven by the activist spiritual ethic that links the personal to the social, collapsing the binary distinctions of private and public interests. "The personal is political" continues to be a formidable statement because it characterizes the activist spirituality that is often at the heart of contemporary social advocacy and defines the full meaning of individuals' humanity.

Material interests and social identities are by no means distinct, competing bases of contemporary social movements. Scholars explain the "new" social movements that have emerged since the 1960s in terms of the ways that the growth and spread of prosperity in postindustrial societies engendered new idealism.[68] However, the spreading affluence in service economies and the decline of Western industrial capitalism cannot explain these movements' lasting influence or the prominence of the individualistic values that inspired them. Instead, those movements should be viewed in terms of much longer trajectory that begins with the religious innovations that became driving forces for social change at the same time that commercial and industrial capitalism began to spread during the sixteenth century.

Since the early sixteenth century, the personal and political have grown closer and closer together because individual spirituality has been linked to social action against established religious and political authorities. Contemporary movements for social transformation share much in common with the earlier moral activism that grew in the nineteenth and twentieth centuries. Spiritual virtuosity is clearly present today, even if many virtuosi activists no longer claim membership in or inspiration from any established faith.[69]

Each of the three movements that we describe offered compelling information that inspired spiritual virtuosi to abandon their purely personal religious paths and minor disagreements. They united (if only temporarily) and engage with the larger society in order to implement their beliefs and democratize access to spiritual resources and new possibilities for sanctification.

In the three movements, activist virtuosi faced opposition from established religious organizations, orthodox theologians, and hostile princes, and each generated a countermovement, the most famous of which was the Counter-Reformation. Antislavery activists encountered family members' disapproval, public disdain from editors and journalists and, in the streets, hostile mobs. Although Human Potential Movement virtuosi did not contend with inquisitors or angry mobs, they had to overcome politicians and conservative clergy's attempts to ridicule and marginalize them. Because the Human Potential Movement challenged established religious culture and mainstream lifestyles, it almost immediately generated a countermovement that brought together conservative Christians and politicians and that has fed the enduring vitriol of subsequent "Culture Wars."[70]

Spiritually charged activism has continued to inform the Western world's reactions to great moral challenges. The ongoing Civil Rights Movement in the United States that began in the twentieth century is unthinkable without a virtuoso religiosity that united older strands of American moral activism, African American religious traditions, and Gandhian nonviolence.[71] And the Human Potential Movement's virtuoso spirituality brought together techniques for self-actualization and larger concerns about racism, sexism, and environmental devastation and technocracy. In the twenty-first century, many quests for personal purification have generated intense concerns about health and nutrition, demands for diversity, suspicion of authority, technology, and scientific expertise, and a reverence for nature.

The Reformation, the Antislavery Movement, and the American Human Potential Movement all had profound, enduring impact that reached far beyond national borders, because virtuosi activists joined together to implement religious change during periods when structural shifts and technological innovations expedited their efforts. While the three movements were dissimilar in their means and specific goals, they resemble one another in terms of a *single* important internal dimension that shaped their success: activist spiritual virtuosi's centrality to their success.

When Martin Luther nailed his *Ninety-Five Theses* to the door of the Castle Church at Wittenberg in 1517, he started an unfinished revolution in Western religion and culture. That revolution has transformed the ways that individuals develop their relationships to a Higher Power and pursue religious virtuosity without abandoning their personal relationships, material goals, and political commitments. Luther's own spiritual virtuosity was the foundation for three significant religious shifts and the millions of lives that they have touched over the centuries.

4 Luther and the Virtuoso Ethic

On July 17, 1505, a brilliant 21-year-old law student entered the friary of the Augustinian Hermits in the German university town of Erfurt. Those closest to him were dismayed, none more so than his father, a prosperous burgher of peasant stock who had invested a great deal in his once-promising son. At his going-away party, the young man told his family and friends, "You see me today and never again."[1]

Martin Luther and his legacy cannot be understood without reference to the role that spiritual virtuosity played in his life.[2] As a young man, Luther became a monk *par excellence*, drawing upon the full range of late medieval spiritual techniques: fasting, prayer, meditation, confession, penance and intense philosophical and scriptural study. And yet the fifteen years that Luther spent as a monk left him spiritually starved and emotionally desolate because piety cloaked what felt like the false assurance of salvation.

Luther's personal struggles brought about a revolutionary new theology that changed the ways that ordinary people understood the world. His breakthrough made him a persuasive and tireless opponent of the Roman Catholic Church. While his sixteenth-century obsessions with sin and justification are almost incomprehensible today, Luther's troubled search for existential meaning and personal redemption have a timeless resonance. At the heart of his revitalized religion lies a virtuoso ethic that insists on everyone's right to seek spiritual freedom that is unbound by external constraints and human institutions.

It is somewhat ironic that a former friar inspired the successful movement for spiritual equality that shook the Catholic world. When Luther turned against Rome, he did so as a spiritual virtuoso who had come to renounce the institutionalization of virtuosity. A professor of theology, he overturned spiritual privilege by affirming religious simplicity and recasting virtuosity as an essential internal transformation that could be available to everyone. An ordained priest, Luther articulated the world-shattering idea that redemption was only possible through personal faith and he called for a "priesthood of all believers" that overturned the clergy's position as a special caste.[3] His vision for true religiosity was centered on the recovery of the Gospel and predicated on the virtuoso ethic that everyone *could* and *should* work toward sanctification by cultivating a personal faith in divine grace.

The religious virtuosi responsive to Luther's call saw themselves as revitalizing Christianity and restoring an authentic popular spirituality rather than developing something new. Having worked ceaselessly toward their own spiritual redemption, clergymen, professors, and theology students began to turn outward to redeem church and society.[4]

Photo 4.1 Young Luther.

They understood that Luther's theology represented a direct assault on the ecclesiastical and academic prerogatives at the heart of the Roman Church's monopoly on salvation. Their principal weapon was placing the salvific Word in the hands and mouths of ordinary people in cities and towns. Viewing themselves as servants of the Gospel, these activist virtuosi sought to enshrine spiritual freedom as a natural human right.[5]

Economic Change and Social Upheaval

In 1483, the year that Luther was born, political, social, and economic changes had profoundly challenged medieval Christianity's fundamental values and teachings. Luther came of age in central Germany, part of the Holy Roman Empire that sprawled across the middle of Europe from northern Italy to the shores of the Baltic and North Sea. It was a loose confederation whose territories included nascent states ruled by dukes and prince-electors, ecclesiastical realms controlled by bishops, petty aristocratic domains, free cities, autonomous cantons, and the direct holdings of the imperial dynasty.

Political order was based on the local sovereignty of territorial rulers nominally united under the imperial crown, but real control lay within the territorial principalities and leading cities. The crown was elected, with a handful of the largest principalities, bishops, and imperial cities having the right to select an emperor's successor and meet with him in annual council or imperial diet (*Reichstag*). In practice, the emperor's authority was limited outside his own finite domains and the princes and free cities continually frustrated all efforts to centralize power. Although the empire proved durable and some of its institutions worked tolerably well, the general failure of imperial reform meant that Germany did not follow France, Spain, and England in centralizing power. Even as the empire weakened, new powers, above all the global Spanish Empire, were also making themselves felt in politics, because New World silver fueled Europe's booming economy and funded its endless wars.[6]

A century of economic growth had enhanced European trade, enlivened its markets, and swelled its cities. Like nineteenth-century America, sixteenth-century Europe was reshaped by a swift increase in wealth and massive, relatively sudden concentrations of financial power. Amid these fierce economic convulsions, new classes rose up to challenge old hierarchies and develop a culture of inquiry and innovative thinking.[7] Growing up in the mining town of Mansfeld, Luther saw his society becoming more urban, more commercial, and more divided.

Knowledge was in a state of flux, as the contours of the known world changed because of the European discovery of the Americas in 1492. The Renaissance and Humanism brought new insights and new kinds of questions that posed deep intellectual challenges to the medieval worldview.[8] And the nascent print industry made intellectual and scientific discoveries, novel ideas, and popular literature widely accessible to an increasingly literate public through inexpensive printing methods and urban distribution networks.[9]

Paths to Virtuosity

Luther's father was an upwardly mobile copper mining proprietor and smelter. He invested in Martin's education, allowing him to attend Latin schools and later enter the university. By the time that Luther began his academic career, there were seventeen universities spread across the empire. Going to the university enhanced career opportunities and much more than that. For the swelling ranks of middle-class students like Luther, university study offered a way around the parochialism, stultifying conventions, and social hierarchies that dominated late medieval life.[10]

Despite all of this change and upheaval, the Church remained the central social institution and shaped the dominant worldview in ways that are hard to imagine today. The monastic orders dedicated to charity and service, clerical vows of poverty and chastity, and the cult of the saints added to its appeal. Moreover, the Church's rich sacramental culture created emotional connections that touched rich and poor alike.[11] But the Church was nevertheless in crisis because urbanization and social mobility had disrupted centuries-old social relations and called their moral underpinnings into question. Money seemed to dominate everything, in both secular and sacred spheres. And the rise of commercial capitalism posed a deep problem for spiritual virtuosi like Luther, because the strict Catholic moral code remained as the ultimate standard for judging all actions and all other institutions.[12]

In late medieval Catholicism, profound fears of death and eternal damnation lay behind individual's quests for holiness and purification on earth. The Church occupied an almost incontestable role as the sole agency that could secure the salvation of souls after life on earth was over. Over the centuries, it had instituted a system that promised earthly sanctification through the sacraments of the Eucharist and penance. Above all, fears of hell inspired sacramental participation and penitential sacrifice. To be forgiven of sins, the believer had to truly feel sorry for a sin (contrition), confess it to a priest, and then make penance by means of payment to the Church for absolution and remission.

The theological claim that Christ, the Virgin Mary, and the saints had left behind an enormous surplus of sacred merit was central to the penitential economy. The Church controlled that store of merit and the pope could draw upon it to shorten the stays of souls in purgatory and hasten their way to paradise. Indulgences from purgatory could be won through good works such as pilgrimages, acts of charity, or monetary payments to benefit the Church. In the 1480s, Church councils declared that indulgences could benefit *both* living and dead souls, an innovation which dangerously strained the idea of voluntary repentance.[13]

Despite its questionable stances on sin and indulgences, as well as the clergy's abuses of power, the Church also gave its adherents immediately rewarding experiences. Preaching foundations and endowed chapels provided opportunities to hear interesting and inspiring sermons. Pious laypeople formed confraternities dedicated to social benevolence. Some embraced the *devotio moderna,* a set of intense practices of prayer, service, and scriptural study. Moreover, expanded theological education produced better-trained clergy, a new humanism among privileged adherents, and broadly improved Biblical literacy.[14] Contrary to the common assumption that the late medieval world was spiritually exhausted, the Church actually remained popular, vital, and responsive to its increasingly diverse adherents in spite of complications of corruption and venality.[15]

Nevertheless, there were deep tensions, because the Church's institutionalized religious monopoly encouraged its worst tendencies and eroded many of its moral claims. Too often ethical and moral guidelines took a back seat to the profitable management of extensive land holdings, lucrative banking interests, and maximum income from the sale of religious services and ecclesiastical offices.[16] Cynicism and corruption seemed to permeate the Church, except possibly within monastic orders. Of all the interdependent abuses, simony, the buying and selling of spiritual offices, was probably the most detested. Many bishops and prince-bishops purchased their miters for lordly sums that they could recoup by selling even more indulgences.[17]

Newly literate audiences were both amused and dismayed by humanist satires that skewered the sorry state of the Church and society as a whole. Humanists such as Erasmus of Rotterdam influenced Luther through their advocacy of more authentic religiosity and a return to original scriptural sources. Luther embraced secular intellectuals like Erasmus because they too abhorred the commercialization of religion as part of the "conquest of society by the merchant and financier."[18] Despite his critical views, however, Luther was no revolutionary.

Luther had a fundamentally conservative worldview throughout his career. The bustling new commercial society alarmed him and Catholicism seemed spiritually inadequate and even objectionable when it supported economic expansion and exploited popular piety for its own gain. The intense competition for profit, moreover, made townspeople selfish and jealous of one another. He observed that wealth produced by honest toil in workshops and farms was used to purchase foreign luxuries and also finance princes' and popes' extravagances. To further its economic and political power, moreover, the Church cynically tolerated "superstition," remnants of paganism, and practices that smacked of heretical magic.[19]

Luther was obsessed with every kind of sin, not only those of a venal Church and a fallen and corrupted world but also his own failings and estrangement from God. He was terrified that death might take him before he had properly made confession and penance. Luther viewed the devil as a very real and frightening presence and feared the grave consequences of sin. He turned away from the corrupt secular world and resolved to become a monk after two near-death experiences while he was studying law: a serious wound and near strike by lightening.[20]

At the university, he had studied the worldliest of medieval subjects. When he rejected legal studies and became a friar, Luther turned away from a compromised world to join the ranks of recognized spiritual virtuosi. Monasticism represented the premiere road to spiritual excellence because it required asceticism and emphasized ethical virtuosity. Monks and friars followed Christ's counsels for a course of frugal living, poverty, chastity, and self-discipline. Although the path was strenuous, the monk belonged to a spiritually privileged category compared with the ordinary adherent and was, therefore, holier and closer to God.[21]

Because of his fierce asceticism and sacrifice, Luther chose to enter an Augustinian mendicant order known for its austerity, discipline, charity, and studiousness. The friars performed services and depended on voluntary donations rather than the Church's largesse. During the period that he wore the cowl, Brother Martin gave sermons, heard confessions, and gave pastoral counsel. His experience as an Augustinian and his heartfelt concern for ordinary Catholics' spiritual welfare inspired his virtuoso activism that was premised on teaching and guiding everyone to understand and live by God's Word.

The ascetic Augustinian path to sanctification made life in the monastery grim. Monks slept alone in bare cells before they woke at two in the morning to begin their seven-times-a-day cycle of prayer that structured daily life. They worked hard, fasted frequently, and ate austerely. Luther tried to perfect these practices. He fasted to the point of emaciation and compulsively confessed sins that required extreme penances, including self-flagellation, but the holiness that he sought still eluded him.[22]

He was deeply afflicted by "spiritual trials" (*Anfechtungen)* that included periods of doubt, desperation, and anger toward God. Some of Luther's despair may have grown from what we would now call "depression." Luther's misery certainly reflected an obsessive fear of a God and an orthodox theology that emphasized judgment and inevitable punishment for sin.[23] Despite countless confessions and acts of contrition, Luther believed that there was absolutely nothing that he could do to overcome his sins or be justified in the sight of God. He later believed that he had tortured his spirit by straining "to do the impossible, namely get rid of sins by running from one good work or penance to another."[24] Even after he was ordained a priest in 1507, Luther was still terrified of finding himself in God's presence.

Luther slowly escaped his despair with support from Johann von Staupitz, a spiritual virtuoso who had become leader of his order in 1506. Staupitz was so patient and tender with Luther that he once soothed him with a six-hour confessional session. Attempting to soothe his troubled acolyte, Staupitz first recommended a mystical path of contemplation and meditation. He counseled Luther to dwell on God's love, rather than on his wrath, but Catholic mystic traditions did not resonate with Luther's pragmatism. Recognizing Luther's earnest piety and impressive intellect, Staupitz counseled him to continue his studies in order to discover more productive ways to direct his spiritual intensity.

His dismay with the state of the Church compounded Luther's private agonies. Northern humanists like Luther had a maxim that a journey to Rome endangered the soul. There was a saying, "The closer to Rome, the worse the Christians."[25] In 1510, Luther nevertheless journeyed to Rome with a petition about a dispute over the governance of his order. The petition was rejected, and his disappointment was magnified by his firsthand exposure to the Vatican's thriving indulgence trade. The provincial monk was overwhelmed by the city's squalor and by Rome's blatant commercialism, venality, and cynicism.[26] Nevertheless, Luther remained eager to cleanse his soul and help his loved ones avoid a future in purgatory, so he sought indulgences by venerating sacred relics. But doubts were creeping in. Clambering up the *Scala Sancta* on his knees in order to free his dead grandfather from purgatory, Luther wondered, "Who knows if it is really true?"[27]

Luther did not break with the Church because of this visit, but his Roman experiences added to his doubts. The same feelings of disappointment and anger assailed him when he listened to ordinary people frightened by hell and desperate to win absolution. Did indulgences give them false confidence in their relationship with God? Could God's grace be chained to payments and pilgrimages?

Seeing that neither asceticism nor mysticism could satisfy Luther's restless spirituality, Staupitz made him his protégé in the Augustinian order and facilitated his academic career in theology and philosophy. Prince Frederick the Wise of Saxony had founded his own university at Wittenberg in 1502 and named Staupitz dean and professor of biblical theology. Recognizing Luther's academic promise, Staupitz called Luther to Wittenberg to continue his studies, and he earned his doctorate of theology in 1512. Then the aged Staupitz resigned his position to clear the way for Luther to succeed him as professor of theology and philosophy.[28]

Mentorship and Discovery

Between 1513 and 1517, Professor Luther was preoccupied with the problem of justification: How could a sinner ever be reconciled to God and be prepared to face His judgment? Luther rejected mysticism because he believed that it promised the impossible, namely a union with God at the divine level.[29] He also rejected the Church's practices of ritual sanctification that allowed individuals to absolve their sins through repentance and good works tied to sacraments. No number of masses attended or heap of good works could ever overcome sin. Sanctification could never be achieved. It could only be God's freely offered gift.

Luther's emotional and intellectual breakthroughs began while he prepared a course of lectures in 1513, principally on the Psalms and on St. Paul's letters to the Romans and Galatians. Luther described his discoveries:

> Night and day I pondered the justice of God and the statement, "the just shall live by faith." Then I grasped that the justice of God is that righteousness by which through grace and sheer mercy God justifies us through faith. Thereupon I felt myself reborn and to have gone through open doors into paradise.[30]

The wider theological implications of this new worldview were profound. No one needed the Church to be saved and enter heaven because holiness could only be found through study of God's revealed Word, true belief in Christ's sacrifice, and inward repentance. Spiritual merit, whether it was earned through moral effort and good works or purchased from the Church, could never gain someone entrance to heaven or stay God's wrath.[31] Luther explained that grace makes union with Christ possible only on God's terms:

> The incomparable benefit of faith is that it unites the soul with Christ, as a bride is united with a bridegroom. By this mystery, as the Apostle teaches, Christ and the soul become one flesh. . . . Accordingly, the believing soul can boast of glory in whatever Christ has as though it were its own and whatever the soul has Christ claims as its own.[32]

The external apparatus of sacraments and works that had evolved under Rome's command had suddenly become an impediment to salvation. These were absolutely radical ideas because reward for good works, the principle of merit, was the foundation of the Church's ethics. Luther's new theology rejected the dogma that salvation comes about when willed human effort (works) joins with Christ's divine grace. Luther asserted that a theology of works is built on straw, because individual will is fragile, the intellect easily deceived, and human nature corrupted. This contradicted both Aristotelian ethics and the teaching of the great twelfth-century Dominican theologian St. Thomas Aquinas. Luther drew upon the Apostle Paul and St. Augustine to support his claim that there was no legitimate foundation for a theology of human works and that, in God's eyes, sin always corrupted human merit.[33]

It was decisive that Luther first presented his new theology at Wittenberg, which was, at best, a provincial university. Before Luther's fame grew, it had few students and so little reputation that one historian characterized it as an "academic Siberia."[34] However, at a more prominent institution, Luther's provocations would have drawn hostile attention, and his theological creativity could have been squelched almost immediately. Because Wittenberg was academically peripheral and protected by Frederick the Wise, Luther had the space and also the patronage that he needed to forge a pivotal intellectual community.

Luther served as professor for more than three decades and shaped Wittenberg to his purposes. He trained his students in rhetoric so that their sermons and speeches could mold public opinion in favor of religious reform. And he hired faculty dedicated to redeeming the Gospel and mentoring a generation that became committed to the Protestant cause.[35]

After they grew convinced that the Church's foundational doctrine was in error, Luther and his followers scrutinized everything that arose from it. This close reading led him to reject ritual sanctification, the integrity of the Catholic sacraments, monastic institutions, and, finally, papal authority. For several years, Luther and his colleagues led a grand seminar in order to assail traditional Catholicism's very foundations.[36] There has probably never been a time when a single university was as influential and exhilarating as Luther's Wittenberg.

Patronage and Opportunity

In June 1520, Pope Leo X issued a papal declaration excommunicating Luther and ordering his writings to be burned. In an act of defiance on December 10, 1520, Luther gathered his colleagues and students outside the gates of Wittenberg in order to burn the declaration. After burning the offending document, they threw Aquinas's *Summa Theologica* and piles of canon law books onto the fire for good measure. As conflict about Luther's innovations spread, books were sacrificed on bonfires throughout Europe. Luther's works had already been burned on Rome's Piazza Navona, and university students at Cologne and Louvain followed suit. However, gangs of students in Leipzig and Erfurt prevented the further destruction of Luther's writings. Book burning continued for some time, and flames even leapt the English Channel when Luther's works burned in London fires in May 1521.

The book burnings made it clear that Luther and his followers had broken with Rome. His emerging movement called itself "evangelical" because of its commitment to the authority of the Gospels instead of the Church.[37] Luther originally intended internal reforms that renewed the Church and made Catholic beliefs and practices more relevant and challenging.[38] Yet, even if Luther had initially tried only to stimulate internal reforms, the Church became increasingly repellent to him, and an absolute break seemed necessary when he thundered that if there were a hell, Rome was built on it.

Photo 4.2 Luther and his students burn the Papal Bull.

However, local events, rather than far-away Rome, provoked the ultimate break between Luther and his followers and the Church. Albert von Brandenburg was already archbishop of Magdeburg when he purchased the office of Prince-Archbishop of Mainz to become one of the empire's supreme prelates and one of three archbishops who could cast a vote to select the next emperor. In order to secure his elevation, Albert borrowed enormous sums that he hoped to repay by issuing papal indulgences. He successfully petitioned Pope Leo X for the right to sell indulgences, as long as he remitted half of the proceeds to Rome.

The Dominican order managed the sales, and Johann Tetzel, an accomplished indulgence preacher, toured Saxony, giving harrowing sermons about the torments of purgatory and the enormous power of indulgences. The indulgences were not sold in the territories ruled by Luther's patron Prince Frederick, but he nevertheless resented the campaign to enrich Albert and the pope. The prince was conventionally pious, but he wanted to curb the bishops' power and safeguard his own revenues from shrines. Frederick's relic collection was inventoried at 17,443 articles, which, if properly venerated, could deduct nearly two million years from a sinner's time in purgatory.

Tetzel preached rousing sermons and sold hundreds of indulgences in ducal Saxony, just a few leagues from Wittenberg. Luther heard about Tetzel's terrifying performances and how ordinary people had been manipulated to make sacrifices in order to buy indulgences and make penance. He was offended by Albert's apparent simony and distressed that hard-earned money would flow to Rome. His pastoral concerns inflamed his theological objections, because Luther feared that instead of bringing people to a redeeming faith in Christ, Tetzel brought them into spiritual error and infantile dependence on the Church.[39]

Luther put his objections about Albert's venality and Tetzel's tawdry manipulation into his *Ninety-Five Theses* of 1517 and sent them to Archbishop Albert. In order to stimulate discussions, he also posted them on the door of Wittenberg Cathedral as an invitation for an academic disputation. Albert ignored his missive and no academics took the bait. Luther denounced indulgences as among the Church's worst offenses because they misled people, encouraged spiritual complacency, and impeded salvation. They were misleading and bad for piety. More broadly, Luther argued that forgiveness of sin is Christ's gift to believers, not something that could be won or purchased.[40]

Within a few weeks, the theses became famous, because the newly inexpensive printing technology transformed them into explosive provocations. Against Luther's wishes, printers arranged to have them translated into German and widely distributed. Tetzel and his fellow Dominicans made the mistake of responding angrily and arrogantly and their unyielding defense of already objectionable indulgences focused the previously diffuse anticlericalism of the age. Indulgences became the symbol of the Church's many transgressions.

Luther quickly recognized the power of marketing, and less than a year later he followed the theses with his *Sermon on Indulgences and Grace*. It was his first popular bestseller, and by 1520 it was reprinted at least twenty times.[41] Luther rejoiced when the controversies surrounding indulgences ignited popular upheavals across Germany; "Printing is God's latest and best work to spread the true religion throughout the world," he declared.[42]

He discovered his métier in short, direct sermons and pamphlets and his output was phenomenal. By the end of the sixteenth century, nearly 5,000 editions of Luther's works were published and he had turned provincial Wittenberg into the cradle of Protestantism and a thriving center of the print industry. He became the most successful author since the invention of printing in terms of his extraordinary output and also his success in the marketplace.[43]

The Controversialists, defenders of orthodox Catholicism, tried to match Luther's blizzard of pamphlets with their own communications. However, they published largely in Latin, while Luther and his supporters intentionally published most of their output in vernacular German and reached many more people than their opponents.[44] This back and forth of pamphlets and broadsides made theological disputes much more interesting; it launched a print war that anticipated today's "Twitter storms" by five centuries.[45]

In 1520, as his conflict with Rome intensified and his fame spread, Luther penned three central treatises that fully defined the emerging Protestant movement. The first, *An Address to the Christian Nobility of the German Nation*, called on the aristocracy to assume responsibility to reform religion by eliminating papal abuses and halting the extraction of tributes and tithes that bled Germany's wealth. In the second, *On the Babylonian Captivity of the Church*, Luther attacked papal institutions, the sacramental system, and the Catholic Mass. Instead of the Church as the essential arbiter between God and the believer, Luther imagined a kind of direct transactional relationship, where Christ takes the place of sinners in exchange for their faith. Every person had to answer to God for himself or herself.

In the third treatise, *The Freedom of a Christian,* Luther proclaimed independence of the spirit. The paradox of spiritual freedom, he argued, is that it is both totally liberating and completely subordinating. According to Luther, "A Christian is a perfectly free lord of all, subject to none. A Christian is a perfectly dutiful servant to all, subject to all."[46] In the realm of conscience, the believer is free, bound only by the Word. In the earthly realm, however, the Christian must serve his neighbors and obey secular rulers who ought to govern by God's law. Good works are not required to win salvation by pleasing God. The Christian does good works for the sake of adoring Him, disciplining the self, and serving humankind, but not in the expectation of the rewards of salvation.

People of all kinds flocked to Luther's cause, pushed by their frustration with the Church and pulled by his compelling arguments.[47] Confession, penance, fasting, indulgences, and pilgrimages to shrines had become more exhausting than spiritually liberating. Above all, Luther's new theology and his passionate call for a simpler religion awakened popular desires for inward spirituality and a new kind of religious virtuosity.[48]

The Church officially responded by insisting on the authority of the papacy and Luther's subordination to ecclesiastical discipline. However, the Catholic controversialists were often ineffective and poorly coordinated. For example, an academic disputation at Heidelberg in 1518 failed to silence Luther and his performance attracted admiration and support from professors and junior clergy. Prelates counted on ecclesiastical discipline to quiet Luther but that discipline depended on secular enforcement that was often unavailable.

The distant, preoccupied Church hierarchy offered little support to loyalists who insisted that papal authority could stop Luther and his supporters. Pope Leo X's death was followed by the election of Pope Adrian VI, who favored internal reforms that might have helped stem the Protestant advance. However, his pontificate lasted only two years and struggles against the Turks and simmering European rivalries preoccupied his successors. In some territories, such as Bavaria and Austria, regional princes enforced Catholic doctrine. Although the emperor's office obliged him to be *defensor ecclesiae,* political circumstances and financial need usually forced him to conciliate Protestant princes and Protestant cities.

In the first decades of the Reformation, Catholic loyalists faced difficult obstacles, despite their many resources. Theologians were hobbled by teachings that kept them from debating heretics or involving ordinary people in doctrinal disputes. The traditional Catholic approach to doctrine combined an academic writing style with stilted, distant preaching that made it difficult for loyalists to reach ordinary Germans and cultivate the populist energy that characterized Protestants. A concerted countermovement did not take shape until after the Council of Trent in 1545 and the beginning of Charles's war against the Protestant princes soon afterward.[49]

Ecclesiastical authorities pressed on Prince Frederick to chastise or extradite Luther from his principality, but he protected the insurgent for a time and spared him the fate of others who had challenged dogma and papal authority. Political patronage repeatedly allowed Luther to avert the full force of a papal reckoning.

When the Church, backed by Holy Roman Emperor Maximilian I, sought approval for a new imperial tax to fund its struggle against the Turks through even more indulgences, Prince Frederick deftly played the situation. He knew that the dying Maximilian needed his support to secure the imperial crown for his grandson, Charles, the King of Spain. He influenced the German princes to compromise by acceding to new taxes, while he denied Rome's ill-timed request for new indulgences. Frederick's clout grew as he positioned himself as a power broker in the looming election of a new emperor, and he could help Luther quietly slip out of Augsburg.[50] But Luther did not leave unscathed, because Staupitz, his old mentor and patron, could not tolerate a break with the Church and expelled him from the Augustinians.

At a second disputation in Leipzig in 1519, Luther faced off against Johannes Eck, a brilliant scholar and papal ally. During the eighteen-day debate, Eck frequently bested Luther. He forced Luther into a corner by making him admit that he agreed with the Bohemian priest Jan Hus, who had been condemned as a heretic by a papal council. Luther stated that Hus was not in error and that papal councils could be illegitimate. Luther declared, "A simple layman armed with Scripture is to be believed above a pope or council without it. . . . For the sake of Scripture we should reject pope and councils."[51]

The new emperor, Charles V, was indebted to Frederick for his election and keeping the imperial crown in Habsburg hands. Following Luther's excommunication, Rome renewed its pressure on Frederick to extradite him, but Frederick again refused and insisted that Luther was legally entitled to a hearing before the emperor and the annual Diet at Worms in 1521. Traveling under an imperial guarantee of safe passage, Luther passed triumphantly through many towns and on his entrance into Worms, crowds demonstrated in his favor. A papal emissary said of the arrival, "Nine-tenths of the people here shout 'hurrah for Luther', the other one-tenth cry 'death to the pope.'"[52]

Despite his exultant entry into Worms, once Luther was in the emperor's presence, he was tongue-tied. His interrogators confronted him with the charges and asked him to recant his works, in whole or in part. Luther requested a recess, but the next day he conceded that his tone was too strident and some of his works were too polemical. However, he would not renounce any part of their substance:

> I do not accept the authority of popes and councils, for they have contradicted each other—my conscience is captive to the Word of God. I cannot and will not recant anything, for to go against my conscience is neither right nor safe. Here I stand, I cannot do otherwise. God help me. Amen.[53]

In his moment of moral and spiritual triumph, Luther unequivocally affirmed the Word as the highest authority and personal spirituality the greatest good. Popes and emperors were no match for the Gospel.

Luther's defiance meant that there could be no compromise, and Emperor Charles responded with the Edict of Worms that declared Luther a heretic and a criminal. Nevertheless, as committed as Charles was to crushing Luther and his reforms, he was in a weak position because he had to rely on German princes to help fund and fight wars in France and Italy and he also needed to be vigilant in the face of the Turks. Political patronage and the nature of the empire's confederal monarchy saved Luther from the flames.[54]

Luther, who defied pope and emperor, had become a popular hero and was sometimes called the "German Hercules." People from every social class and condition projected their hopes onto Luther, and he symbolized diverse movements for reform in Central Europe. However, many of those who hailed Luther as hero in the early 1520s would come to be disappointed. Luther absolutely rejected a mantle of charismatic leadership, because he wanted to lead by example, not exhortation. He insisted that he was neither the message nor the messenger of the vast spiritual awakening that was under way. In 1522, at the height of his acclaim, he wrote:

> Make no reference to my name; let them call themselves Christians, not Lutherans. What is Luther? After all, the teaching is not mine. Neither was I crucified for anyone. . . Let us abolish all party names and call ourselves Christians, after Him whose teaching we hold.[55]

Although they had initially embraced his ideas, humanists, like Erasmus, came to scorn him because they viewed Luther's movement as too radical. For other adherents, Luther's reforms were not radical enough. Nationalists among the lesser nobility wanted Luther to lead an uprising that would unite the empire, but he refused to take up the cause. Between 1524 and 1526, peasants staged rebellions across southern Germany because they saw Luther's ideas about Christian liberty and the equality of believers as a template for social justice. Luther, however, denounced them as deluded criminals who deserved to be put down by the sword, because his first interest was always religion and his priorities were always spiritual. He insisted on internal routes to sanctification and cared little about secular institutions. Many early supporters who wanted Luther to support radical political or social transformation were gravely disappointed.

Democratizing Spiritual Privilege

After Worms, Prince Frederick knew that Luther was in mortal jeopardy. Acting cautiously, the prince had Luther spirited away from Worms to the Wartburg, a lonely mountaintop castle in his Saxon territories. Luther battled his isolation and depression through prayer and work. He wrote furiously and made his influential German translation of the New Testament from Greek into his own Saxon dialect

The reform movement continued to spread across the empire and Prince Frederick worried that Luther's absence made it possible for radical students and professors to press for greater reform in Wittenberg's religious institutions. Luther heard about the radical innovations that were sweeping Saxony and feared that an overly

Photo 4.3 Wartburg Castle.

"enthusiastic" sectarian church might prevail. He jeopardized his safety to return to Wittenberg after a year's seclusion in order to advocate for his spiritual ideals and vision of a new church.

Luther envisioned the new church as both spiritually demanding and religiously egalitarian. He wrote: "God has given every saint a spiritual way and a special grace for living according to his or her baptism."[56] Monks, the old church's spiritual elite, would be freed from vows and the cult of the saints would be abolished. Instead of a spiritual aristocracy of canonized saints, Luther preached the communion of saints, where every baptized Christian who lives by faith is sanctified. The pastor was not outside and above his parishioners but was to live among them. Moreover, clergy could and should marry. Luther wrote, "Ordaining is not consecrating. We give in the power of the Word what we have, the authority of preaching the Word and giving the sacraments; that is ordaining."[57] So he saw every Christian as equally exposed to God's grace and argued that work in the world was no less a path to holiness and no less bound by duty to God than spiritual vocations.

Luther gave new ethical meaning to family life by arguing that spouses and parents held holy offices and that sex and childrearing were noble and pleased God. He lived out his ideals by marrying Katherina von Bora, a former nun who had been smuggled out of a convent in a herring barrel. They enjoyed a lusty sex life, and Luther spoke very directly about the trial and joys of marriage. Katie and Martin had six children and also raised several orphans. They became models for good marriages and of the partnership between a pastor and his wife. Middle-class newlyweds in the emerging Protestant world sometimes hung engravings of the pair as reminders that good marriages and many children were part of God's plan.

Luther's spiritual equalitarianism inspired Anabaptist sects that he quickly detested because he saw them as radicals who had abolished the pastoral role,

Photo 4.4 Luther and his large family: A popular image.

rejected hierarchy, and despised secular governments. Along with other moderates, he wanted to balance a personal virtuoso ethic that was based on direct relationship with God with orderly institutions and pastoral guidance grounded in Protestant doctrine. The Word had to be taught to all. It was a "people's church" (*Volkskirche*) where sinners, saints, and hypocrites worship side by side. By being baptized and asserting his or her faith in Christ, each believer could drive away the Devil by affirming, "I have been baptized, I am a Christian."[58]

As a scholar of Biblical theology, Luther was acutely aware of the scriptures' limitations and contradictions. However, it was a pastoral duty to safeguard them, so that the scriptures would not be used to support dogmatism or error. What really mattered was that everyone found his or her own way to Christ and the Gospel through the text itself.[59] The emphasis on personally reading the Word had profound, long-lasting implications for spreading spiritual privilege and laid the groundwork for eighteenth- and nineteenth-century evangelical awakenings, as well as the twentieth-century Human Potential Movement.

Luther's wildly popular translations of the Bible into colloquial German made the scriptures vivid and immediate. He explained that his translations were based on the simple premise of bringing the Word of God to everyone:

> We must ask the mother in the home, the children on the street, the common person in the market about this. We must be guided by their tongue, the manner of their speech, and do our translating accordingly. Then they will understand it.[60]

Johann Cochlaeus, one of Luther's earliest and harshest opponents, complained:

> Luther's New Testament was so much multiplied and spread by printers that even tailors and shoemakers, yea, even women and ignorant persons who had accepted this new Lutheran gospel, and could read a little German, studied it

with the greatest avidity as the fountain of all truth. . . In a few months such people deemed themselves so learned that they were not ashamed to dispute about faith and the gospel not only with Catholic laymen, but even with priests and monks and doctors of divinity.[61]

To Cochlaeus's frustration, Luther's Bible translations became best sellers along with his pamphlets. And during his lifetime, he authored more than 2,000 printed sermons.[62]

In order to underscore everyone's equality before God, Luther did away with all but two Catholic sacraments. Moreover, he modified Baptism and Holy Communion, the remaining ones. Infants would be baptized as an expression of the ineffable and limitless grace of Christ, not because they had somehow qualified for it. Their baptism made them part of the invisible church—the body of Christ—and united them in the community of believers. And during Communion, every baptized believer could share the Lord's Supper of bread and drink from the cup of wine. Both revised rituals underscored the importance of community in God and did away with the miracle of transubstantiation whereby the priest transformed the bread and wine into Christ's actual body and blood.

Luther emphasized preaching on the scriptures, making the sermon the pivotal event in Protestant worship services. In fact, he revolutionized the art of preaching and conceived of sermons as the best vehicles for God's Word in a society that was still largely illiterate. He was also a prolific, powerful hymnodist. He made sure that sacred music would be one of the new church's enduring glories, and it reached a zenith in the next century in Johann Sebastian Bach's cantatas, which were often based on themes from Luther's hymns.[63]

Luther's myriad critiques of the Church and its monastic orders created a quandary for him. If Roman ecclesiastical order and radical sectarian Protestant organization were discarded, where could Luther's church find institutional support? Because of the need for organizational stability, Luther was willing to allow secular magistrates to rule as God's providential agents, and he turned the governance of his church over to territorial princes.[64]

By linking Protestantism with the governments of rising principalities, Luther ensured the survival of his reforms, but this strategy ultimately blunted the Reformation's full democratic potential in Europe. Luther had imagined that the church and secular state would exist in separate realms, but in practice he and his successors had established a church–throne alliance. Dependency on monarchial states made Lutheranism increasingly conservative and beholden to its own orthodox theology.[65]

Pivotal Communities

Conventional wisdom holds that Luther, Melancthon, Zwingli, Calvin, and other great reformers were heroic virtuosi who were primarily responsible for the Reformation. In reality, Luther and other visible leaders initiated a religious movement that succeeded by inspiring hundreds of virtuosi disciples to spread the new theology and implement the Reformation.[66] They inspired students, clerics, and former monks to embrace a virtuoso path based on ideals of spiritual freedom and interior sanctification. After discovering their own paths to redemption, the virtuoso activists turned outward and made the communal Reformation.

Who were these virtuoso activists? The collected biographies of over 200 men active in the early Protestant movement provide some of the answers.[67] The first wave of activist virtuosi came from relatively privileged ranks. Most of them were highly educated and about 80 percent of them matriculated at one or more universities during their formative careers. Wittenberg University's centrality to the early Protestant movement is unmistakable, because nearly 40 percent of the first generation of Protestant activists spent at least some time there before spreading the new theology elsewhere.

In the years before 1517, there had been a mismatch between expanding educational possibilities and limited opportunities to join the ranks of the elite clergy. Spiritual virtuosi drawn to the Protestant cause had the humanist educations that made the new theology accessible to them, but they lacked the economic and social capital that would have most likely made them support the spiritual *status quo*. It is not surprising that only 15 percent of the first generation of Protestant pastors had the financial means that could allow them to earn their doctorates.[68]

Because less affluent students, however brilliant, could not earn their doctorates and acquire the necessary credentials, they could neither secure endowed university positions nor gain high-ranking government posts. Such frustrating experiences made German universities fertile ground for activism, as similar limitations have in other historical contexts.[69]

Like Luther, nearly half of the Protestant activists came from the middling social ranks of growing towns, with only a quarter of them from the families of urban patricians and the nobility. In 1517, on average they were about twenty-seven years old; Luther was less than a decade older than his early followers. The new activists were still students or in the early stages of their clerical or academic careers when the movement began.

Students in the early modern era were uniquely positioned to take the path of virtuoso spirituality and commit themselves to a movement for spiritual equality. They had frequent opportunities to read, travel, and encounter new ideas. Moreover, the young men trained in emerging centers of evangelical theology, especially in the universities of Wittenberg and Basel, had access to distinctive intellectual communities where the exciting new Protestant theology was the center of attention. They could quickly form a group with extensive social network ties, common experiences, similar theological concerns, and religious zeal.

Between 1515 and 1520 enrollment at Wittenberg shot up 70 percent. In 1518, one of Prince Frederick's advisors reported that 400 students regularly attended Luther's theology seminar and 500 to 600 went to each of his colleague Melanchthon's lectures.[70] The university became a center of an emerging movement, converting students to its cause and drawing others to its halls. One noted historian described the university and its students: "Wittenberg was Luther's city, and we cannot overestimate its importance as a center of the Reformation."[71]

Leading theologians were vital to the Protestant movement's social networks, and they encouraged and coordinated outreach and action for religious and social change. Melanchthon and Luther both maintained voluminous correspondence with Protestant activists and their patrons across the empire. Luther alone built a sprawling network of friends, former students, and collaborators. There are eighteen volumes in the German edition of his correspondence.[72] His former students fanned out across the empire, often returning to their hometowns, where they preached to the widest audiences possible, seeking to build a movement that united them with disaffected clerics and townsmen.[73]

Around the same time, spiritual movements in the Swiss regions and the German Southwest formed around Ulrich Zwingli and his followers. The University of Basel and later Heidelberg served as key centers for Protestant theological training. It was at Basel that Erasmus published his influential annotated Greek New Testament in 1516, and many young men went to study with him and other Biblical humanists. However, humanism merely "laid the egg that Zwingli hatched."[74] Zwingli and his allies went beyond the new pedagogy to cultivate a corps of young preachers willing to throw themselves into the battle for Reformation and carry it forward to their own towns.[75] Basel and its university were far more bitterly divided than Wittenberg, and it was not until 1529 that the Zwinglian party could oust the Catholic faculty, including the famed Erasmus.

Social Networks and Bridging Activism

The first generation of Protestant activists made the growing towns the central arenas where they hoped to convert individuals and motivate them to redeem the Gospels through institutional reforms. Most activist virtuosi from universities returned to their old towns and cities, where they successfully linked their new theology to the local burghers' grievances and hatched a significant political and social movement that reached beyond religious institutions. For the emerging Protestant movement, students became the link between universities and the towns, especially when they returned home to serve as preachers and agitators.

Protestants demanded profound changes in collective piety and the civic constitution of the towns. Persuading individuals was not enough, because during the Reformation's early years Protestants could only overthrow the church by converting almost everyone in a town or city or somehow compelling its civic elite to institute reform. Not surprisingly, the demands for change often sparked bitter battles, growing into what some historians labeled a veritable culture war between Protestants and defenders of Catholic orthodoxy.[76]

Towns that enjoyed the formal status of city were self-governing communities with their own laws and civic administration, and they could be persuaded to support Protestant innovations because their governing councils were broadly accountable to their residents.[77] In some places, agitators and preachers quickly won support from prominent citizens or territorial princes and introduced reforms, but there was substantial opposition in other cities. When they were challenged, activist virtuosi and their supporters took to the streets in order to press for reforms. In the 1520s, mob violence, anticlerical rioting, and pillaging of monasteries and abbeys were common. However, some Protestants conducted peaceful protests which were the spiritual forebears of later religiously inspired social movements such as Abolition and the US Civil Rights Movement.

The urban elite often proved easy to sway, because literate townsmen shared many of the grievances that motivated Luther and his supporters. They eagerly sought opportunities to shake off the Church's extractions of their wealth and possibilities to seize control of ecclesiastical assets. Moreover, since Protestants proposed unified legal authority and civil judiciary that could improve urban governance, their messages meshed with the civic republicanism favored by many urban burghers.[78] Once reform triumphed or Catholic loyalists prevailed, the defeated partisans were expelled from a town because in either event, there were no precedents for religious pluralism.[79]

If rulers like Prince Frederick could profit from seizure of Church resources or envisioned a better share of religious revenues, they tended to favor the Reformation. However, if regional princes had substantial control over those resources or advantageous alliances with the Church, they tried to hold back the Protestant cause.

Nevertheless, the influence of elites can be easily overstated, because elite support did not determine the movement's early successes and failures. At its outset, the Protestant cause had to overcome enormous skepticism, if not outright hostility, from political elites. In the early 1520s, the princes did not initiate the Reformation movement and did not desire it, though they could not stop it.[80]

In the towns, activist virtuosi threatened the authority of city councils that often opposed the movement at first, until the middle-class townsmen who had become Protestant advocates swayed them. Activist virtuosi won townsmen's support when they strategically linked their new theology to popular grievances, general anticlericalism, and established ideals of civic autonomy and good government.

Virtuosity and Vulnerabilities

The Church and its allies were by no means Luther's only antagonists. Like other successful movements for religious and social change, its internal schisms widened as the movement gained ground. The common experience of studying with spiritual leaders and forging ties with fellow activists created a sense of collective identity and shared purpose during the Reformation's first years. Over time, however, activists' loyalty came into increasing tension with their individual spiritual virtuosity.

Protestantism's original message was spiritually and intellectually liberating, but political conflict and religious partisanship hardened some of its theological innovations into new orthodoxies. Andreas Osiander's career as a virtuoso activist and emerging critic of Luther's illustrates the tensions that almost inevitably develop within significant spiritual movements. Although he was one of bright lights of the early Protestant movement, Osiander experienced profound tensions in navigating between authentic virtuosity and religious partisanship. In the end, he was left isolated and embattled.

Osiander was born near the imperial city of Nuremberg, received a humanist education at the university in Ingolstadt, and was ordained as a priest. Because he was a recognized talent in Greek and Hebrew, Luther's old order of Augustinian friars hired him as a language teacher. In 1522, Osiander established his scholarly credentials by publishing a well-regarded revision of the Latin Vulgate Bible that was based on his improved translation of original Hebrew sources.

However, despite recognition from the Church, Osiander was soon in the thick of the theological and social upheavals that were wracking Nuremberg. After his 1518 visit to Nuremberg, Luther's supporters in monasteries and among the city's wealthy, well-educated elites convinced the city council that clerical vacancies should be filled with disciples from Wittenberg. Osiander, at this point an enthusiastic proponent of Luther's cause, was named the priest of the parish church of Saint Lorenz.

At Saint Lorenz, he was at the forefront of a "devoted and zealous band of preachers" that expounded the Protestant cause and he became the first priest in Nuremburg to offer the laity both the bread and the cup at the Lord's Supper (communion).[81] Osiander soon followed Luther's example by renouncing his priestly vows and marrying. Protestants recognized him as the city's leading reformer. Their support put him in the first rank of movement activists. In short order, with Osiander's leadership, Nuremberg's Protestants compelled the town council to abolish the Roman mass, expel defenders of Catholic orthodoxy, dissolve monasteries, and prohibit monks and priests from preaching.

In addition to his theology and preaching, Osiander cultivated his own virtuosity through a number of spiritual and intellectual pursuits that sometimes led him to take unpopular stances that smacked of dissent from Lutheran orthodoxy. Hebrew scriptures fascinated Osiander, and he also dabbled in the Kabbala's Jewish mystical tradition. Inspired by his profound interest in Judaica, Osiander sharply opposed the hatred and intolerance of Jews that was common among leading Protestants. His stance antagonized Luther, whose anti-Jewish polemics grew increasingly bitter as he aged. Osiander refused to condemn the Jews for rejecting Christ as the messiah and used his pulpit to preach against vilifying them.[82]

Osiander also took the humanist's view that while only religion could offer ultimate truth, science could produce different, valuable insights. Fascinated by the natural sciences, Osiander supported astronomy, going so far as to arrange for the publication of Nicholas Copernicus's revolutionary work about the earth and planets

Photo 4.5 Andreas Osiander among the heroes of the Reformation.

revolving around the sun. When *De Revolutionibus Orbium Coelestium* appeared in Nuremberg in 1543, it included Osiander's unsigned preface. He hoped to ease its acceptance among religious leaders, including a skeptical Luther, by explaining that the work proposed hypotheses, not revealed truths.[83]

Protestant leaders quickly drew sharper party lines, however, because the theological latitude that they had given virtuosi activists like Osiander was quickly narrowing. The emerging orthodoxy was obvious in the rivalry between the Lutheran and Zwinglian wings of the Reformation. The Zwinglian virtuosi were more politically radical than the Lutherans, and they were more militant in instituting reforms, even when they were faced with armed opposition. Instead of deferring to princes' goals, the Zwinglians emphasized the civic republicanism of the self-governing free cities and the Swiss cantons. In southwestern Germany, the Lutherans and Zwinglians engaged in bitter rivalries for supremacy and offered different liturgical and institutional reforms.

The Protestant princes were eager to reunite the movement and they hoped for reconciliation between Luther and Zwingli. Unity was urgent because war with papal and imperial forces seemed increasingly likely and the princes and free cities wanted to form a defensive league. Nevertheless, serious theological differences divided the two factions. In 1529, the opposing camps agreed to meet at Marburg, with Osiander and other leading Protestants in attendance. Luther and Zwingli agreed on many points but remained fundamentally divided on their most serious theological conflict about the Lord's Supper. While Luther insisted on the real presence of Christ in the sacrament, Zwingli maintained that the feast was a memorial that united the Christian community rather than a mystical conjoining between Christ and the elements.

No matter how high the stakes, Osiander never supported conformity at the price of virtuosity and he publically criticized Luther and Melanchthon about the emerging Lutheran consensus. While he agreed with Luther about the Lords' Supper, Osiander broke with him about the practice of public confession, as well as other points. Luther eliminated private confession as a sacrament, but Osiander insisted on it and ensured that it would be required in Nuremberg. Osiander was a relentless critic and he refused to be silenced. In 1537, he was even sent home in disgrace from a Protestant conference because of his strident, unyielding attacks on a sick and weakened Luther.[84]

Zwingli fell during a battle with Catholic forces in 1531. Melanchthon became the new leader of the Lutheran camp after Luther died in 1546. Osiander spoke for many other dissidents when he remarked, "The lion is dead; now I have only to do with foxes and hares."[85] Dissent among Lutheran virtuosi activists grew and the disaster that some had foreseen at Marburg came to pass. In 1546, the Catholic Holy Roman Emperor Charles V invaded Germany and, for a short time, prevailed against the Protestant movement and its supporters. Like many other activist virtuosi, Osiander was embittered when Melanchthon and his party decided to submit to his rule.

In 1549, Osiander fled eastward and found refuge in Prussia, where a sympathetic prince appointed him as a professor of theology at the University of Königsberg. From this refuge, Osiander engaged in one last assertion of his independence and reexamined Luther's doctrine of justification, a teaching at the very heart of the emerging Lutheran consensus. Osiander argued that Luther's original conception of justification included spiritual renewal through mystical unity with Christ. When sinners experience the indwelling of Christ by faith, they are regenerated as copies of Christ and restored to the true humanity possessed by Adam before the fall. The believer is justified, in short, because God finds Christ in him or her.[86]

Osiander's apparently outrageous speculations alarmed many other Protestant virtuosi. The idea of a mystical pathway to sanctification that overshadowed the crucifixion was absolutely outrageous. Osiander seemed to repudiate Luther's foundational belief in the sinful depravity of all humans and undermine the sacrificial interpretation of Jesus' gift of grace. Twisting his message, his sharpest critics charged that Osiander wanted to be God.

Compared with the other Protestant activists of his generation, Osiander had always been an unconventional thinker and troublemaker, but this final heresy made him a pariah. In 1552, soon after he was condemned as a mystic and fanatic, Osiander died. Fifteen years later, Prussia censored Osiander's thought and put three of his followers to death for heresy.[87] Rapid institutionalization and growing rigidity weakened the Protestant cause almost as much as external opposition.

Emperor Charles V's military victory over the German Protestants was short lived, because the princes rebelled against his attempts to impose imperial authority and restore a unified church. Finally, the exhausted parties ratified a peace treaty in Augsburg in 1555. The empire would remain religiously divided under the principle of *cuius regio, eius religio* ("whose realm, his religion"). Local secular rulers, whether Catholic or Lutheran, could decide the religions of the empire's various territories. Another century of religious strife followed the Augsburg peace treaty, but in 1648, the Peace of Westphalia effectively ended the wars of religion. It reaffirmed the earlier formula of local rule and also admitted Calvinism to the ranks of acceptable confessions.

As established Protestantism hardened into competing confessional camps, it would afford ever less tolerance to creative and independent figures like Osiander. Doctrinal conformity, social closure among the newly minted Lutheran clergy, and party spirit trumped spiritual and theological creativity.[88] The space for independence and exploration that originally attracted so many virtuosi to the movement narrowed.

The great promise of Luther's Christian liberty was that each person would have the right to interpret the Word. Although spiritual virtuosity was not extinguished in the conservative Lutheran tradition, it was diminished. In coming centuries, enforcement of orthodoxy in Lutheran lands came to be obsessive.

Lutheran virtuosity found its most authentic expression in Pietism, a spiritual movement at the faith's margins. Pietist leaders advocated for active, vital personal religion against the academic orthodoxy and conservatism of the newly established Protestant churches. They published moving appeals, created charitable institutions, and organized devotional networks, but refrained from breaking with the established churches. Even so, Lutheran officials viewed even this mild nonconformity with suspicion. In some instances, enforcing orthodox theology became something of a science. The Swedish monarch who presided over a Lutheran state, for example, sponsored the first quantitative content analysis of religious texts in order to root out nonconformity in hymn books and devotional materials.[89]

Subordination to the state made it increasingly difficult for spiritual virtuosi to take activist paths within the Lutheran tradition. Some brave virtuoso activists, such as the extraordinary Dietrich Bonhoeffer, were pushed to act against the absolute depravity of Nazi totalitarianism. Bonhoeffer's virtuoso ethic and call to activism boldly rejected Luther's subservience to secular authority and affirmed activist spiritual virtuosity as the moral obligation of twentieth-century Christians.[90]

Going forward, Luther's fundamental message of Christian liberty and the virtuoso ethic flourished not in his early vision of a unified people's church but through struggles with the divisiveness and sectarianism that were unintentional but logical consequences of his doctrine of Christian liberty. The Pietists, not the orthodox Lutherans, inspired the evangelical awakenings in an eighteenth-century Anglo-American Protestantism that was outside the limits of state control.

The unbridled ethic of spiritual virtuosity stimulated a proliferation of rival churches and sects that propelled evangelically inspired movements for religious and social change.[91] In the nineteenth century, the virtuoso ethic was decisive for religious innovation. With increasing force those ideas empowered people, regardless of their social status, to assert their spirituality and claim a voice in public affairs. As the radical abolitionist and feminist Sarah Grimké declared in 1837:

> I . . . claim to judge for myself what is the meaning of the inspired writers, because I believe it to the solemn duty of every individual to search the Scriptures for themselves with the aid of the Holy Spirit, and not be governed by the views of any man, or set of men.[92]

Conservative Protestant critics could not silence Grimké. Her bold spirituality and commitment to act on it reflected Luther's lasting influence and the spiritual virtuosity that shaped his ideas and was at the heart of the American Antislavery movement.

5   Grimké, Weld, and the Antislavery Movement

Black and white abolitionists crowded into the parlor of Mrs. Anna Frost's Philadelphia row house in the spring of 1838. They gathered to witness the marriage of the renowned antislavery activist Theodore Dwight Weld and the notorious feminist Angelina Grimké. Although they were ardent Christians, the couple sealed their wedding in the private home of the bride's sister.

It was an unmistakably abolitionist affair! Their friends had received an invitation engraved with an image of a slave in chains. A black and a white minister presided jointly, but did not officiate. The tiny bride wore a plain brown dress and the lanky groom a matching brown coat. Instead of the traditional Protestant wedding liturgy, the pair improvised their vows. Theodore promised that the only power he would ever exercise over Angelina was the power of love. Angelina pledged to be guided by God's love as long as their shared pilgrimage lasted.

Their "soul marriage" was the result of an extraordinary courtship. A few years earlier, Weld had recruited Grimké as a public speaker and organizer for the American Anti-Slavery Society. Although she had proved to be a dynamic and effective orator, she provoked bitter controversy among Protestants because of her unabashed feminism.

As they fell in love, Weld and Grimké had poured out their souls to one another, and had resolved to base their life together on the same spiritual ideals that motivated their antislavery activism. Attaining holiness necessitated putting down the soul-crushing domination that they perceived in both slavery and in patriarchy. She exhorted Weld to recognize that antebellum womanhood "robbed woman of her essential rights" and denied her "the right to fulfill the great end of her being, as a moral, intellectual and immortal creature."[1] He promised to "forget sex" in their romance and make a marriage between unsexed souls. They both resolved to temper their ardent desire for each other and have a new kind of holy and egalitarian marriage that promised mutual sexual and spiritual satisfaction.

The ceremony's greater significance was that it united two radicals who insisted that the American republic was drowning in the evil of slavery and demanded its immediate abolition. They agreed with the great abolitionist William Lloyd Garrison, who stated plainly, "We are all alike guilty. . . Slavery is a national sin."[2] Grimké and Weld were activist spiritual virtuosi inspired by the faith that they could help redeem America of her collective sin. They were exceptional members of a cohort of virtuosi driven to purify themselves and their society by committing their lives to overcoming collective sins. Their abolitionism united personal spiritual imperatives with the desire for collective redemption. Grimké and Weld used revivals and the culture of evangelical religion to harness widespread personal guilt about slavery into activism that would negate acquiescence to the national sin.

Nineteenth-century American activist religious virtuosi believed that righteous Christians could not escape the insidious reach of slavery because their guilt and shame inevitably corrupted the holiness and spiritual repose that they craved. As public awareness of the scale and horror of slavery grew, their claims gained greater resonance. Religiously inspired activists made increasingly unreasonable demands on other citizens and the government, insisting that the vehicle for national redemption had to be a great popular movement.

As an abolitionist from an elite Southern slaveholding family, Grimké testified that slavery required not only personal atonement but also collective struggle. Acknowledging her special burden in speeches and pamphlets, Grimké nonetheless went beyond her own testimony when she insisted that the slaveholding South's sin fell just as squarely on Northern listeners, because they were ensnared in slavery's commercial and political web.[3]

During the 1830s when Weld and the Grimkés were at the peak of their influence, they convinced supporters that faith and action were inseparable. The new Antislavery Movement that Weld did so much to mobilize was different from what had preceded it. It treated slavery as a collective sin. This great national sin had poisoned America's republican experiment, and it was abolitionists' Christian duty to bring the national sin to everyone's attention. Weld wanted all Americans to recognize that complicity with slavery brought guilt and shame to every Christian. The first step in advancing a plan for the spiritual equality of all races was overturning slavery, but the ultimate aim was the full vindication of human rights.

Radical abolitionists like Weld differed from their predecessors by insisting that the republic must immediately abolish slavery without compensating slaveholders for the loss of their "property." They categorically rejected any partial or gradual plans for emancipation as well as colonization schemes that would free slaves but deposit them in Africa or Haiti. Their stance antagonized moderate abolitionists and the Protestant establishment because it charged them with complacency, white supremacy, and unwillingness to embrace integration and reconciliation. This struck many white Americans as an unconscionable endorsement of interracial society, which they denounced as radical race-mixing.

Activist virtuosi in the Antislavery Movement combined religious and secular thinking in new ways. They drew from evangelical Christianity but moved beyond conventional religion when they embraced universal human rights. They connected Enlightenment ideals to the religious conviction that not only slavery but also any racism was a sin because whites and blacks were spiritual equals in God's eyes. Grimké and Weld were among those who went even one step further. The feminist wing of the radical Antislavery Movement insisted that sexism, like slavery, was an affront to human dignity and God-given spiritual equality. By rejecting the conventional Protestant understanding of women's circumscribed roles and by insisting upon their civil rights, feminists

Photo 5.1 Theodore Dwight Weld.

provoked hostile reactions from many evangelicals whose support for the antislavery cause was necessary. Conflicts about feminism ultimately split the movement and revealed the limits of religious mobilization in nineteenth-century America.[4]

Religious mobilization was essential to the radical abolition movement because it sprung from a ground seeded with evangelical awakenings and intense moralism. As foreign visitors like Alexis de Tocqueville observed, evangelical religion animated antebellum America to a remarkable extent and spurred a host of morally charged reform movements. But the Antislavery Movement stood out among them. It was the most radical and divisive public cause because the implications of immediate abolition were nothing short of revolutionary. Nevertheless, a peaceful revolution of the spirit, not a violent one, seemed eminently possible to activists steeped in evangelical culture.

People like Grimké and Weld had experienced personal rebirth and they felt the power of Holy Spirit. In the revivals and camp meetings that spread from England to the American frontier in the eighteenth and nineteenth centuries, evangelicals had

Photo 5.2 Angelina Grimké.

seen massive conversions from sin and passivity to a true, energetic religion. They believed that when the Gospel truth was recognized, conversions would be swift and sweeping. The radical abolitionists trusted that evangelical religion had remade the culture so that everyone—man or woman, free or slave—could obey what Angelina Grimké called the "small still voice" of the soul. Once that voice was unleashed, it would be part of a chorus of the faithful united in redemptive struggles.[5]

Evangelical religion brought together the Protestant devotion to spiritual cultivation with a freshly charged moral activism. In the hands of activists it radically recombined Luther's concept of virtuosity with outspoken, passionate, and uncompromising moral advocacy.[6] Abolitionists mounted a sustained and organized challenge to existing institutions, powerful stakeholders, and conventional beliefs. Blocked from advancing their crusade through standard politics, the activist virtuosi leading the antislavery cause invented a new vehicle to pursue holiness and assail spiritual privilege that was neither church nor state—the morally driven social movement. Evangelical religion had produced paths to spiritual virtuosity that required an end to slavery and embraced racial and gender equality. The radical abolitionists forever enlivened democracy by making morally driven social movements permanent features of the modern social landscape.

Economic Expansion, Slavery, and Social Upheaval

The English-speaking world experienced dramatic economic expansion and social upheaval in the late eighteenth and early nineteenth centuries when the industrial revolution combined astounding technological advances with a rational division of labor. Factories replaced farms and workshops as steam power altered textile manufacturing, mining, and iron working. Although the fruits of the new prosperity were unevenly shared, productivity improved so much that millions escaped from the misery of bare subsistence, and England's urban population nearly doubled between 1700 and 1800.

In the decades after independence, the American economy also grew rapidly and the population moved beyond the coastal eastern seaboard into the continent's interior. Manufacturing expanded, particularly in the New England and Middle Atlantic States. Pulled by opportunity and pushed by population growth and poor soil, American farmers moved westward. Population growth was explosive: the new republic had five million people by 1800 and twenty million by 1845. With its high birthrate, America was a society of young adults who were drawn into public engagement through religious revivals, election rallies, and parades.[7] Despite being spread out as they moved west, Americans were integrated into national affairs by the recent proliferation of railroads, telegraphs, canals, and steamboats. However, the new prosperity challenged the conservative religions that were the bedrock of the early republic.[8]

For all of its astounding success, Anglo-American capitalism exacted an appalling moral price. For many people, money had become society's "common whore" and its "visible divinity."[9] Radical evangelicals believed that the economic development stained every purchase and tainted each financial gain with sin, and they saw slavery as a particularly odious and inescapable element of the market economy. The transatlantic trade in millions of captured Africans fueled eighteenth-century prosperity because slaves were essential to the sugar production at the center of the commercial web that entrapped Britain, New England, and the West Indies.

In Britain, abolitionism found mass support. Led by the famous evangelical politician William Wilberforce, the Antislavery Movement succeeded spectacularly in abolishing the trans-Atlantic slave trade by Act of Parliament in 1807. Afterward, activists kept up a continual fight for the total abolition of slavery in the British Empire that they won in 1833.[10]

English Quaker and evangelical Christian activists were the first to draw attention to slavery's centrality to economic exchange. They urged the righteous to forgo goods produced by slaves and pioneered the use of consumer boycotts. The Quakers even shunned fellow members who would not divest from slavery-related enterprises. Portraying slavery as an evil that demanded political redress, the Christian Antislavery Movement made a critical innovation. While English antislavery activists mobilized moral unease behind a concrete public campaign for political action, Americans were denied the legislative route to abolition. Instead, they relied on a social movement which involved hundreds of thousands of ordinary people in petition drives, demonstrations, and underground networks to assist escaped slaves.

Nevertheless, slavery, particularly in North America, continued to thrive. Some had hoped that factory production and the creed of free trade would make slavery an anachronism.[11] However, slavery proved far too profitable. As sugar's importance receded, the cotton that slaves cultivated and picked became the world's most important commodity, and textiles were the first mass-produced good.

Cotton linked the plantation field to the factory floor and the clothing shop in ways moralists found impossible to ignore. Domestic slavery undergirded American prosperity and King Cotton demanded it. In the colonial era, the center of slave production in the United States was in the tobacco and rice fields of the eastern seaboard, but the newly invented cotton gin increased efficiency and made more widespread cotton growing profitable.

In 1800, only one in ten American slaves worked cotton but a half-century later more than 60 percent did and cotton comprised half of the value of all American exports. Slaves became the most substantial stock of physical capital in the United States and a pillar of its financial system. Worse yet, the suppression of the international slave trade gave rise to flourishing internal markets and slave prices ballooned. Between 1800 and 1860, more than one million slaves were sold and transported (many by forced march) from Virginia, Maryland, and other declining plantation regions to the Deep South and the Gulf Coast. The expanding slave market increasingly separated families and that was particularly troubling for evangelical Christians.[12]

No one could ignore the reciprocal relationship between the slaveholding and nonslaveholding states. William Lloyd Garrison stated plainly what many felt when

THE REV. JOHN WESLEY AND HIS FRIENDS AT OXFORD.
(From the Historic Painting by Marshall Claxton, Esq.)

Photo 5.3 The Wesleys and the Holy Club at Oxford.

he declared that everyone—whether in the North or South—had become slavery's "partner in iniquity."[13] Because slavery was so central to the prosperity of the republic, practical politicians and advocates for national development did not make the case against slavery. The antislavery argument was the province of "impractical" religious idealists committed to abolition at whatever the cost.[14]

The radical abolitionists cared little for the conventional give-and-take of politics. Garrison rejected American institutions entirely, condemning electoral politics as a wicked farce and Independence Day as "a day of great lamentation."[15] Weld dismissed arguments that immediate abolition was impractical by explaining, "As a question of politics and national economy, I have passed it with scarce a look or word believing that the business of abolitionists is with the heart of the nation, rather than with its purse strings."[16]

Angelina Grimké and her older sister Sarah were intimately aware of slavery's evils and willing to speak against it. Slavery brought bitterness to their family because their father was a prominent judge who hailed from one of Charleston's most respected plantation dynasties. The Grimké sisters were deeply pious and their consciences were stung by the ways that slaves were treated.

The Grimkés' parents condemned Sarah for secretly and illegally teaching a slave to read the Bible. In sympathy, Angelina repeatedly rebuked her other siblings and her mother over their moral indifference, mourning how slavery's corrupting power "works such fearful ruin upon the hearts of the slaveholders."[17] Sarah was so distressed by home life that she abandoned the South, became a Quaker, and moved in with relatives in Philadelphia. When she reached her early twenties, Angelina, the baby of the family, followed Sarah into exile despite the pain it caused their mother. Neither sister was permitted to return home.[18]

These experiences made the Grimké sisters unusually impassioned witnesses against slavery during times when all outspoken abolitionists were unusual. Even as

Photo 5.4 A slave auction.

Photo 5.5 William Lloyd Garrison making an anti-slavery speech on Boston Common.

it became the bleeding sore of the republic, most white Americans either supported or tolerated slavery. Antislavery voices could trouble the conscience of the nation but cotton's profitability inspired Southern politicians to flex "slave power" in Congress. Southern states effectively controlled the Senate, and both the Democrats and the Whigs accommodated slavery's legal and political prerogatives. Southern politicians demanded the strengthening of slavery and pushed for its continual western expansion. On the other side, "free soil" Northerners insisted upon containing it.

The matter came to a head in the Compromise of 1850, in which Congress limited the expansion of slavery in exchange for a robust Fugitive Slave Act that obliged Northern authorities to assist in the arrest and return of runaway slaves. In 1854, the Kansas-Nebraska Act nevertheless upset the consensus and threatened the creation of yet more slave states. It had become unmistakably clear to almost all Americans that the politics of slavery, like its economics, had drawn everyone into its orbit as the country bitterly divided into pro- and antislavery camps.[19]

Paths to Virtuosity

The rise of radical abolitionism as a social movement was only possible because evangelicalism had changed Protestantism and God had become more personal, imminent, and concerned with earthly affairs. Evangelicalism championed the spiritual autonomy of each believer and was radically democratic in its organization. In America, evangelicals created a thoroughly populist religion that was guided by common sense, Bible reading, and personal experience.

The origins of the evangelical upsurge in Anglo-American Protestantism can be traced to the Reformation grown cold. In the eighteenth century, theologians of the state churches in Europe stressed duty and morality over spirituality and the quest for redemption until economic and social change threw the establishment into crisis.

In England, as the population shifted to towns and cities, the parish system was neglected. Ordinary people saw institutionalized religion as stale and torpid. Critics charged that the Church of England was resistant to reform and insensitive to the pastoral needs of its flock. Poor attendance rates at worship services reflected a church that offered ordinary people too little fellowship, too little opportunity for religious expression, and too little spontaneity.[20]

In America, the established Episcopalian (Anglican), Congregationalist, and Presbyterian faiths of the Colonial era were similarly unable and unwilling to meet the shifting religious needs of a frontier population. At the end of the eighteenth century, less than a fifth of Americans regularly attended church. The established churches huddled on the coasts, employed few ministers, and rarely missionized.[21]

Stagnant faiths in England and America were ripe for the waves of evangelical innovation and social mobilization known as the "Great Awakenings." In the 1730s, John and Charles Wesley gathered a group of like-minded students and theologians into a Holy Club at Oxford. They studied the lessons of continental Pietism and the spiritual revivals developed by the Moravian sect. Against established churches that were preoccupied with doctrine and conformity, they insisted on inward spiritual transformation that could be fostered by prayer, devotion, and selfless service. The Wesleys inspired a network of young preachers and supporters pledged to religious revitalization. Methodism grew out of this network and thrived because it recruited lay preachers. Although founded as an Anglican movement which invited all believers to "advance in holiness toward perfection in Christ," by the end of the century Methodism was evolving into a separate faith.[22]

The Anglo-American revival that began with the Wesley brothers at Oxford and with Jonathan Edwards in New England was premised on an ethic of spiritual virtuosity. Each soul needed to experience a "new birth," a spiritual conversion that would forge a personal bond between the believer and a redeeming God. It was not enough to count on God's grace and defer to ministers: evangelicals insisted on the convert's active holiness. Everyone could preach and lead a life of mission.

Evangelicals employed a direct and emotional style. George Whitefield was an exemplar of the new type of preaching. Already a sensation in England before his first tour of America, the evangelist gave hundreds of sermons to thousands of American listeners. His heartfelt, energizing sermons described the terrible burden of sin and the urgent need for new birth in the spirit. Unlike the solemn assemblies that prevailed in the established churches, Whitfield's were grippingly entertaining and worshippers shouted, swayed and wept during his widely promoted and advertised evangelical meetings.[23]

The popular response to Whitefield's preaching shocked the Protestant establishment. He reached out to lowly classes and even to slaves. Orthodox theologians concluded that unseemly evangelical revivals were bad for church discipline. They gave undue license to the enthusiasm of unlettered laymen in gatherings where races mixed and women spoke publicly. In time, English authorities checked the Methodists' democratic enthusiasm.

The situation was different in America, however, because of its weaker institutions and scattered government. American Christians were difficult for established church leaders to discipline because they had little influence outside of coastal areas. This enabled the upstart sects to remake the American spiritual landscape. In 1776, there were a few dozen Methodist congregations in North America. In 1850, there were 13,000 Methodist congregations with nearly three million members. By the mid-nineteenth century, Methodists and the Baptist sects commanded a much larger share of religious adherents than the old denominations.[24]

In the United States, the empowerment of lay preachers and leaders was especially important in creating the new activist spirituality. Antebellum America had more preachers than Europe and they were young, energetic, and enterprising. They generated publicity, traveled tirelessly to preach or attend camp meetings, and founded a host of religious periodicals. Many were like Theodore Weld, who was an adept preacher and gifted organizational entrepreneur despite the fact that he never graduated from a seminary or university.

In the 1820s and 1830s, the evangelical awakening stirred widespread commitments to improve public morality. At the same time, American clergymen founded a proliferation of advocacy groups with the support of wealthy benefactors. The men at the helm of this organized benevolence were determined to remedy a host of social ills that needed to be confronted in order to truly Christianize America. Rather than slavery, they claimed that greatest of these sins were alcoholic drink, work on the Sabbath day, physical sloth, illiteracy, and sexual vice.[25]

Like their Reformation forebears, the activists in the Antislavery Movement were unsatisfied with churches that focused on narrow reforms, charity, and obedience. They denounced religious orthodoxy for favoring social hierarchy and moral regulation over spiritual engagement. They attacked the clergy and the organized benevolence institutions for complacency, pragmatism, and racial superiority. Moreover, they decried conservative clergymen's tepid reformism and their willingness to countenance slavery and racial injustice. And they contested the role of women in the churches and public life, contending that they should speak and play leading roles.[26] Critics of mild change drew together in intellectual communities committed to institutional reform that eliminated the bastions of spiritual privilege.

Pivotal Communities

In contrast with the Reformation, universities were peripheral to the evangelical movement and the rise of abolitionism. The Wesley brothers and their Holy Club at Oxford helped stimulate evangelicalism and encouraged lay ministry and popular preaching, but Methodists, Baptists, and other evangelical sects spread a simple message that did not require academically trained clergy or even churches because many revivals took place at open-air events and camp meetings.[27]

Informal intellectual communities, however, played a pivotal role in the Antislavery Movement. A determined antislavery subculture thrived in cities like London, New

York, Philadelphia, and Boston, where black ministers, white moralists, writers, and journalists created a space that was unusually open to thoughtful conversations about race. Black congregations, Quaker meetings, and free-speech halls hosted lively debates about the values and tactics of the emerging movement.

When Garrison's militant abolitionist newspaper, *The Liberator*, appeared in 1831, it drew upon and fostered this diverse intellectual community. Garrison had the financial assistance of antislavery businessman Arthur Tappan in launching his paper, but *The Liberator* relied on free African Americans as readers and writers as well as for the greatest share of its financial support. Garrison's paper and the emerging activist network that it sustained brought militant abolitionism to a national audience.[28]

In the West, some frontier seminaries became hotbeds of the activism that grew into a national Antislavery Movement. The Lane Institute, for example, was a new Presbyterian seminary in the western state of Ohio. Funded by Christian philanthropists, Lane was founded as an outpost of respectable Protestantism on the wild frontier and the famed theologian Lyman Beecher became its first president.[29] Encouraged by the Tappan brothers, who were not only his patrons but among the seminary's major contributors, Weld enrolled in Lane's first theology class in 1832.

Weld preferred activism to ordination, and when he arrived, he was already well known for public speaking and organizing of revivals. His father was a Congregational pastor in Connecticut who wanted his son to follow a traditional path that led to ordination. However, the younger Weld was miserable at Andover seminary and dropped out after a year. Despite suffering from memory problems and other infirmities, Weld was determined to find his own way. He worked hard to become an outstanding public speaker and his talent for oratory attracted Lyman Beecher's support and encouragement.

In the 1820s, after he was converted to evangelical Presbyterianism, Weld spent several years assisting with evangelical revivals and moral advocacy campaigns. Like many Christians who were uneasy about slavery, Weld had once supported colonization societies that hoped to gradually emancipate slaves and settle them abroad in black societies like Liberia, Sierra Leone, or Haiti. By the time that Weld enrolled at Lane, however, he had undergone a profound spiritual reckoning with slavery. His travels in the South intensified his long-standing unease and convinced him of the shallowness and mendacity of pro-slavery arguments. He had absorbed William Lloyd Garrison's radical abolitionist thought and concluded that racism was an affront to human rights and that slavery was the root of the racist vine. The various colonization schemes now struck Weld as cruel and unjust.

Presbyterians, like other denominations, did not take a clear antislavery stand.[30] Beecher counseled his fellow clergymen to ban discussion of abolition in their congregations, lest the "silken ties" that bound Northern and Southern Presbyterians be frayed. Rather than fighting slavery, Beecher hoped for eventual colonization and proclaimed that the foremost goal of Christian advocacy should be legislative changes that established the sacredness of the Sunday Sabbath. He asserted that the moral priority eclipsing all others was reversing danger to the nation's soul that a seven-day-a-week mail delivery system represented.[31]

Weld wanted to force confrontation on the slavery issue on fellow Presbyterians and bend the faith toward abolition. When he arrived at Lane, he was the only student with outspoken antislavery views, but he soon converted his entire theology class. Like Weld, most were already experienced preachers and a dozen had been agents of various benevolent societies. They were predominantly New Yorkers and New Englanders, well steeped in the culture of the Second Great Awakening.[32]

Employing revivalist tactics, Weld focused first on converting the most abject sinners to abolition—the Southerners—because their conversion would have the biggest effect on the others. Weld's first Southern convert amazed his classmates, as "his noble soul broke loose from its shackles."[33] Despite the opposition of his professors, Weld built on that early momentum by initiating a grand debate that involved students from across the school. This fusion of an academic seminar and a religious revival went on for eighteen days. Propelled by raw emotional energy, the debate progressed swiftly from resolving that slavery was evil, to agreeing that colonization compromised with that evil, and, finally, to dramatic public confessions to the sin of slavery and promises of personal dedication to abolition.

In the heat of the debate, Lane's students pledged to battle racism. Afterward, they made good on their commitment by reaching out to Cincinnati's embattled free black community with charitable assistance and a school staffed by volunteers. Weld and some of his followers stopped worshipping alongside white Presbyterians and resolved to attend only African American churches. All of this alarmed Lane's trustees who prevailed upon Reverend Beecher to discipline Weld's band and halt their racial outreach. But Weld and his companions stood fast. Garrison's *Liberator* praised the rebels and denounced Lane as a "Bastille of oppression." Rather than submit to Beecher's ruling, the rebels withdrew en masse from Lane. Most of the students quickly reenrolled at Oberlin, which immediately made the college an abolitionist stronghold. Inspired by Lane, uprisings against conservative clergymen and professors erupted at colleges and seminaries across Ohio, New York, and New England.[34]

After Lane, Weld discovered his vocation as a full-time abolitionist for the new American Anti-Slavery Society, which he helped found in 1833 with the support of the Tappan brothers. He set about shaping a cadre of activists who would become the voice of the movement and organizers of local antislavery societies. Weld drew on the culture of mentorship and spiritual discovery that were part of evangelical Christianity.

Mentorship and Discovery

Deep spiritual bonds based on intimacy, confrontation with sin, and self-scrutiny characterized the process of evangelical conversion. Close spiritual partnerships between its leading theologians and their protégés followed that model and shaped the emerging Antislavery Movement. Because radical abolitionism involved calls for active holiness and training in oratory and organizing, mentorship played an unmistakable part in its growth and spread

Weld entered Hamilton College in upstate New York in 1825, but he did not remain long. Academic studies were far less appealing to him than the religious awakening that was sweeping upstate New York under the leadership of the brilliant Presbyterian revivalist Charles Grandison Finney. Finney was an emotional and strident preacher, roundly criticized by conservative clergymen. At first, Weld joined the critics, but then he witnessed the "wonderful outpourings of the Holy Spirit" that Finney awakened.[35] A public confrontation between the two men led to a tearful embrace. Finney called on Weld to commit totally to "unselfish benevolence" and a life of holiness. Weeping with joy, Weld responded by joining the band of young men who assisted Finney in organizing his revivals. Finney's mentorship provided Weld with the revival techniques that lifted his antislavery work to new levels.

Weld's experience with mentors was common among abolitionists. Quaker activist and publicist Benjamin Lundy, for example, inspired many abolitionists, philanthropist Arthur Tappan and William Lloyd Garrison among them. However, Sarah and Angelina Grimké may have had the most intimate and intense mentoring relationship of any abolitionists.

Since she was thirteen years older than her sister, the Grimkés made Sarah Angelina's godmother, a lifetime duty that she took quite seriously. The sisters were very close and Angelina followed Sarah into evangelicalism and then into Quakerism. She also emulated Sarah's bold decision to abandon the South in order to escape from the pressures of a slaveholding family. Sarah supported Angelina's public career and, moving in with her sister and brother-in-law, helped them through three difficult pregnancies and the trials of child rearing. Angelina and Sarah had an intense, frequently troubled, but nevertheless supportive relationship that nurtured their spirituality. They inevitably held each other to the highest standards of moral integrity.

Mentors helped abolitionists find their public voices and William Lloyd Garrison's mentorship was crucial for Angelina Grimké's public career. Once she settled in Philadelphia, Angelina avidly read the abolitionist press. *The Liberator* won her to the cause of immediate abolition and she wrote to Garrison explaining her conversion. Recognizing a person of uncommon intellect and experience, Garrison published the letter.[36] Garrison also mentored Frederick Douglass in his rise from obscurity as a runaway slave to one of the most worlds' most influential antislavery intellectuals.

Although her Quaker meeting rebuked Angelina for vanity after her article appeared, Garrison pressed her to continue writing. In 1836, she authored a brilliant essay, "Appeal to the Christian Women of the South." In the wake of the public attention it drew, Weld recruited Angelina and Sarah to become antislavery activists and public speakers for the American Anti-Slavery Society. Now it was Angelina's turn to mentor Sarah. She fostered her older sister's political conscience, persuading her to break with orthodox Quaker conventions and become an outspoken abolitionist and feminist writer. In 1837 and 1838, the sisters took to the road, attending antislavery conventions, speaking to racially mixed audiences across New England, and helping organize women's antislavery societies.

Social Networks and Bridging Activism

The activist virtuosi of the nineteenth century moved between the high culture of established Protestantism with its seminaries, benevolent societies, and civic associations and the popular religiosity of small town revivals. No one excelled at this bridging more than Weld. In building the American Anti-Slavery Society, he brokered an alliance between the elite moralists and philanthropists at the helm of benevolent associations and the radical publishers and lay preachers outside of orthodox ecclesiastical control. Weld had strong ties to elite philanthropists like the Tappan brothers and was a respected minister's son raised in the heart of New England Protestantism. An effective ambassador to religious bodies and reform societies, he could debate Calvinist theology as easily as he could speak plainly from the heart.

Radical abolitionism became a social movement in large part because Weld bridged the empire of benevolent organizations on one side and popular religiosity on the other. Weld learned the techniques and language of the frontier revival from no less a master than Finney. Never ordained, he had retained the independence and spontaneity of an extemporaneous lay preacher. Personally committed to manual labor and a frugal lifestyle, Weld could relate to workers, backwoodsmen, and African Americans.

His most impressive innovation was constructing a network of professional antislavery agents. As the American Anti-Slavery Society's lead organizer, Weld carefully selected and trained agents from a new generation of activist virtuosi dedicated to the cause of racial equality that had emerged in the wake of the Lane Rebellion. Weld drew the most able into the Society's network and brought a new level of organization and sophistication to their activism.

Unlike previous American reform groups that had relied on local notables and clergymen to spread their message, Weld cultivated a cadre of professional, paid agitators. They could bridge the social gap between the radical spiritual and ideological innovations being made by the Antislavery Movement and the local faith communities that would provide abolitionist foot soldiers. Perfecting techniques that had been honed in the evangelical revival, Weld taught his disciples to bring people to a public confession of the sin of slavery and a pledge to redress it.

The image of seventy righteous disciples going forth to spread the word of God had deep Biblical resonance.[37] Having secured elite patronage to pay their salaries, Weld called his own disciples the "Seventy," and they were among the first professional social movement activists in American history. He selected some of them from among his Lane classmates and some from other provincial seminaries. Weld also included experienced antislavery speakers and revivalist preachers without seminary training. Most of the Seventy were New Englanders or New Yorkers who were well versed in the organization of evangelical revivals, but he also recruited several Southerners. Weld made sure that his activist network cut across lines of religious difference. Many agents belonged to respectable Congregationalist and Presbyterian churches, but Weld also recruited a dozen from the upstart Methodist and Baptist sects. Most had middle-class backgrounds and many had attended universities or seminaries. He boldly included the Grimké sisters among them.[38]

Until their funding ran out, the Seventy set America afire in the mid-1830s. They attracted extensive publicity and, not infrequently, hostile mobs in Northern towns. Weld and his agents won respect for enduring insults and injuries with resolution and Christian forbearance. The Seventy used dramatic revivalist techniques to compel people to confront slavery and their sinful acquiesce to it. Portraying slavery as a collective sin that imperiled the soul of every American, they urged men and women alike to undergo a conversion to free their spirits and allow them to dedicate their lives to the holy cause of abolition.

Weld's mobilization of professional agents immersed in evangelical culture was a brilliant organizational strategy. Like the revivalist preachers whose techniques Weld had learned, the Seventy left behind converts in their wake and they built on their public commitments by founding local antislavery societies. In 1835, there were around 200 local antislavery societies across the country. A year into Weld's professional organizing drive, there were more than 500 societies. By 1838, there were more than 1,000 auxiliary societies boasting more than 100,000 members.[39]

Opportunity and Opposition

It is almost axiomatic to observe that social movements arise when their leaders perceive an opportunity to influence politics or when new openings allow them to spread. However, in the radical Antislavery Movement's case, the picture is murkier. Opposition to the movement was always much more severe in America than it was in England, because English antislavery societies could count on friends in Parliament and the judiciary. Moreover, British abolitionism capitalized on well-institutionalized moral advocacy networks that included the Anglican Church.[40]

In the United States, where domestic slavery reigned and racism was normative, abolitionism faced far more substantial obstacles. Abolitionists had few legislative allies in Congress, while slavery's defenders counted on a solid bloc of Southern congressmen and their Northern allies who continually sought to expand slavery and opposed any legal check on it. In America, most churches either supported slavery or tolerated it.

All of this meant that American abolitionists faced a level of hostility and public rejection unlike anything in Europe. The 1830s were years of growing momentum for the Antislavery Movement, thanks in large part to Weld's organizational strategy. However, even as the Antislavery Movement's resources, public visibility, and outreach efforts surged, a great wave of repression limited its gains. Slavery's friends

ATTACK ON THE POST OFFICE, CHARLESTON. S.C.

Photo 5.6 Pro-Slavery Rioters in Charleston Destroy Antislavery Tracts.

used both law and lawlessness to blot out abolitionism. Widespread racism fueled resistance to African American rights and advancement. Besides throwing up political hurdles, pro-slavery forces drew upon bigotry to organize large-scale violence against abolitionists.

Southern members of Congress imposed a gag rule that prevented the presentation of antislavery petitions. Southern states forbade antislavery activities and their local postmasters, with the backing of President Andrew Jackson, refused to deliver "seditious" antislavery material. In the Grimkés' hometown of Charleston, 3,000 men stormed the central post office to burn parcels of abolitionist tracts that were part of the American Anti-Slavery Society's campaign to distribute millions of pieces of literature across America.[41]

During the 1830s, mob violence and intimidation abetted by men of property also stalled the Antislavery Movement's progress in Northern states. In New York City in 1834, rioters assaulted African American leaders' homes and sacked Lewis Tappan's residence. In Philadelphia, pro-slavery mobs attacked free blacks. In Boston, a mob beat and nearly succeeded in lynching William Lloyd Garrison. In 1837, an Illinois mob murdered abolitionist printer Elijah Lovejoy. In Troy, in upstate New York, a mob assaulted Weld when he attempted to give a lecture series, leaving him shaken and badly injured.

There were more than seventy instances of collective violence that targeted American abolitionists in the 1830s. The violence reached its peak between 1835 and 1836, precisely when antislavery organizing was at its most active. The repression was intentional, targeted, and effective. In most instances, local authorities and

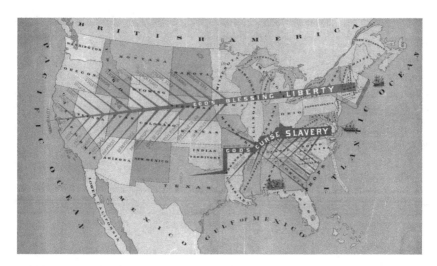

Photo 5.7 Abolitionist map of the USA.

political notables either backed rioters or did nothing to stop them. Northern newspapers and politicians typically blamed abolitionists for the disorder, variously accusing them of being anarchists, socialists, British agents, or race mixers. Conservative clergymen were scarcely more sympathetic. In New England, the Congregational Church banned abolitionists from the pulpit.[42]

Although abolitionism influenced the public understanding of slavery and contributed to growing political divisions between North and South, abolitionists had reason to be deeply disappointed. Between 1830 and 1860, the Antislavery Movement could claim little legislative success at the national level. In 1790, there had been eight slave states, and in 1860 there were fifteen. In the same interval, the number of slaves in America had more than doubled to four million. Abolitionists had failed to stop the war against Mexico that expanded slavery, impede the passage of the hated Fugitive Slave law, or stop the Supreme Court's Dred Scott Decision, a ruling that denied blacks basic human rights. An antislavery political party in 1840 found little support, despite its wealthy patrons. In the national elections of 1840, 1844, and 1848, the Liberty Party never won more than two percent of the national vote or carried a majority in a single county.

Evangelism generated the commitment to enact holiness that made it possible to mobilize people behind the righteous cause no matter how unlikely its realization. And faith nurtured resolution. The violent repression of the 1830s shook radical abolitionism but did not destroy it. In its darkest moment, Angelina Grimké was among those who resolved to risk everything by committing herself publically to the Antislavery Movement.

As violence against Northern abolitionists spread, she wrote a letter of support to a shaken William Lloyd Garrison, who had recently escaped a lynching in Boston. She implored him to remain resolute: "The ground upon which you stand is holy ground; never—never surrender it."[43] He, in turn, invited her to join the cause.[44] Scores of

American abolitionists' stories reveal a similar theme of highly religious people who imagined the struggle as a righteous crusade. For activist virtuosi, the Antislavery Movement was less political than spiritual. They energetically sought holiness and moral purity as they made ending slavery their great cause.

Outside of some Northern and Western states, antislavery forces only had success when they insisted on limiting the expansion of slavery, not when they called for its abolition. The radical abolitionists remained a widely despised minority until eleven Southern states had seceded from the Union and Southern rebels attacked Fort Sumter in 1861, triggering America's Civil War. Four months before the war ended in 1865, Congress passed the Thirteenth Amendment to the US Constitution and abolished slavery.

Publicity and the Limits of Moral Persuasion

One prominent German historian asserted: "No printing, no Reformation."[45] We can add: "No printing, no antislavery movement." Traveling speakers like Weld and his Seventy were effective but antislavery writers reached wider audiences through national distribution of newspapers, magazines, and pamphlets.

The expansion of print capitalism in the eighteenth and nineteenth centuries had made communication cheaper and more accessible than in Luther's day. In Britain, the trans-Atlantic publishing trade brought evangelical texts to audiences across the empire and antislavery activists followed suit. During the Great Awakenings, evangelicalism produced a flood of printed sermons, journals, and conversion memoirs.[46]

In America, the government accidentally subsidized evangelism and moral advocacy through laws designed to nourish a free press, stimulate civic life, and inform voters on the frontier. In 1792, Congress established a national postal service and set low postal rates for printed materials, and eighteen years later, the government mandated daily mail deliveries. However, if national leaders hoped to create a strong sense of unified American identity through a national postal service, they would be disappointed. Flourishing media markets actually accelerated diversification and contention, as publishers exploited the regional, sectarian, and political diversity of antebellum America.[47]

Evangelists and moral reformers found the press to be a powerful instrument because of America's low population density. Settlers who lived on isolated farms were eager for national news as well as personal communications. The press helped to fulfill the need for news and made rural Americans available to activists who wanted to inform, evangelize, and mobilize them. Just as sixteenth-century Protestants had helped ordinary people read the Bible for themselves, evangelists supported universal literacy and Bible reading so there would be more support for their upstart faiths.[48]

Inspired by evangelicals' successful conversions, abolitionists were convinced that information and argumentation would be sure weapons for the crusade against slavery. They had faith that moral persuasion could convert slaveholding America to the abolitionist cause. If Americans of every class and condition really knew the horror of slavery and its utter sinfulness, they would turn away from it. Weld declared:

> The old falsehood that the slave is kindly treated, shallow and stupid as it is, has enabled to sleep four-fifths of the free north and west; but with God's blessing the sleep shall not be unto death. Give facts a voice, and cries of blood shall ring till deaf ears tingle.[49]

The abolitionists' evangelical republicanism led them to believe that the nation could be redirected through an epidemic of spontaneous moral conversion. But slavery proved intractable and it was not easy to spread the liberating word.

The massive abolitionist publicity campaigns that distributed antislavery materials yielded limited political gains and triggered violent backlash. Intolerance and stubborn racism spurred attacks on speakers, printers and presses, as well as public burnings of antislavery literature. Worse yet for people convinced of the ultimate authority of the scriptures, persuasion and the "Gospel truth" were not enough to convince a majority of white Christians to turn against slavery.

Evangelicals of all stripes agreed that everyone was spiritually empowered to read and understand the Bible. Guided by common sense, every soul could ascertain God's will with no need for religious authorities or elaborate theology. Despite works such as Weld's learned and passionate 1837 treatise, The Bible against Slavery, abolitionists did not clearly prevail in the resulting debate on scripture. Even the Bible proved to be a dull weapon, because few evangelicals embraced the value of racial equality. While Southern Christians claimed that the Bible obviously justified the perpetuation of slavery, most Northern Christians struggled with their unease and moral ambivalence.[50] Only a stubborn minority who were already committed to abolition persisted in claiming that the Bible obviously forbade slavery.[51]

Even while they sought to win over public opinion through their interpretations of scripture, abolitionists struggled to maintain their identity as a cohesive movement. With a limited market and narrow subscriber base, the abolitionist press relied heavily on subsidies. William Lloyd Garrison, for example, founded The Liberator with assistance from the Tappans. Despite the remarkable ideological clarity and moral force that made The Liberator the leading antislavery newspaper, almost thirty years after its founding in 1831, it had only 3,000 subscribers.[52] Like The Liberator, most American antislavery newspapers barely had enough subscribers to remain in print, because there were relatively few committed abolitionists and ideological differences fragmented the appeal of its media.

Despite the hurdles, the abolitionist press, with The Liberator as the standard bearer, helped make a coherent Antislavery Movement possible. Garrison sagely built a shared identity among the groups by publishing and republishing a wide range of news related to the cause, by reporting on state- and national-level politics, and by commenting on the conference reports and proceedings of antislavery societies. Newspapers and magazines were lifelines for the embattled movement because they helped different groups communicate with each other, defined a general movement identity, and reached far-flung supporters.

More profoundly, the abolitionist press allowed the Antislavery Movement to exert a surprisingly strong cultural influence in shaping nineteenth-century America's national literary canon and moral imagination. In 1839, the newly married Grimké-Welds wrote what they believed was the definitive portrait of America's national sin. *American Slavery as It Is: Testimony of a Thousand Witnesses* became one of the most influential works that preceded the Civil War. With Sarah as their research assistant, they carefully assembled diverse accounts describing the practice of slavery. Along with harrowing first-person narratives, the book presented mountains of facts that they had combed from thousands of Southern newspaper stories and advertisements. Combining objective and subjective depictions of slavery, the book demolished most of the myth-making and deception that upheld the institution.

The book was an unexpected triumph for the American Anti-Slavery Society. Selling 100,000 copies, *American Slavery* became abolitionism's first best seller and influenced all subsequent antislavery literature. The Grimké-Welds believed that once Americans woke up to the hard facts about slavery and its material and moral consequences, decent and honest people would wholeheartedly reject the institution. In the Introduction, they wrote:

> Reader, you are empaneled as a juror to try a plain case and bring in an honest verdict. The question at issue is not one of the law, but of fact—"What is the actual condition of the slaves of the United States?" A plainer case never went to a jury. Look at it. Twenty-seven hundred thousand persons in the country, man, woman, and children are in SLAVERY. Is slavery, as a condition for human beings good, bad, or indifferent? We submit the question without argument. You have common sense, and a conscience, and a human heart; pronounce upon it.[53]

This was something new. Steeped in evangelical culture, the book united a systematic refutation of pro-slavery arguments with gripping personal stories intended to awaken its readers' empathy.

In the wake of *American Slavery*, abolitionists expanded their canon by creating a genre of slave narratives that further humanized and personalized the cause. *The Narrative of the Life of Frederick Douglass, an American Slave* was the most popular slave narrative, selling 30,000 copies between 1845 and 1860. Perhaps most important, abolitionist literature engendered Harriet Beecher Stowe's *Uncle Tom's Cabin*, the most influential antislavery work ever written. She was Lyman Beecher's daughter, but her husband, a Lane theologian, converted her to the abolitionist cause. In composing her melodrama, she drew on the testimonials and materials collected in *American Slavery*. After its first appearance in serial form in 1852, *Uncle Tom's Cabin* went on to sell hundreds of thousands of copies. Beecher Stowe concluded her book by imploring Americans to repent of the national sin of slavery. No work did more to awaken sympathy for the enslaved or trouble white readers' consciences.[54]

Despite the Antislavery Movement's limited political gains, the abolitionist press helped develop national debate and sustain an embattled cause. In a deeply Protestant culture where reading was the center of devotional life, the printed word brought abolitionism home. It shocked whites with the cruelty of the internal slave market, the separation of families in its service, and the bloody reality of cotton cultivation. Abolitionist writers were unique in portraying African Americans as people deserving of recognition and sympathy. They inflamed many white Americans' moral sympathies and convinced some that slavery corrupted the nation and imperiled its soul. The true power that the Antislavery Movement achieved was cultural, because it changed how many people on the sidelines of the struggle thought and felt about slavery.

Democratizing Spiritual Privilege

In the spring and summer of 1837, Sarah and Angelina Grimké made an unprecedented speaking tour of New England on behalf of the American Anti-Slavery Society. As two women born to the Southern plantation elite, their personas were enough to attract attention. But Weld had chiefly selected them to be among his Seventy because Angelina was a brilliant, emotionally affecting writer and speaker. Despite being slight and fragile looking, she was a powerful and magnetic presence whose careful deployment of rhetoric that emphasized guilt and conscience was perfectly crafted to affect Protestant audiences shaped by the culture of evangelicalism.[55]

Nevertheless, prominent women in the Antislavery Movement were lightning rods that attracted not only public condemnation but also criticism within antislavery ranks. In February 1838, Angelina crowned the two sisters' speaking tour with an appearance before a special committee of the Massachusetts Legislative Assembly. Invited to give testimony and present antislavery petitions, Angelina became the first woman in American history to address a legislature, a full decade before the first women's rights convention in Seneca Falls. In testimony that stretched over two days, she made the case for immediate abolition and insisted on the religious and moral duty of all Americans to oppose slavery. Angelina implored the lawmakers to recognize that women's partnership in a nation's guilt obliged them to take public action against slavery. Women's petitions as citizens of the republic had to be acknowledged, although they lacked the right to vote.

Feminists in the Antislavery Movement applauded Angelina's courage and eloquence. But pro-slavery journalists attacked the Grimké sisters as fanatics and ridiculed the 33-year-old Angelina and 46-year-old Sarah as "old hens." The New England clerical establishment was nearly unanimous in denouncing them. Conservatives condemned the "Devil-ina" whose unseemly conduct in political settings and before "promiscuous assemblies" ignored Christian teachings about modesty and feminine subordination. The bitterest criticism, however, came from fellow abolitionists who charged the sisters with endorsing a feminine immorality that was sure to destroy the foundations of society.[56] Angelina wittily dismissed the critics, noting, "We have given great offense on account of our womanhood, which seems to be as objectionable as was our abolitionism."[57]

The controversy created by the Grimkés's speaking tour and the crisis it provoked in the Antislavery Movement reveal much about the contours of spiritual privilege in American Protestantism. Despite championing the general ethic of virtuosity, for most evangelical Protestants, cultivating piety and reforming public morals took precedence over removing barriers to equality. In spite of drawing overwhelming support from women, evangelical leaders were reluctant to empower them. Talented women could be effective lay preachers and wealthy women might be valuable patrons, but evangelical leaders would not ordain them for ministry or leadership. And what historian Mark Noll has observed in nineteenth-century evangelical sects, "Traditional gender roles tended to reassert themselves as the heat of the early revivals cooled," also applied to the conservative wing of the Antislavery Movement.[58] As evangelicalism shifted in antebellum America from a religion of upstart sects to respectable churches, its leaders reemphasized women's subordination and sought to silence their voices as moral advocates.[59]

Many white evangelicals were also ambivalent about race. While British Methodists supported the antislavery cause, American Methodists divided on the issue. Baptists and Methodists encouraged free black preachers, but they wanted them to form their own churches and missionize only to African Americans. Their preaching to whites was as unacceptable as interracial worship or marriage.

Further compromising their own egalitarian ideals, many evangelicals were slaveholders and remained so after their spiritual conversions. Church leaders of all denominations were reluctant to force a slavery debate that might be internally divisive or undermine the republic.[60] Garrison's and the Grimké-Welds' insistence on inhabiting racially integrated worlds deeply offended racial sensibilities and unnerved some supporters. Growing support for radical abolitionism within the Methodist Church led it to split into Northern and Southern wings in 1844. The Southern Methodists were resolutely pro-slavery; many of its clergymen and all of its pre-Civil War bishops were slaveholders.[61]

Whatever its institutional shortcomings, the ethic of virtuosity at the heart of evangelicalism was hostile to spiritual privilege and nurtured egalitarianism (at least among white Americans). Although evangelicals shrank from confronting the inequalities in race and gender that undercut their assertions about spiritual equality, they tried to realize the Reformation's goal of universalizing access to spiritual virtuosity. They made personal conversion and a life of holiness an imperative for ordinary people, gave women a voice, and encouraged religious expression among slaves and free people of African descent.

The Antislavery Movement pressed evangelicals to take action against privilege and helped initiate the transformation of womanhood. For many white women of middle- and upper-class origins, evangelical religion was the road that drew them to abolitionism. With increasing confidence, American women engaged the public about slavery, distributed abolitionist literature, and, because they were denied the vote, drafted and distributed petitions. Besides membership in formal societies, the movement drew upon much wider support from sympathizers, chiefly women. Recognition of women's leading role came in 1837 when abolitionists held the Anti-Slavery Convention of American Women in New York City, which offered a prominent platform for women as public speakers and leaders.[62]

The Grimkés were among the women who discovered that confronting slavery had made them acknowledge women's subordination. As Angelina explained, "The investigation of the rights of the slave has led me to a better understanding of my own."[63] Without losing sight of the unique evil that was slavery, the Grimkés were part of a generation of spiritual virtuosi that connected spiritual equality and universal human rights.

Virtuosity and Vulnerability

Just a few days after her wedding in 1838, Angelina spoke at an abolitionist conference at Pennsylvania Hall, Philadelphia's free-speech temple. A mob assaulted the hall, and, although she was showered with broken glass, Grimké continued her speech. The next day, the hall was burned to the ground. Shocked by the violence and by the unwillingness of government officials to stop it, this proved to be Angelina Grimké's last major public address.

After the incidents at Pennsylvania Hall, Weld and Grimké largely retreated from public activism about slavery. In the following years, childbearing extracted a frightful physical and emotional toll on Angelina, but the constraints of domesticity did not lead to diminished public roles. Activist battles had worn down Theodore and ruined his voice. Angelina, who had never been physically robust, had spoken and traveled tirelessly in the years before her marriage and a bout of typhoid fever when she was on the road had nearly killed her. After the Philadelphia debacle, the family turned to farming and teaching as ways to make a modest living and enact their spiritual virtuosity more privately.

Throughout their lives, Theodore and Angelina were nourished by religious experiences and spiritual relationships that grew out of evangelical awakenings. Yet both had been profoundly disappointed with evangelical Christianity, which they came to see as constrained by stifling orthodoxy, particularly regarding women's emancipation. They lost confidence in the belief that confronting the sin of slavery would be enough to trigger national conversion to abolitionism. Without abandoning their pursuit of spiritual truth, they stepped away from the active leadership in the Antislavery Movement and sought an alternate to traditional Protestantism.

They were deeply discouraged by the infighting and schisms within the American Antislavery Society. In 1839, the movement split over issues of feminism and political strategy. The claim that the democratization of spiritual privilege included feminism was one of the major issues dividing abolitionism, although the Grimké sisters had sacrificed their reputations and religious standing for the cause.

William Lloyd Garrison was resolute in his defense of women's active role in the movement. However, while Garrisonian abolitionists, including many prominent women activists, embraced sexual equality, most evangelical abolitionists, including the leading philanthropists, opposed it. Feminism simply unnerved the evangelical wing of the Antislavery Movement that was led by the Tappans and supported by Finney. They publicly worried that the movement had grown too radical on questions of race and sex.[64] They favored a more moderate strategy focused on third-party politics and conciliating influential clergymen and church leaders.

The polarization of the movement was painful for Weld and the Grimké sisters. Weld was personally close to the conservatives and the schisms within the movement tore his friendship network apart. He also questioned Garrison's radical rejection of politics, so he had few places to turn. The criticism that they had faced from church leaders and from evangelical women in the Antislavery Movement wounded both of the Grimkés.

When they withdrew from active leadership, Weld and the Grimkés endured painful reproaches from their friends. Feminists visited the sisters and rebuked them for stepping aside, and Garrison's *Liberator* publically condemned the Grimkés and Weld for abdicating leadership. Weld was offended by the insensitivity of the critics who ignored their struggles to support themselves by their own labors and who overlooked their less visible work on behalf of the cause.

In the great struggle against slavery, American evangelicalism had sorely disappointed Weld. He lost confidence in conversion as a force to remake self and society. Moreover, his old evangelical friends, including Finney and the Tappans, scolded him for taking on heretical views and falling away from the church. They warned him that his salvation was in peril. But the inability to bring white America to confession and atonement for the sins of slavery and racism had shaken his faith. Adding to the pain caused by feminist criticisms, Sarah and Angelina's strict Quaker meeting expelled them because of their habitual nonconformity and immodesty. Deciding to find their spiritual way without the church, the Grimké-Welds explored a nondenominational Christianity—a "home religion"—of their own making.[65]

For the next two decades, the Grimké-Welds tended their spiritual garden in a new vocation as parents and householders. They supported themselves as farmers and teachers. They established a progressive school and tried in vain to help sustain a small utopian commune. They explored a wide range of spiritual and physical disciplines and observed Graham's diet of temperance and vegetarianism. However they were not completely apolitical. Theodore worked briefly as an antislavery researcher and lobbyist in Washington. Angelina and Sarah contributed to the ongoing feminist conversation and the family hosted political salons.

The Grimké-Welds pioneered a vision of peer marriage based on spirituality and a partnership of like-minded souls. It served as a model for other abolitionist couples and influenced the nineteenth-century women's rights movement.[66] In stepping away from lives given entirely to the Antislavery Movement, the Grimké-Welds defended the right of a spiritual virtuoso to withdraw from political contention when it threatened the soul. As Weld explained to a young abolitionist who came to visit their farm,

> there is a fighting era in everyone's life. While you feel it so, fight on; it is your duty, and the best thing you can possibly do. But when your work in that line is done, you can reach another and higher voice.[67]

Virtuoso Legacies

The Grimké sisters have become contemporary feminist icons because of their eloquence and courage as advocates of the women's cause. Theodore Weld is largely forgotten. One biographer called him the most important neglected figure in nineteenth-century history.[68] Although the most active and influential part of their careers lasted just a decade, during that time they were outstanding members of a generation that helped remake religion and society.

Antebellum America was set afire by a thirst for spiritual perfectionism. The Protestant revival created a new class of spiritual activists that was drawn into the public sphere by their belief that their private salvation was imperiled by shared sins, the national sin of slavery first among them. The demand for immediate abolition brought together a diverse set of activists and focused their attention on a single great and nonnegotiable cause. They became convinced that the road to personal sanctification ran though collective redemption. They sought to politicize everyday life and draw everyone into a grand struggle against collective sin.

In the late eighteenth and nineteenth centuries, evangelicalism strengthened the links between American politics and religion. Like their Reformation forebears, the activist virtuosi in the Antislavery Movement broke with the leading institutions. They assailed the Protestant establishment for conservatism and complacency. Because slavery divided American religion and neutralized the churches, activist virtuosi were compelled to organize America's first modern social movement.

Radical abolitionism's political influence was indirect but its cultural influence was profound. In the confrontation with slavery, the search for spiritual virtuosity informed a new understanding of personality that united intense, personal religious devotion with fervent public engagement. For people like Weld and the Grimkés, personality was the product of intense cultivation of an authentic spiritual self that had to express itself by taking public stances. Sanctification could be approached by confronting the iniquities of a corrupted world and tearing down spiritual privilege.

Since the nineteenth century, the great egalitarian causes of the modern era owe something to the powerful blending of spirituality and public engagement that began with the American Antislavery Movement. When they moved beyond the boundaries of traditional religion, abolitionists started to speak a new language of human rights. In the twentieth century, diverse and personalized forms of spirituality took flight in movements that went even farther by linking human rights to a notion of human potential that owed little to conventional religion.

6 Corita and the Human Potential Movement

On a cold but sunny January day in 1967, more than 20,000 spiritual seekers, neighborhood residents, stoners, and political activists crowded onto Golden Gate Park's Polo Field for the Human Be-In. People spilled over the park's edges listening to the Grateful Dead, Jefferson Airplane, and other local rock bands that were destined for international fame. The crowd heard speakers ranging from political activist and comedian Dick Gregory to Zen poet Gary Snyder. But psychedelic guru Timothy Leary stole the show when he shared his personal mantra: "Turn on, Tune in, Drop Out!"

Photo 6.1 The Human Be-In.

Soon after Leary captivated the crowd, the sun began to set, and Allen Ginsberg and Snyder asked everyone to turn toward the sea and intone a much older mantra—the Buddhist refrain "Om Sri Maitreya." The crowd came together to chant and sway before gathering up their colorful banners and packing up their cushions and blankets. They left the pungent scents of weed and patchouli oil behind as reminders of a day designed to animate every aspect of human potential: mind, body, psyche, and soul.

The following May, Sister Mary Corita helped sympathetic clergy, flower-bedecked nuns, and hundreds of students from Immaculate Heart College honor the Virgin as an empowered, vital "real woman of Nazareth."[1] They commemorated Mary's Day with folk songs, prayers, dancing, and an explosion of imaginative banners. Late in the afternoon, a joyful procession traveled from one end of the campus to the other. They closed the festive occasion with a celebratory mass. In this case, the drugs of choice were deep faith in God and optimism about human possibilities.

Both events honored spiritual experience and personal authenticity, and both angered conservative critics who feared that festivities like these undermined their authority and led to orgies.[2] The underlying similarities between the two festivals that seemed so far apart at first glance illustrated the ways that the movement's expansive influence inspired many kinds of spiritual virtuosity.

For the span of a decade, from the mid-1960s through the early 1970s, the movement functioned as a coalition of virtuosi with diverse religious, political, and professional agendas. Activist virtuosi from many faiths introduced new approaches to inclusive spirituality and social justice and challenged religious and political institutions.

Photo 6.2 Immaculate Heart College's 1964 Mary's Day Parade.
Copyright Corita Art Center, Immaculate Heart Community, Los Angeles, used with permission.

Sister Mary Corita combined her religious and artistic virtuosity when she silk-screened posters for different groups that were associated with the movement. Her posters about spiritual diversity, a loving Higher Power, peace, and social justice made an impact on both established faiths and alternative religions. Corita's art reflected her deeply felt hopes that the Catholic Church could someday accept the Human Potential Movement's values of experimentation, religious tolerance, and social action to make the world better for everyone.

Corita was neither at the forefront of a rebellious religious movement like Luther nor an outspoken agitator like Grimké and Weld, but she nevertheless inspired other spiritual virtuosi to bridge organizational boundaries and to challenge anything and anyone that stood in the way of spiritual equality and social justice. She shared Luther's foundational belief that people could pursue holiness and purification without formal intercession by any church.

By the end of the 1950s, Mary Corita was well known to progressives in the American Catholic world and also to artists in Los Angeles and New York. In 1964, she became better known and also more controversial, when one of her mentors asked her to paint a forty-foot-long banner for the Vatican Pavilion at the 1964 World's

Photo 6.3 Sister Mary Corita in 1966.
Copyright Corita Art Center, Immaculate Heart Community, Los Angeles, used with permission.

Fair. And by the end of 1967, Sister Corita was close to becoming a national celebrity when *Newsweek Magazine* featured her on the cover of its December 25 issue with the caption, "The Nun: Going Modern."[3]

In the early 1960s, before the Vatican Pavilion displayed her work or Sister Mary Corita appeared on the cover of *Newsweek*, influential Human Potential Movement virtuosi took note of the ways that her art communicated fresh approaches to spirituality and personal growth. George Leonard, the former *Look Magazine* editor who defined and popularized the movement, reached out to Corita and introduced her to his extensive networks.

In the fall of 1967, he invited Corita to help inaugurate the San Francisco branch of Esalen Institute, the esoteric think tank and personal growth mecca located on the central California coast near Big Sur. At that moment, Esalen was the epicenter of the Human Potential Movement, and its founders hoped to spread spiritual privilege and virtuosi techniques to more people by bringing their workshops into the city and establishing a branch in San Francisco. Leading off the weekend event, Corita stood beneath the vaulted ceiling and stained glass windows in the First Unitarian Universalist Church on San Francisco's Cathedral Hill and briefly addressed hundreds of listeners who were interested in social, spiritual, and personal transformation.[4] Later that evening, Abraham Maslow, President of the American Psychological Association and the movement's best-known academic supporter, pondered the meanings of beauty, wisdom, and social justice in his lecture, "The Farther Reaches of Human Nature."[5]

Corita did not participate in the following night's boisterous festivities, which were "a splendid evening of religious razzmatazz."[6] A former Episcopal priest, Alan Watts, who was a best-selling writer about Zen and a flamboyant advocate for psychedelic drugs, orchestrated an "ecumenical liturgy."[7] Incense, candles, and conga drums enhanced a service that included Hindu, Buddhist, and Gregorian chants along with Watts's sermon on "Joy to the World." One of his many assistants for the evening, Timothy Leary, wore ecclesiastical robes and sang, drummed, and murmured his approval throughout the event.

The differences in the two celebrations reflected the surprising range of spiritual virtuosi who contributed to the movement's success. On the first night, academics, professionals, and people from mainstream religions presented new ideas about religiosity, personal growth, and social transformation. On the second, Watts and his entourage offered direct experience, mystical moments, and sudden insights. The movement honored both intellectual and experiential approaches, drawing together rationality and absurdity in ways that altered America's spiritual landscape.

The Human Potential Movement

The Human Potential Movement attracted virtuosi from dozens of religious traditions because it embraced every spiritual system that enabled individuals to create more vital, meaningful lives on earth and improve the world. Its ecumenical spirituality drew seekers from marginal faiths like Americanized Zen Buddhism and also disaffected members who wanted to reform and revitalize established religious traditions. It attracted progressive religious virtuosi like Sister Mary Corita because it affirmed their beliefs that everyone could find God in their own ways and improve their lives on earth as well as the lives of others.

During the early 1960s, Corita, along with most of the other sisters in her Los Angeles order, welcomed the Second Vatican Council's call for respectful recognition of all faiths, including non-Christian religions and even nonbelievers.[8] Because of the Council's call for renewal and reinvention, many women in the Order of the Immaculate Heart of Mary (IHM) began to challenge the scope of their subordination within the Church, and Corita welcomed the movement's emphasis on social and spiritual equality, even though most of its leaders were men.

Every group in the movement was grounded in assumptions that people could achieve some degree of spiritual virtuosity and develop the enhanced capacities for spontaneity, creativity, and social responsibility that Abraham Maslow, the father of humanistic psychology, associated with the ideal of full self-actualization.[9] Some psychological approaches added a transpersonal dimension to self-actualization and explicitly affirmed the importance of a Higher Power, while others made spirituality implicit in their ideal of full personal authenticity.[10] The heady mix of possibilities for personal and spiritual growth attracted seekers like Steve Jobs who experimented with quirky innovations in psychology, like Primal Scream Therapy that involved reliving the moment of birth and Yoga, Hindu meditation, and Zen Buddhism. Embodied spirituality was another facet of the Human Potential Movement that included massage therapy, dance, sensory awareness exercises, and holistic medical practices in settings that ranged from mountain meadows to luxurious spas.[11]

Philosopher-poet Allen Ginsberg casually described the movement's foundational assumption about spirituality when he lolled in the hot springs at Esalen Institute along with a group of visiting Episcopal clergymen and their wives. His companions queried Ginsberg about his religious beliefs and he told them that he saw himself as a Buddhist Jew with attachments to Krishna, Allah, Shiva, Coyote, and the Sacred Heart. He said, "I figure one sacrament's as good as the next one, if it works!"[12]

Deep faith in one or many distant, benevolent Higher Powers was embedded in the movement's paths to self-awareness, spiritual growth, and ultimate social evolution. Supernatural forces both outside and within people granted them the possibility to become their best selves and contribute to the advancement of all humankind.

Ginsberg's conversation in the hot springs could never have occurred without George Leonard's efforts to make the Human Potential Movement an important force for social and religious change. In the early 1960s, he helped his best friend, Esalen's cofounder Michael Murphy, organize the institute and cultivate affluent donors, private foundations, and institutional allies. He hoped that the pursuit of full human potential should become a national priority.[13] Because of Leonard's persuasive arguments, the National Council of Churches, a consortium of liberal denominations, dispatched representatives to Big Sur so that they could have first-hand experiences of movement workshops and encounter groups that might help them develop innovations to motivate old members and bring new ones into their congregations.[14]

The Human Potential Movement's loosely coupled collection of interest groups and aspiring spiritual virtuosi were already coming apart at about the time that ordinary Americans had learned the meaning of "human potential." By the end of the 1970s, most humanistic psychologists, holistic healthcare workers, religious personnel, and educators had incorporated movement techniques into their professional roles, and they were no longer engaged with it. Other spiritual explorers charted riskier paths and dropped out of the social and economic mainstream to follow gurus or pursue enlightenment through psychedelics. Most of the movement's followers, casual participants, and eager audiences utilized some things that they had learned about personal and spiritual possibilities but never dedicated their lives to the pursuit of spiritual virtuosity.

And yet the movement's influence continues to ripple through twenty-first-century social life. Products and services for personal and spiritual expansion are available throughout the United States or on the Web. Educators, therapists, massage and bodyworkers, popular writers, and founders of personal growth retreats and spas monetized the virtuoso practices that they had learned at Esalen and other movement centers. And goods ranging from meditation cushions to sage sticks fill an ever-more crowded marketplace for spiritual connections.

The movement's spiritual innovations changed both mainstream and marginal faiths. In the late 1970s, liberal denominations incorporated some of the movement's ideas into their doctrines and practices, while more conservative churches reprimanded or cast out persistent advocates for ecumenical doctrines and new ways to reach toward God. Occasionally, activist virtuosi like members of Corita's order departed from their faiths *en masse* and joined more inclusive, politically committed denominations or formed their own religious groups with loose ties to their previous religions.

Economic Expansion and Religious Transitions

Like the Reformation, the Human Potential Movement rallied ordinary people who had been swept up in the wake of economic expansion and the mass migration to cities that accompanied economic shifts. California had attracted migrants seeking jobs from the late 1930s onward, but after the Second World War the state experienced extraordinary population growth. The unanticipated twenty-year economic boom that began after the Second World War did not touch everyone, but Californians were fortunate, because the state's aerospace, electronics, and entertainment industries dramatically expanded after the war and created new economic opportunities and widespread optimism about the future.[15]

In the 1960s, the California-based Human Potential Movement offered spiritual seekers like Steve Jobs dozens of spiritual options, while it provided committed religious virtuosi like Corita with possibilities to discover new meaning within their faiths. At the time that the Human Potential Movement peaked in the late 1960s, a modicum of economic security and relatively comfortable lifestyles had already spread down as far as the lower middle classes on the West Coast and much of the rest of the country as well. Relative affluence made it easier for the first wave of postwar spiritual insurgents to attract supporters who had begun to believe that they could control their destinies on earth and come to terms with death.[16]

Since the 1849 Gold Rush, people had migrated to California because of economic opportunities but they usually paid significant social costs when they moved. Although their transitions frequently disrupted long-standing personal support networks, religious congregations could offer new arrivals spiritual continuity and friendship networks that linked their old and new homes.[17] Corita, who was christened Frances Elizabeth Kent, grew up in a Catholic neighborhood that revolved around the parish church of the Blessed Sacrament.[18]

Frances was six years old when she moved to Los Angeles with her parents and five brothers and sisters. Her working-class family crowded together in a three-bedroom apartment that opened onto the courtyard of a modest Hollywood complex that her mother's parents owned. Bob Kent, an Irish immigrant, had difficulties holding down his earlier jobs, but he found work with the Payne Furnace Company through the Church. In a few years, however, he lost his job because of the economic downturn that preceded the Great Depression. Despite free rent and Edith Kent's home laundry business, the Kent family barely had enough to eat.

During the hard years before the Second World War, the Church subsidized all of the Kent children's educations until their family's finances and local social standing grew more secure after Bob Kent found another job. The family was less pressed after Corita's older brother, Mark, became a priest and her older sister, Ruth, entered the Order of the IHM. Religious community created an emotional and material safety net that allowed the Kents to survive the Depression and help secure their children's futures.

Until the end of eighth grade, Frances and her friends walked four blocks to Blessed Sacrament Elementary School, where almost all the teachers were Immaculate Heart sisters. Blessed Sacrament was a Jesuit school, so it was shaped by a tradition that stressed education, the arts, and social justice.[19] The nuns who staffed its classrooms had no formal connection with the Jesuits, but their order, IHM, also emphasized critical thinking, the value of arts, and the importance of fairness and equality.

Frances was one of ten girls in her class who went to Catholic Girls High School, where nuns from a number of different orders taught. After her senior year, she took summer courses at Otis Art Institute, while waiting for the September ceremony when she would join a cohort of other young women entering the IHM as postulants.

When Frances told her friends that she wanted to become a nun, they were shocked, because she had never mentioned that she hoped to dedicate her life to the Church. She took it for granted that she was destined to join the Order of the IHM because she loved God. Moreover, IHM nuns had been her grammar school teachers and her older sister's mentors and they embodied her aspirations to find sanctification and serve her community.[20]

During the 1930s, many Catholic girls entered the Church because of their childhood experiences and because taking vows represented not just an act of faith and a commitment but also one of Catholic women's few plausible avenues to vocations in higher education, healthcare, or management.[21] Opportunities like those may explain why the number of nuns in the United States grew to a peak of 182,000 in 1965.[22] About two years after she entered IHM as a postulant, Frances became Sister Mary Corita and made her first formal vows of poverty, chastity, and obedience.

When she changed her name to Mary Corita, Frances formally signified that she was a committed spiritual virtuoso, who lived among other virtuosi dedicated to education and arts, service to others, and social justice. Three decades later, when she exited the world of institutionalized virtuosity and reentered the secular world, Sister Mary Corita again thought about what it meant to transform herself. She considered reclaiming her old name and starting over as Frances or Frannie Kent. Her close friends persuaded Corita that a different name might blur memories of her selfless dedication to her former order and also confuse the art world. Their arguments persuaded her to drop "Sister" and "Mary" and simply become "Corita." She only added "Kent" to her name when it was a requirement for something like signing a lease, opening a bank account, or writing a check.[23]

When Corita left IHM in the summer of 1968, she was absolutely exhausted after years of sleep deprivation from serving God every waking moment. On typical weekdays during the school year, Corita attended morning mass at 6:30, then meditated and said prayers, taught half a dozen college classes, and served dinner in the priests' dining room. After quickly eating her own dinner, she convened adult extension classes and later monitored the dormitory. On weekends and during the summer, she stole time to paint and make prints and serigraphs.[24]

The Second Vatican Council's calls to make the Church more responsive to contemporary life and its challenges forced her to rethink her vocation and her relationship to God and also complicated her hectic life with meetings and private conversations.[25] Long before Pope John the XXIII opened the first council meeting in 1962, however, IHM leaders had urged members of their order to consider ideas from every philosophy and faith, in order to make their teaching and service more spiritually meaningful and effective.

Beginning in the late 1930s, the Immaculate Heart faculty invited controversial Catholics to lecture and discuss social and political issues with the nuns and students at the college. Well-known visitors ranged from the pacifist Dorothy Day who founded the Catholic Worker Movement to the ultraconservative politician and playwright Clare Booth Luce, who was married to the publisher of *Time, Life, Fortune, and Sports Illustrated*.

The college's supporters and also its detractors recognized that the sisters, particularly the teachers at the college, were dedicated to critical thinking and rigorous debate about contemporary social issues. The 1960 Immaculate Heart College' catalogue described its mission "to stimulate awareness, awaken imagination, deepen reflection and equip students to define their areas of social responsibility."[26] Students considered diverse perspectives in their classrooms and explored Los Angeles in order to experience the world around them and understand the need for equality and social justice.

During the five-year term that began in 1958, Immaculate Heart College's outspoken president Mother Mary Humiliata, who went on to become the order's Mother General, stressed intellectual rigor and creativity. In 1967, 313 sisters taught full time in Catholic elementary and high schools in the Los Angeles area. Most received their bachelor's degrees from Immaculate Heart College, where they had learned to interrogate Church dogma and explore other spiritual traditions.

Immaculate Heart sisters were among the hundreds of nuns, priests, and bishops in the Americas who viewed the Church's inflexibility and separation from the secular world as a drain on its vitality. Pope John XXIII responded to mounting worldwide pressure to make the Church more responsive to contemporary issues when he summoned over 2,000 bishops from around the world to the Second Vatican Council. He charged them with modernizing doctrines in order to reflect decades of cultural and political transformations that had unfolded since Vatican I had met from 1869 to 1870.

Under a new pope, the council concluded in December 1965 and mandated sweeping change. It relinquished its claim to be the only true religion and encouraged dialogues with other faiths. Priests would face their congregations, not their altars and conduct services in their parishioners' own language rather than Latin, so that worshippers could better understand the full content and message of the liturgy. Over three years, the council liberalized rules dictating what women wore to church, the frequency of confession, proofs for the annulment of marriages, and restrictions like meatless Fridays. Most important, Vatican II challenged the Church's moral absolutism, redefining it as community of God's people charged to understand and implement His will.[27] It soon became clear that the full scope of the council's innovations represented the most dramatic change within institutionalized religion since the sixteenth century. Some of its reforms resembled Luther's.

Most Immaculate Heart sisters supported the changes and welcomed them as affirmations of their own practices and also as invitations to experiment with more flexible ways of honoring the sacred. Most believed that they could understand and communicate with God without a priest's intercession and that the privilege to reach toward spiritual virtuosity could and should be available to everyone. Vatican II encouraged them to look not just upward but also inward and experiment with new ways of developing their personal spiritual virtuosity.

Mother General Humiliata interpreted the council's call for every religious order to renew its spiritual life as an invitation for Immaculate Heart to continue developing new ways of doing God's work through liberal education and social justice advocacy. The sisters also discussed simplifying or even eliminating their nuns' habits and making private devotions an alternative to masses. Most radically, the majority wanted to make decisions as a community rather than obey all of the orders from the conservative Archdiocese of Los Angeles.[28]

Before Vatican II, some older members of the order were shocked by IHM's liberalization and concerns with poverty and discrimination. In order to heal the divisions, Mother General Mary Regina invited the founder of the psychology department at the University of Montreal to guide one of the order's weeklong spiritual retreats in 1961. However, Father Noel Mailloux profoundly disappointed the traditionalists when he discussed the interpersonal dynamics of building spiritual community in terms of issues like passive aggression and fear of change. The conservative nuns felt lost when there were no conversations about penance, sacraments, or grace.[29]

The master of the next retreat was another professor who drew psychology and religion together in terms of Abraham Maslow's humanistic approaches. Maslow's theory of self-actualization led Father Adrian Van Kaam to question dichotomies between sacred and profane. He used the hierarchy of needs to explain spiritual virtuosity. According to Maslow's paradigm, people had to be sure of their material security before they could live the spontaneous, creative, and fully moral lives. Van Kaam's religious interpretation of Maslow's ideal grounded IHM's five-year plan for spiritual renewal in 1963, "challenging each sister to develop her fullest capacity as a person."[30]

Maslow's vision of self-actualization was the Human Potential Movement's touchstone. He offered workshops at Esalen in Big Sur, and along with Corita he had participated in the official opening of its San Francisco branch. However, Maslow was

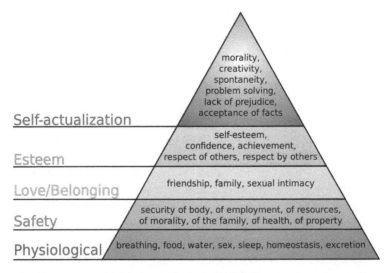

Photo 6.4 Human potential: Maslow's Hierarchy of Needs.

uninterested in living at Esalen or any other movement center. He was committed to refining his theory and testing clinical approaches that supported personal flexibility, ethical virtuosity, and social responsibility, so he continued as a professor of psychology at Brandeis University until shortly before his death in 1970. He hoped to reinvent clinical psychology and supported the movement in order to persuade Americans that everyone was entitled to physical security, social esteem, and elements of spiritual privilege.

Maslow's descriptions of self-actualization appealed to individuals who were loosely affiliated with established faiths or who saw themselves as spiritual but not religious. They felt morally and mystically impoverished in a land of material plenty, and they critiqued both liberal religions' vapidity and also conservative faiths' rigidity.[31] While he did not call himself religious, Maslow's recognition of a mysterious connection between an individual and the cosmos made his work accessible and attractive to progressive Catholics, Protestants, and Jews.[32] After Corita learned about humanistic psychology, she leaped into the Human Potential Movement, and George Leonard was ready to catch her.

Spiritual Privilege and Pivotal Communities

Leonard was the relatively unknown spiritual virtuoso who had popularized the term "Human Potential." He was a senior editor at *Look Magazine and* a prolific writer of popular articles and books who was often described as Esalen Institute's third founder and the Human Potential Movement's master communicator.[33] Leonard was the skillful broker who identified and fashioned the loose coalition of alternative religions and professional groups interested in spiritual and personal growth that became the movement.

Leonard worked behind the scenes to craft a decades-long public relations campaign that brought the movement national prominence and made people like Maslow popular heroes and personal growth centers like Esalen famous. While he was skeptical about traditional religions, Leonard believed in forces beyond human comprehension and possibilities for mystical transformations through the kind of sustained practice that he described in his book, *Mastery*.[34]

Born into an upper-class Georgia family, Leonard served as an Air Force pilot during the Second World War before finishing his undergraduate studies at a top public university. In 1953, he moved to New York City to work at *Look*. During his seventeen years as one of the magazine's senior editors, Leonard cultivated his relationships with writers and editors from magazines like the *New Yorker* and the *New York Times Magazine* and television networks like NBC. When he became a central figure at Esalen in the mid-1960s, Leonard invited useful acquaintances to sample Big Sur's splendors and they helped him create the media buzz about the movement that continued until the beginning of the twenty-first century.

Leonard was affluent, worldly, and well connected. Those three elements of spiritual privilege compensated for his unfocused spiritual affinities and allowed him to work toward a sense of connection with some Higher Power. He differed from many

Photo 6.5 George Leonard at the Whole Earth Jamboree in the 1970s.

other movement virtuosi, however, because he tried to implement his conviction that full personal and spiritual development required commitment to collective social action so that *everyone* could realize their full human potential. He believed that the movement would not truly succeed unless it addressed the collective wounds of racism and poverty.[35]

After the 1965 Watts uprisings in Los Angeles, Leonard worked with black psychologists to create a short-lived program of interracial encounter groups. Although well intentioned, the program completely failed to bridge the divides between their white and black participants. However, he also helped a group of educators develop enduring classroom exercises that could be incorporated into low-income schools.[36]

Leonard appreciated Corita's celebrity status and saw her as a comrade, albeit an unlikely one. In a special 1966 *Look* issue about California as America's future, he described her as one of twenty "turned-on people":

> Long before those young men in New York invented pop art, a small nun in Los Angeles was showing her students at Immaculate Heart College how to discover the novel and beautiful in popular magazines and packages from the supermarket. But Sister Mary Corita is a different kind of pop artist. Whereas the New York boys deal in a certain brittle archness (they are chic), Sister Corita and her

students unabashedly affirm and celebrate the here-and-now glories of God's world—the words of Beatles' songs, the pictures on cereal boxes, the sheen of stamps, the typography in movie magazines.[37]

From the time that she first grasped a crayon, Corita's spiritual affinities compelled her to imbue her art with sacred meaning. Before she started kindergarten, she sat in her apartment's courtyard and drew both the world around her and the sacred one that she could sense. Although the nuns at Blessed Sacrament School tried not to single anyone out, her sixth-grade teacher recognized Corita's ability as a God-given gift. After school, Sister Noemi tutored her with course materials from the graduate classes that she was taking at UCLA.[38]

When she finished elementary school and went on to Catholic Girls High, Corita was disappointed that her art teachers had students copy historic religious works. However, her father and some IHM nuns understood that Corita's originality expressed her dedication to God. They encouraged her to continue to explore new ways of depicting religious themes.

Corita was both a spiritual and an artistic virtuoso, and she expressed her religious virtuosity through her art. Unlike Hildegard von Bingen who used her artistic talents as a means to power, Corita saw her art as a way to become closer to God and encourage people to find sacred meaning in their everyday lives. Corita's religious affinities were the foundation of her spiritual privilege, and she wanted to share them with everyone.

The contrasts between Leonard and Corita illustrate the ways that spiritual privilege is a mixture of religious affinities and material, social, and cultural resources. Robust religious affinities can facilitate spiritual virtuosity when other elements of spiritual privilege are minimal. And conversely, even with limited religious talents, someone like George Leonard could have the financial, cultural, and social resources to pursue virtuosity on his own terms.

Before Corita finished college, she was assigned to substitute regularly in her order's Los Angeles elementary school. She made up for her lack of experience and self-confidence by drawing pictures of Bible stories rather than talking about the Gospel. She was so successful that she was appointed first-year teachers' official sponsor. One of them remembered, "Corita's advice and help consisted of ideas for brightening up the room and giving little ones love."[39]

After completing college, Corita continued teaching elementary school and also attended graduate-level studio art classes at the University of Southern California. But her studies ended abruptly in the early 1940s, when she was posted on a mission to teach in two different schools in British Columbia. When IHM called Corita back to Los Angeles, she was assigned to be an instructor at Immaculate Heart College and also study for her master's degree at the University of Southern California.

Corita left Canada because IHM called her back when a state accreditation committee noted that the college's art department needed more than one permanent faculty member and specified that the new member had to have a master's degree or higher. The nun who chaired the department, Magdalen Mary, who was called

Mag, already had an advanced degree from UCLA, so she dispatched Corita to USC. With characteristic humility, Corita could barely believe that she had been selected to attend graduate school because of her abilities and thought it was probably because she already had "the most points toward a degree."[40] At first, Corita was so anxious about graduate school that Mag rode on the city bus with her and stayed at USC until they could ride back together. Corita soon took the bus by herself as she grew more confident about her skills.

Determined to make Immaculate Heart's art department famous, Mag encouraged Corita to expand her artistic reach and assert herself in Los Angeles's arts community. Soon after Cortia graduated from USC, Mag submitted her work to several competitions and her serigraph titled *the lord is with thee* won first prize in the Los Angeles County Museum's 1952 print competition and at the California State Fair. After Corita's talent was publicly honored, Mag arranged exhibitions for her in Catholic colleges and churches all over America and placed it in private galleries on both coasts.

Corita started to use words and phrases in her serigraphs in the mid-1950s. She received wider national recognition in 1958, when the Container Corporation of America commissioned a serigraph for its "Great Words of Western Man" series of advertisements in major magazines. More commissions and artistic freedom followed, but before Corita was dispensed from her vows in 1968, the money from her sales and commissions went directly to the college.

The Order of the IHM and its college in particular were the pivotal communities that nurtured Corita's spiritual virtuosity and supported her artistic innovations and political convictions. The order was flexible enough to allow nuns to read materials that the Church forbid like Hobbes' *Leviathan* or Ray Bradbury's *Fahrenheit 451.*[41] In the 1950s, liberal Catholic educators across America respected Immaculate Heart College because it nurtured creativity, encouraged critical thinking, and advocated for social justice. A number of graduates who did not join the order became activists for social justice in different contexts.[42]

Colleges were also pivotal communities for the Human Potential Movement, housing intellectual pioneers like Maslow and hundreds of part-time spiritual virtuosi who reached out to the wider culture through brief strategic alliances with other movements for social change, notably the anti-Vietnam War movement. The first generation of Human Potential activists, like the first members of Luther's movement, were drawn primarily from elite universities that housed both virtuosi professors and dedicated seekers.

In the 1950s and early 1960s, many Americans believed that social engineering could solve both material and existential problems. Intellectuals and scholars enjoyed wide public recognition, media attention, and social influence.[43] The movement emerged from informal groups interested in personal and spiritual growth that had sprung up around universities in the Boston area near Harvard, MIT, and Brandeis and in the San Francisco Bay area around Stanford and Berkeley.[44]

By the end of the 1960s, pivotal communities of spiritual virtuosi had developed in major cities and university towns on both the East and West Coasts. Thousands of accomplished virtuosi and interested seekers lived in the Boston area, New York City, the San Francisco Bay area, and west Los Angeles near UCLA.[45] Virtuosi in different locations collaborated on projects, offered workshops, and gave talks, when they traveled along a Human Potential "trade route" that stretched across the continent and often ended at Esalen in Big Sur.

A wide range of virtuosi and charismatic leaders briefly came together at Esalen to plan conferences, develop joint projects, and lead workshops. After they left Big Sur, they formed temporary alliances to advance their shared objectives. However, they rarely developed extended relationships unless they collaborated on specific long-term goals. The sisters of the Immaculate Heart were at the periphery of the movement, but individual movement virtuosi and humanistic psychologists' talks and workshops at the college influenced them.

Because of her national fame, Corita facilitated relationships among Catholic social activists, humanistic psychologists, and other individuals and groups associated with the movement. She attended events and worked on movement projects, allowing knowledge and opportunities to flow more freely. Moreover, as a bridging virtuoso, Corita modeled the possibilities for new kinds of spirituality that crossed social and religious boundaries.

Patrons, Mentors, and Opportunities

A handful of wealthy patrons gave the Human Potential Movement direct financial support and political protection that were unavailable to progressive Catholic orders within the Church. For example, Laurance Rockefeller, heir to one of America's great fortunes, donated tens of millions of dollars to the movement through his Fund for the Advancement of Human Spirit. His major beneficiaries were the San Francisco Zen Center, the California institute of Integral Studies, and especially Esalen.[46]

The Order of the Immaculate Heart had no such generous patrons and had to depend on the Archdiocese of Los Angeles for almost all funding. The sisters had neither powerful patronage within the church nor significant external backing that might allow them to effectively challenge the hierarchy, although a small number of progressive allies from distant parishes sometimes advocated for them with Rome. They scratched together extra funds from regular sales of faculty and student art and small donations that sustained their progressive agenda without attracting adverse attention from Church officials. Beginning in the late 1950s, Corita's serigraph sales, commercial commissions, and public installations generated resources for guest speakers and funded special faculty projects that would have upset their archbishop.

Immaculate Heart's highest officers and its college officials backed all of Corita's projects and encouraged her to develop new ways to communicate messages of hope and possibilities for sanctification. And from the moment that Corita joined the art department faculty in 1947, Mag was her advocate and supporter in Los Angeles's emerging art scene.

Despite her good intentions, Mag overwhelmed and ultimately alienated Corita with demands to accompany her on trips, to give talks at galleries, Catholic colleges, and seminaries across the country, and to produce more and more saleable art. In some ways, Mag resembled George Leonard because she molded public perceptions of the college as a cohesive, creative academic community that defined what both the National Gallery and the Metropolitan Museum of Art labeled "the IHC style."[47]

Mag had a great eye for art and for interesting artists as well. Long before it was highly valued by galleries, she collected folk art that she displayed in her office and classroom in the college's basement "catacombs." She also contacted well-known artists and shamelessly coaxed them to visit her classes. When the music department refused to invite composer and artist John Cage to speak, Mag arranged for him to talk with art classes. And one day she simply called famed architect Charles Eames and set a time for a group of students to see his famous hillside house in nearby Santa Monica. The field trip became an annual occasion and Eames became one of Corita's artistic mentors.

Because of possibilities for torrents of hostile publicity and serious Church sanctions, Mag was more cautious when she asked Henry Miller to stop by the college some morning and chat with her about his films and novels. This was an incredibly audacious invitation, because some of Miller's work was not only on the Church's list of banned books but also censored for obscenity by the American government. Early one Friday, a student heard several of Mag's folk art music boxes playing at once. When she entered the art studio, she saw Miller and Mag waltzing. The student remembered, "Maggie was dancing with Henry Miller and they were whirling about and her veils were flying."[48]

Corita learned from Mag's excursions to exhibits, movies, and artists' houses. After Corita became a regular faculty member, the two nuns collaborated on class trips that ranged from the then little-known Watts Towers to posh openings at the avant garde Ferus Gallery, where Corita discovered Andy Warhol's work and started giving commercial logos spiritual significance in her own serigraphs. In spite of being Corita's teacher and patron, Mag was never one of her artistic mentors.

The teacher who most inspired Corita was a part-time faculty member who had been the director of the National Gallery in Berlin. Alois Jacob Schardt escaped to America in 1940, after Hitler forbade him to speak publicly.[49] Corita described Schardt as the person who helped develop her visual sensitivity and release her imagination.[50]

Corita wanted her students to be able to see holiness everywhere and express their wonder at the ordinary. To help them discover that art should never remain static or limited to traditional materials like paint or marble, she asked them to make puppets based on the Old Testament's book of Ecclesiastes, do a hundred drawings overnight, sew dozens of banners in a day, or focus attentively on a single blade of grass and then return to class and talk about what they experienced. Some students never adapted to her calls for creativity, but her supporters helped Corita write out an iconic list of art department rules that could inspire inventive teaching and learning everywhere.[51] The list was a call for intense commitment and hard work and a reminder that virtuosity in art and spirituality requires absolute dedication.

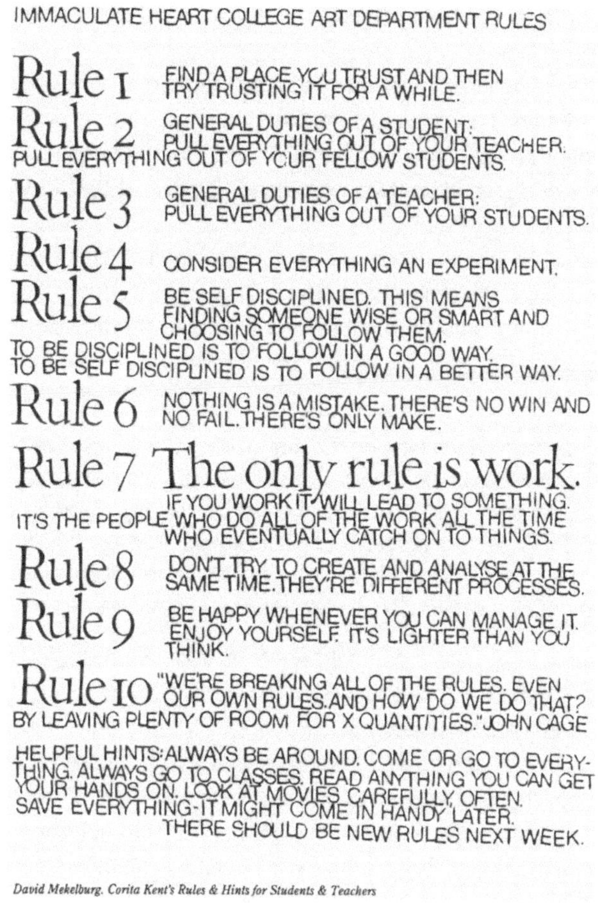

IMMACULATE HEART COLLEGE ART DEPARTMENT RULES

Rule 1 FIND A PLACE YOU TRUST AND THEN TRY TRUSTING IT FOR A WHILE.

Rule 2 GENERAL DUTIES OF A STUDENT: PULL EVERYTHING OUT OF YOUR TEACHER. PULL EVERYTHING OUT OF YOUR FELLOW STUDENTS.

Rule 3 GENERAL DUTIES OF A TEACHER: PULL EVERYTHING OUT OF YOUR STUDENTS.

Rule 4 CONSIDER EVERYTHING AN EXPERIMENT.

Rule 5 BE SELF DISCIPLINED. THIS MEANS FINDING SOMEONE WISE OR SMART AND CHOOSING TO FOLLOW THEM. TO BE DISCIPLINED IS TO FOLLOW IN A GOOD WAY. TO BE SELF DISCIPLINED IS TO FOLLOW IN A BETTER WAY.

Rule 6 NOTHING IS A MISTAKE. THERE'S NO WIN AND NO FAIL. THERE'S ONLY MAKE.

Rule 7 The only rule is work. IF YOU WORK IT WILL LEAD TO SOMETHING. IT'S THE PEOPLE WHO DO ALL OF THE WORK ALL THE TIME WHO EVENTUALLY CATCH ON TO THINGS.

Rule 8 DON'T TRY TO CREATE AND ANALYSE AT THE SAME TIME. THEY'RE DIFFERENT PROCESSES.

Rule 9 BE HAPPY WHENEVER YOU CAN MANAGE IT. ENJOY YOURSELF. IT'S LIGHTER THAN YOU THINK.

Rule 10 "WE'RE BREAKING ALL OF THE RULES. EVEN OUR OWN RULES. AND HOW DO WE DO THAT? BY LEAVING PLENTY OF ROOM FOR X QUANTITIES." JOHN CAGE

HELPFUL HINTS: ALWAYS BE AROUND. COME OR GO TO EVERY- THING. ALWAYS GO TO CLASSES. READ ANYTHING YOU CAN GET YOUR HANDS ON. LOOK AT MOVIES CAREFULLY, OFTEN. SAVE EVERYTHING-IT MIGHT COME IN HANDY LATER. THERE SHOULD BE NEW RULES NEXT WEEK.

David Mekelburg, Corita Kent's Rules & Hints for Students & Teachers

Photo 6.6 Corita's art department rules.
Copyright Corita Art Center, Immaculate Heart Community, Los Angeles, used with permission.

Corita attended to Rule Five in 1960, when Jesuit renegade Dan Berrigan visited the college for the first time. Cardinal McIntyre had ordered the nuns to cancel Berrigan's official visit, but they invited him to come anyway and meet with small groups in the basement art studios. Corita and Berrigan bonded immediately.[52]

Five years later, she saw him again when he led an IHM Holy Week retreat shortly after the Church censured him and his brother Philip, a Josephite priest, for signing pledges to resist the military draft. Dan talked persuasively about living out Christ's teachings of radical peace and charity. A small number of conservative sisters made a formal complaint to the cardinal and Dan was reprimanded for conducting illegitimate services.[53]

Mother General Humiliata was not intimidated by the complaints or the cardinal's reprimand. The next year she asked Berrigan to collaborate with Corita and lead a summer retreat at the order's novitiate near Santa Barbara. It was an IHM tradition that sisters who had been in the order for at least a decade could take an occasional summer away from regular duties to reflect, meditate, and pray about their past and future spiritual journeys.

Dan celebrated Eucharist every day and led discussions about war, racism, and poverty. That summer transformed Corita's art and also her political engagement because up until that time, she had viewed herself as someone "with no guts at all." With humor and discretion, Dan convinced Corita that her art was brave and profoundly political.[54]

Although they lived thousands of miles away from each other, they collaborated on the themes for antiwar and civil rights posters. Dan wrote a poem as the introduction to the only book that Corita both wrote and illustrated, *Footnotes and Headlines*. Later, he reflected on the ways that they joined forces to interweave art, religion, and activism:

> [We had] a common understanding, East and West Coast, that We couldn't just lose oneself in harsh realities of war and survival, but we had to say "Yes" that was a little louder than "No" . . . "Yes" involved poetry, music, Corita's art, all the ways we were trying under pressure to celebrate our lives—the lives we wanted to lead. . . . The art of Corita became part of understanding that unless the movement were producing celebration, it was not a pro-human movement."[55]

Dan drew Corita into a greater commitment to activist virtuosity in the larger world and she brought that standpoint to IHM's 1966 and 1967 chapter meetings. After Pope John died in 1963, his successor, Pope Paul VI, embraced his predecessor's pledge to renew the Church so that it welcomed everyone, spread spiritual privilege, fought against poverty, and allowed nuns new freedoms.[56] IHM organized its chapter meetings at the Santa Barbara retreat to discuss and write out detailed Decrees of Spiritual Renewal in terms of Pope John's vision. During one of the most acrimonious disputes between the liberal majority and a forceful group of traditionalists, Corita spoke up and asked, "Can't we just keep it simple: Love one another and do good."[57]

The progressive majority that included Corita shaped a set of detailed decrees about restructuring their order. They advocated for flexible possibilities for worship, modified nuns' habits or modest secular dress, financial support for nuns to earn graduate degrees at secular universities, opportunities for sisters to work at spiritually meaningful vocations other than teaching in parochial schools or nursing, and broad replacement of the Church's "narrow legalism" with the Holy Spirit's guidance. All of these innovations meant that the order could have far greater autonomy and independence from hierarchical control.[58]

The personal and political tensions within the order and her anxiety about the renewal process made it difficult for Corita to fulfill her duties as a teacher or create much art. As she stood before the crowd welcoming the new Esalen Center to San Francisco, she was emotionally drained. Corita questioned her own commitments and wondered if the foundations of her beliefs had somehow slipped away.[59]

Like some other nuns that she was close to, she had begun to see a therapist in order to decide what she really wanted to do next. Corita underwent Jungian analysis

we carry within us the wonders we seek without us

Photo 6.7 Corita's 1972 serigraph about the spark of divinity in everyone.
Copyright Corita Art Center, Immaculate Heart Community, Los Angeles, used with permission.

and explored her dreams. She discovered that she might not want to be a nun anymore but instead hoped for marriage and a less-restricted life.[60] Corita's chronic insomnia, depression, and anxiety grew worse, so in the fall of 1967, the Mother General insisted that Corita take a six-month sabbatical the following summer.

During a quiet summer making serigraphs and painting watercolors at an old friend's vacation house on Cape Cod, Corita realized that she could no longer represent IHM to the public and serve as a bridge among radical Catholics, political activists, and disparate groups in the Human Potential Movement. And she had discovered that she saw God as a cosmic presence that no institution could limit.[61]

At the end of the summer of 1968, she returned to Los Angeles to gather her few possessions and say goodbye to a community that meant everything to her. The Mother General sent Corita on her way with a blessing and a thick pile of undeposited checks from sales of her art. Corita was taken aback, because at age fifty, she had no idea how to open a checking account. She would also need to learn how to drive, shop for groceries, and cook.

Corita's host at Cape Cod was Celia Hubbard, an old friend who owned a contemporary religious art gallery that was named after St. Botolph, the patron of wayfarers. After spending two summers on the Cape and more than a year sleeping on a couch at Celia's Boston apartment, Corita was able to function as a "civilian." She rented a small place of her own near the gallery, where she welcomed old friends from IHM. Like Weld and Grimké before her, Corita moved to the sidelines of religious and political movements, while she continued to dedicate her life to sanctification. She designed free posters and serigraphs for progressive groups like Plowshares and

Physicians for Social Responsibility, while supporting herself with well-paid commercial commissions, including designs for the decoration of a huge gas tank on a major expressway outside Boston.

A rainbow similar to the gas tank design appeared on a US stamp with the word "Love," in 1985. The ceremony marking its issue was held on the set of the cheesy prime-time television series called *Loveboat*. Corita was furious, because she wanted to inspire love that unites everyone with one another and leads to world peace.[62]

Although she had hoped that she might marry after leaving IHM, Corita remained single. Dan Berrigan was her soul mate and probably her great love, but he was absolutely committed to celibacy and political activism and Corita understood that was how he sought unity with God.

In April 1967, Dan and Philip Berrigan and seven others entered a draft board in Catonsville Ohio and seized hundreds of young men's selective service information, while astonished clerks looked on. In the building's courtyard, the resisters used napalm to set fire to over 300 files and waited to be arrested for their war protest. All nine were tried and found guilty, but they were freed on bail while they appealed their convictions. After the Supreme Court refused to hear the final appeal in April 1970, Dan went underground to avoid jail. A network of antiwar activists and fellow priests sheltered him until August, when he was captured and sent to serve sixteen months at a minimum-security federal prison.[63]

Throughout the time that he was in jail, Corita sent Dan art and long letters and he wrote poems for her. Catonsville was just the beginning for Dan. He went to prison for civil disobedience against war, racism, and poverty countless times. At age ninety, he joined an Occupy Wall Street demonstration in Zuccotti Park in lower Manhattan. Corita, however, avoided large crowds and demonstrations, and enacted her spiritual virtuosity through her art.

In 1974, Corita was diagnosed with ovarian cancer. She temporarily returned to Southern California for surgery and chemotherapy along with guided meditation and massage. She went into remission, but in 1986 her annual medical examination revealed terminal liver cancer. Her small Boson circle cared for her during the final months and old friends from IHM came to say goodbye.

Over the years, Dan Berrigan kept in touch long distance and visited Corita occasionally. About a week before she died, he went into her hospital room and she started to weep, something that she had rarely done throughout her painful illness. She also found it almost impossible to sleep. As he held her, Dan thought:

> She was the guardian angel of the world, and therefore, she's called to be sleepless.[64]

Virtuosity and Vulnerability

Corita was a spiritual virtuoso, not an angel, and she had human flaws. She hated conflict, and when she felt hurt by friends, she might suddenly drop them altogether.[65]

She was so adverse to conflict that the final battles about the future of her order might have destroyed her.

The large progressive faction that drafted IHM's Chapter Renewal Decrees expected that Cardinal McIntyre would criticize their proposals, but they believed that the Vatican's mandates could allow them to negotiate with him. When they presented the decrees in October 1967, they were not prepared for him to draw a line in the sand. He responded ferociously, and, in private, he bitterly asserted, "They want a fight and so I will fight to the finish."[66] He was not only battling IHM, but also Vatican II.

IHM's Decrees of Renewal represented everything that the cardinal detested about the Second Vatican Council.[67] McIntyre was part of a dissident group of influential traditionalists who failed to slow the council's progressive momentum but continued to operate after the council concluded. The International Group of Fathers or *Coetus Internationalis Patrum* believed that the Council represented "an enterprise of subversion of the doctrine of the Church of a kind that the Church has never seen throughout its history."[68]

IHM's proposal for renewal tested Cardinal McIntyre's ability to resist Vatican II and keep his diocese from liberalization. In 1924, IHM was constituted as a papal institute that was under the auspices of the Sacred Congregation in Rome. However, IHM was required to cooperate with the local prelate and abide by his wishes. The conflict was an important test of McIntyre's independent power, and he treated it as a battle that would justify his many earlier skirmishes with IHM. Moreover, by absolutely rejecting IHM's Chapter Renewal Decrees, he could underscore his control over all independent papal orders and institutes that he was assigned to oversee.

Outsiders described Cardinal McIntyre as "the most reactionary prelate in the Church" and IHM was by no means his only target.[69] However, he kept an especially close eye on IHM because its members staffed over 300 classrooms in the Los Angeles area, and one of his long-term objectives was to provide a parochial education for every Catholic child in his diocese. Because the school represented the summit of Catholic education in Los Angeles, the cardinal routinely scrutinized the instructors, classes, books, and guest speakers at Immaculate Heart College.

McIntyre was personally disturbed if instructors went anywhere other than Catholic universities for their graduate work, if John Locke or other Enlightenment thinkers were assigned in philosophy or political science courses, and if Immaculate Heart professors lectured at the University of Judaism or other local non-Catholic institutions.[70]

For more than two decades, IHM leaders tried not to distress McIntyre. They were usually able to move forward with their plans after writing long explanatory letters or meekly meeting with his representatives. In some cases, they simply went ahead without consultation and politely accepted reprimands about speakers like Dan Berrigan or about Sister Corita's art.

McIntyre's anger with IHM intensified over the years as he watched Sister Mary Corita become the order's public face. The cardinal believed that her work was blasphemous and demanded that she refrain from creating abstract images of holy figures. After the 1966 Mary's Day celebration, he insisted that Sister Corita confine all of her art to the classroom unless the Church's committee on art approved it. By that time, however, IHM was hopeful that its Decrees of Renewal would liberate them from his oversight, so they did not pay much attention to the edict.

Both IHM's Mother General and its college president had interpreted the Vatican's Decree on the Adaptation and Renewal of Religious Life as an invitation to experiment with new ways to assert their autonomy and work to implement social justice. They were further buoyed a year after the close of the Vatican Council, when Pope Paul VI explicitly encouraged women's religious communities to experiment with their dress, their living arrangements, and their vocations.

Years before Vatican II convened, some American bishops had backed women's religious orders that had quietly modernized.[71] Those orders and their bishops supported IHM's plans for change and rallied around them throughout a battle that lasted for well over a year. The progressives in IHM had staked their hopes on the pope's calls for renewal, support from Catholic clergy and nuns across North America, and on the fact that IHM was a pontifical community that was formally under Rome's auspices, not Cardinal McIntyre's.

During his meeting with a small delegation that came to discuss IHM's plans for renewal, McIntyre stated that he would never allow any nuns into his classrooms unless they wore a full religious habit. In less than an hour, the cardinal had used the issue of dress to put hundreds of women on notice that he could and would fire them. Moreover, he implied that no IHM nun could teach in Los Angeles' vast archdiocesan school system after June 1968 unless she repudiated the Decrees of Renewal.

In the wake of the cardinal's ultimatum, the sisters affirmed their decrees in a tense meeting. Many immediately reached out to sympathetic California bishops and queried them about teaching positions. In December, they sent letters and information to every one of their students' families about the fact that they might not return the following year, which fueled a huge protest and a publicity storm.

As the battle progressed, the Vatican supported Cardinal McIntyre's authority, and its investigating committee recommended that only the fifty-one nuns who had voted against the reforms could work in the diocese's schools after the spring term ended. The conservatives assumed their order's original nineteenth-century name, the California Institute of the Most Holy and Immaculate Heart of Mary, and their small canonical community moved into a spacious house that the diocese had purchased for them. The other 455 women became the largest single group that the Vatican had ever formally released from their vows.

About a third of them, including Corita, chose to move on to new places and start new lives, but they still kept in touch. Many found jobs fairly easily because of their previous experience as teachers and administrators. Some taught in parochial schools outside of Los Angeles and a large contingent worked in public schools or community colleges in Southern California whether or not they joined the newly formed Immaculate Heart Community.

The expelled sisters founded the Immaculate Heart Community in 1970 as an ecumenical Christian religious group grounded in faith that obedience to God's wishes absolutely superseded the Church's hierarchical authority. Some members shared a large residence but most of them lived with other women or with their new husbands and families. Everyone agreed to contribute 20 percent of their wages to support the community's work for social justice and equality.

The new Immaculate Heart Community began with financial resources because the institutions that the order had built over many decades belonged to them. The sisters who voted to leave were majority shareholders in the nonprofit corporations that constituted most of the order's assets. Their legal team negotiated a division of property that allowed the new community to retain control of Immaculate Heart College, Immaculate Heart High School, Queen of the Valley Hospital, and the order's retreat center near Santa Barbara. Moreover, it was agreed that the new community would staff all four institutions. Cardinal McIntyre approved the generous settlement quickly, in order to avoid further contact with the insurgents.[72]

The new community needed immediate help, and many of their families and friends provided it. For example, Mag, who had taken an extended leave, returned to auction her treasured collection of folk art at Sothebys and donated everything to the struggling college. Nevertheless, it closed in 1980 because of deficits and diminishing enrollments.

Virtuoso Legacies

No one from the secular Human Potential Movement came forward to support the community. But it did receive help from some of the priests who had introduced the sisters to humanistic psychology. IHM had developed a relationship with the Human Potential Movement in the early 1960s, when the visiting priests who were professors at Catholic institutions brought humanistic approaches to the order's spiritual retreats. Cardinal McIntyre did not approve of either humanism or psychology, but he only voiced his wrath publicly after Carl Rogers, a respected academic researcher and clinical psychologist, led a set of workshops before and after the 1967 chapter meetings that crafted the final version of IHM's Decrees of Renewal. One of Rogers' former assistants charged that humanistic encounter groups had fueled the nuns' rebellion and also fostered lesbian relationships.[73] Although they were false, the charges added to the cardinal's animosity and provided him with ammunition.[74]

Humanistic psychology was a lightning rod for cultural backlash of all kinds. It was lampooned in movies like *Bob and Carol & Ted & Alice* and *Semi-tough* and dissected in Tom Wolfe's article on the "Me Generation."[75] Some evangelical Christians saw the movement as a force that could lead to America's moral disintegration. As evidence for their claims, they observed that evil institutions such as liberal churches and academic disciplines had adopted its theories and techniques.[76]

Humanistic psychology thrived in the wider culture and in a handful of universities, but marginality and lack of professional legitimacy of any kind weakened the far corners of the movement. Anticult groups successfully tarred a number of alternative religious movements and encouraged government intervention against them.[77] President

Nixon's "War on Drugs" criminalized most psychedelics and funded enforcement of new laws that affected some of the movement's most publicly visible virtuosi.[78]

The Human Potential Movement was short lived, but it spread a durable message of personalized spirituality that linked individual divinity with powerful Higher Powers and created a handful of lasting organizations. Influential supporters like Laurance Rockefeller, pioneering software entrepreneur Frederick Lenz, and California politician Jerry Brown helped sustain it and protect the movement from negative publicity. The California Institute for Integral Studies, Saybrook University, the San Francisco Zen Center, Esalen Institute, and Naropa University survived for decades because of powerful patrons and because of resourceful virtuosi in their founding generations.

George Leonard remained Esalen's loyal spokesman until he died, and he kept the memory of the Human Potential Movement alive in the twenty-first century. He developed a new path to spiritual virtuosity called Leonard Energy Training, a spiritual and physical practice that was based on the martial art of Aikido and promised growth and harmony with the universe.

The Human Potential Movement was shaped by vague spiritual ideals that God was both transcendent and also within everyone. Corita, who had long placed her faith in an omnipotent God that could only be reached through a priest's intercession, became convinced that a spark of divinity was part of everyone.

The women in the Immaculate Heart Community believe that all people can strive to understand God, but God is not within them. About 160 members remain, some of them men, who are dedicated to a flexible Christianity, seeking sanctification by living simply and doing God's work for equality and social justice. The community operates housing for disadvantaged families, retirement residences, and the former IHM retreat and conference center in Santa Barbara. They also administer and help staff six institutions including Immaculate Heart High School.

The Corita Art Center on the High School grounds has been a moving force in her recent rebirth as a significant American artist displayed at major museums, including London's Victoria and Albert, Paris' Centre Pompidou, and the San Francisco Museum of Modern Art. In 2000, as part of a Lenten service, the archbishop of Los Angeles, Cardinal Roger Mahoney, repented for the Church's sins and issued an apology for the ways his predecessors had treated the women who left their order in 1970.

Leaders in the Human Potential Movement and the Sisters of the Order of the Immaculate Heart of Mary were spiritual virtuosi. Their different paths suggest that the pursuit of virtuosity can involve asceticism, moral influence and outreach, and political activism. Contemporary searches for holiness and purification are rarely linear or confined to one type of virtuosity.

Corita and her art connected her order with the Human Potential Movement and radicals in the Catholic peace movement. Those virtuosi-led movements were only possible because of America's vital, pluralistic spiritual marketplace. However, within that marketplace, power and patronage often shaped a group's success.

The men at Esalen and in some major universities rarely worried about political vulnerability or economic survival because of their spiritual privilege and their patrons' power. They sought sanctification in an economic context where almost anything seemed possible. The IHM women were far more vulnerable because they tried to redefine the meanings of their spiritual virtuosity within the boundaries of the Catholic Church.

Although Vatican II had invited women in the Church to explore and expand their spiritual practice, Cardinal McIntyre saw innovation as a challenge to his authority and a threat to his values. The Church supported him, despite the Second Vatican's calls for experimentation and modernization, because he was allied with influential traditionalists in Rome and also because of his authority as archbishop of Los Angeles.

Corita and her message have become internationally renowned because of the small Corita Art Center that is part of her legacy to the IHM Community. Because of her art, the breakaway group has had a lasting influence on contemporary spirituality. Corita's contribution may foreshadow the future of virtuosity in small groups of activists who drive the expansion of spiritual privilege and extend possibilities to become spiritual virtuosi.

7   Conclusion: Virtuosity and Its Possibilities

Virtuoso Legacies

Martin Luther sparked a spiritual revolution with theological innovations that removed the institutional barriers between believers and God. Supported by other spiritual virtuosi, theology students, and ordinary townsmen, he launched a religiously driven social movement that overturned established religious and political institutions. Luther's late medieval world was not poised for immediate religious revolution, but the novelty and force of his spiritual breakthrough combined with the advent of inexpensive printing, rapid urbanization, and political opportunities to fuel the Reformation.

Because the Reformation opened possibilities for sanctification to everyone willing to pursue holiness with self-discipline and humility, personal agency became central to spiritual virtuosity and the quest for sanctification. Luther envisioned a restoration of Christianity based on a relationship with the divine that unfolded through an individual's private Bible study and spiritual struggles. Although this ideal reflected his own uncompromising intellect and deep religious affinities, Luther believed that everyone could, by faith and through grace, attain salvation and amass enough spiritual privilege to live a life of holiness on earth. This virtuoso ethic became part of Protestantism and, ultimately, Western culture, because it emphasized individual freedom and planted seeds for new kinds of morally committed social and political activism.

For centuries, it was widely assumed that the Reformation represented a giant step in the relentless Western march toward modernity, rationality, and science.[1] From this perspective, Luther was not merely a spiritual virtuoso. He was also a prophet who foretold the Enlightenment. Some critics, however, never accepted the idea that the Reformation ushered in centuries of progress. Historian Brad Gregory argued that it destroyed a Catholic world that was philosophically, morally, and institutionally coherent and replaced it with secularized societies that grew deformed from their members' egoism and materialism.

According to Gregory, when Luther and other reformers insisted that conscience and personal interpretation of scripture were the highest ethical authorities, they unintentionally shattered possibilities for moral and cultural consensus. Since then, Western society has endured a long descent into the perpetual twilight of personal isolation that reflects the decline of religion and the cultural emphasis on possessive individualism.[2]

The vision of a unified Catholic world in the Middle Ages and the picture of an increasingly fair and rational post-Reformation West both distort complicated social processes and their consequences. There was no cohesive Catholic world before the sixteenth century, because as small as Europe was at the time, it was still politically and ethnically diverse. Economic growth fostered further social differentiation. Moreover, most of Central and Northern Europe were only nominally Christian and vernacular paganism remained the dominant religious practice during the Middle Ages.[3]

Idealization of the Reformation is equally skewed, because its successes were neither inevitable nor part of an unstoppable march toward personal freedom and social progress. As we noted in Chapter 4, when political patronage strengthened the sixteenth-century Church, it successfully resisted reform. Wars, plagues, poverty, and irrationality did not fade away after Luther posted his *Ninety-Five Theses* on the door of All Saints. The Reformation's successful challenge to Catholic hegemony emerged in the context of changing economic, political, and social arrangements that it did not create. In the wake of the Reformation, Protestant princes instituted strict confessional churches that implicitly constrained the religious liberty the new theology promised.

In the sixteenth century, spiritual privilege spread because fiscal expansion, urbanization, and introduction of inexpensive printing enabled people to add to their economic, social, and cultural capital, at the same time that corruption and stagnation weakened the Church. Luther's theological innovations allowed people to leave the Church, become part of emerging Protestant congregations, and devote themselves to understanding and implementing God's Word in their lives. The Reformation expanded the accessibility of all four elements of spiritual privilege as it revitalized and reshaped Western religion so that many more ordinary people could aspire to spiritual virtuosity.

The religious diversification that began with the sixteenth-century Reformation has made it easier for twenty-first-century Americans to develop eclectic, personalized spiritual worldviews and practices that are not necessarily antireligious. Because they were no longer dependent on priests to map their paths to sanctification, in the wake of the Reformation individuals could start to select their own routes to purity and holiness. As we observed in Chapter 5, those paths multiplied in the eighteenth century with the revivals that generated upstart Christian sects like the Methodists. In the twenty-first century, established faiths and confessional traditions no longer dominate the religious landscape in the same ways that they did in the past, but people still search for direct relationships with a transcendent God or some other Higher Power.

Since the 1970s, the share of Americans that describes their religious affiliation as "none" has increased to a fifth of all adults. And over 40 percent of Americans over eighteen change their formal membership at least once in their lives. However, the diminishing strength of traditional faiths and denominational groups does not mean that people have abandoned spirituality. For instance, more than half of self-described

American "Nones" believe in a Higher Power and about the same percentage of them believe in some kind of afterlife. And while younger Americans are especially prone to disaffiliate from traditional religious organizations, 80 percent of those born between 1971 and 1994 believe in life after death. The ranks of convinced atheists remain very thin.[4]

Moreover, possibilities to experience something sacred continue to multiply as extraordinary experiences are available outside of explicit religious contexts. Established faiths have by no means disappeared from the religious marketplace, but when popular interest in them grows, it is often because energetic independent denominations provide intense spiritual experiences that allow their members to feel a sense of transcendence in their bodies and souls.[5] Religious participation can grow when liberal and conservative faiths institute flexible boundaries that permit tinkering with practices drawn from different religious traditions. Christian Yoga, Episcopal labyrinths, or Congregationalist sermons about Zen koans are some examples. As people become unmoored from lifelong attachments to exclusive religious organizations and start to diversify their religious portfolios, they often integrate varied religious, scientific, and embodied approaches into their daily lives. They seek out and discover new communities of purpose like the Sunday Assembly or mindful meditation groups that can support their personal quests for some kind of sanctification. In contemporary America, innovation and creativity continue to flourish in spiritual expressions that lie at and beyond the margins of conventional religion.[6]

The Virtuoso Idiom

Over the centuries the pursuit of spiritual virtuosity has increasingly shifted its emphasis from searching for personal holiness and purification in order to attain salvation in the afterlife to making sanctification on earth a primary goal. Since the Human Potential Movement flourished in the twentieth century, spiritual virtuosity has become a widespread goal. This transformation is grounded in historical differences in the ways that aspiring virtuosi have come to view their relationships to God or some Higher Power and the centrality of personal agency in their spiritual lives.

Luther's groundbreaking doctrine affirmed everyone's right to pursue virtuosity and seek spiritual freedom without intervention from human institutions. They could reach toward sanctification and ultimate salvation by reading the Word and doing God's will, but their fates after death were uncertain and no one could know about personal salvation in advance because it was a gift of God's grace.

The distant, powerful God was always righteous and fair, but nevertheless everyone trembled before Him. Without priests to intervene, they were unmasked and their souls were naked, standing alone before God as He inscrutably decided if they were to be included among the saved. No specific deeds or prayers could sway God's judgment, because there was no bargaining of any kind. This position of spiritual loneliness, however, was offset by confessional faiths that offered hope of salvation and communities of purpose.[7] Beginning in the eighteenth century, those Protestant communities were the places that the virtuoso ethic expanded and embraced activism.

Communities of purpose were vital to Angelina Grimké and Theodore Weld, but their God was very different from Luther's. They believed that God was a loving, personal deity that wanted everyone to attain salvation. At the same time, God demanded righteousness and justice on earth. No one had to accumulate a lifetime of good works for the purpose of redemption, purchase indulgences for their past sins, or have special knowledge of the Word. Moreover, the New Light theology made women and men equally free to choose salvation or damnation to hell.

Confessions of past sins and the full acceptance of Christ into their hearts were all that people needed to purify themselves and receive the blessings of spiritual rebirth. However, this new understanding of God demanded more of people than faith in God and dedication to a vocation. The new evangelical Christianity expected believers to lead lives of active holiness that might stir them to moral advocacy.[8]

Charles Grandison Finney, Theodore Weld's early inspiration, added a social component to the new evangelical theology and speculated that collective effort could recreate pure Christianity within the kind of simple, equalitarian society that Christ had envisioned.[9] Although Finney ultimately shied away from radical abolitionism and feminism, Weld expanded his implicit criticism of inequality so that spiritual virtuosity necessarily embraced social justice and universal human rights.

Grimké and Weld reasoned that everyone should have equal human rights, since they had equal opportunities to be reborn and saved by accepting Christ. They extended their interpretation to assert that in a truly Christian world, no one could become another's property, whether by slavery or by patriarchy. The radical Antislavery Movement created a new virtuoso idiom by combining Luther's ideal of a private relationship to God with collective activism grounded in religious principles. Personal purification and sanctification required virtuosi to struggle against injustice and unearned privilege.

The Antislavery Movement unfolded in a society that was far more complex and diverse than Luther's had been. New kinds of communication such as newspapers, popular magazines, and sentimental novels described the brutality of slavery and also its significance to Anglo-American economic life. Distant strangers and their fates acquired an immediate moral urgency. The new theology's emphasis on the importance of personal faith and force of will in realizing God's purpose underscored the role of individual agency in fully accepting Christ and implementing His hopes for humanity.

Personal action was as important to the Human Potential Movement as it was to the antislavery cause, but sanctification involved cultivating mind, body, and psyche, as well as the soul, rather than depending on grace or being reborn through Christ. The movement included myriad spiritual traditions, some with one true God like Corita's or Berrigan's, and some with only diffuse supernatural forces such as Steve Jobs' Americanized Zen or George Leonard's Aikido. However, there was a shared recognition that everyone possessed a divine spark that connected them with one another and with something beyond themselves. God—or some Higher Power—was both transcendent and within everyone. Supernatural beings or forces were implicitly optimistic about human possibilities.[10]

The movement rarely addressed salvation or the afterlife in anything but very vague terms, because the groups that came together under its canopy emphasized personal agency in life.[11] In an era of remarkable prosperity, many seekers who were drawn to the movement sought new kinds of spirituality that could enhance their experience of the world. No matter how strongly they felt about peace or justice, movement virtuosi and seekers shared beliefs that everyone had to move toward self-actualization before they could fight for social justice. Movement virtuosi called on people to live simply and work toward becoming their best possible selves so that they could slowly improve the lives of people who were less fortunate. As he drew closer to self-actualization and personal purification, George Leonard spoke about how his spiritual virtuosity compelled him to move beyond his own concerns. He both needed to and felt obligated to change the world since "I was somehow different and special."[12]

Until Cardinal McIntyre denounced her art and the Church limited the ways that the Order of the Immaculate Heart of Mary (IHM) could change or respond to Vatican II's calls for renewal, Corita had been dedicated to Catholic rules and traditions. Her order's relationships with humanistic psychologists and with Dan Berrigan allowed Corita to discover new ways to see and serve God. She began to experience something sacred within herself that nurtured her growing activism in movements for peace and social justice.

Contemporary quests for sanctification are shaped and supported by recognized religions as well as by diverse groups that encourage self-discovery and personal commitment to virtuoso practices rather than to specific doctrines. Amid every kind of social stimulus, twenty-first-century Americans seek meaningful moral and spiritual foundations for their lives. Although many people abandon traditional religion, the desire for meaning and purpose persists. Even a fifth of the relatively few Americans that define themselves as atheists or agnostics still note that they are spiritual people. Despite growing disappointment with institutionalized religion, especially among younger Americans, many still crave a spiritual purpose and a sense of holiness for themselves and for the next generation.[13]

Individuals may hope for ethical certainty within conservative faiths or simply seek spiritual direction through events like Oprah's "The Life You Want Weekends." For half a dozen years in the early twenty-first century, the larger-than-life celebrity, Oprah Winfrey, drew thousands of Americans into huge stadiums. Those weekends brought

Photo 7.1 Oprah's 2008 "Life You Want Weekend" with Elizabeth Gilbert and Rob Bell.

people to tears and to euphoria by relaying possibilities for new beginnings. The participants, primarily women, wanted to discover the spark of divinity within them so that they could find and live out their life's purpose. Notably, there was deference to God or other Higher Powers, but there were no references to sin.

In some ways, Oprah's intensive, and expensive, weekends resembled the dramatic revivals and camp meetings that spread from England to the American frontier in the eighteenth and nineteenth centuries, when preachers shepherded mass conversions from sin and passivity to true, energetic religious commitment to Christ and a better world. Their religious dedication persisted because of the rise of Methodism and other new faith communities that people could join, but political activism often burned away because morally driven social movements did not offer them either protection from their adversaries or sustained local social support.

Similarly, the feelings of joy and collective purpose that spread through events like the 1967 Human Be-In were seldom transformed into either sustained religious commitment or dedicated activism, because there was little institutionalized support for either alternative religions or progressive politics. Nevertheless, Americans still flock to contemporary events like Burning Man and new versions of Oprah's "The Life You Want Weekends" that offer entertainment alongside possibilities for greater spiritual virtuosity.[14]

Uncovering Sin, Discovering Indulgences

Oprah was uninterested in sin or divine punishment, because her buoyant spirituality mirrored contemporary attitudes about the sacred. While the overwhelming majority of Americans continues to believe in God and an afterlife (usually heaven), the number of people that are sure that sinners and nonbelievers will go to hell has declined dramatically since the 1970s to include barely half of the adults in the United States.[15]

Without clear concepts of sin, however, the road to spiritual virtuosity can be treacherous. There are few obvious signposts that indicate where to go and where to keep out. In the twenty-first century, "sinful" is often as likely to describe a very rich chocolate dessert as it is an act that offends God, yet a considerable body of scholarship indicates that people still create and respond to clear moral boundaries.[16] Over the centuries, spiritual virtuosi have given sin different meanings but justice and morality are crucial to the virtuoso idiom.

Spiritual freedom does not necessarily atomize society or dissolve its moral boundaries. While the Reformation made salvation an individual obligation and emphasized the importance of private conscience, it by no means eliminated either personal or social responsibility.

In late medieval Europe, Martin Luther and other religious virtuosi believed that sin was inescapable and the devil was a tangible presence that could tempt or taunt someone at any time. Sin and its punishment by eternal damnation to hell were central elements of Catholic doctrines and vividly depicted in the art of the times. Hell and the devil terrified Luther all of his life. When he first became an Augustinian friar, Luther attempted penitence for his sins by nearly starving himself to death and flagellating his flesh, but he was never reassured that his prayers and sacrifices could merit God's mercy. After becoming a professor of Biblical theology, he developed and refined his understanding of sin throughout his life.[17]

According to Luther, sin could lead to damnation for eternity, yet no one could ever predict whether they would be saved or damned because of their actions. Although people with wholehearted faith in God avoided the greatest sin of all—disbelief, they could not help but engage in minor transgressions or major sins against God, so salvation always depended on His grace.

Luther's theology rested on his assumption that God alone fully understood and judged each person's merit. Salvation was up to Him alone and no one could influence the final decision about her or his fate in the afterlife. Luther believed that everyone had an individual responsibility to God and must bow before his judgment, so his new theology absolutely undercut the role of the Church as an intermediary and a broker between God and man and challenged its lucrative trade in indulgences.

Luther was incensed that the Catholic Church encouraged people to believe that purchasing indulgences could allow them to avoid hell, shorten their time in purgatory, and speed their way to heaven. As we noted in Chapter 4, feeling truly sorry about sins or spiritual shortcomings and confessing them to a priest were preconditions, but payment for indulgences was the most important part of the transactions that guaranteed absolution and remission of sins.

He was sure that the penitential economy rested on false theological claims that the Church alone had access to a stupendous stockpile of sacred merit that had been left at its disposal. Although the faithful could receive absolution through good works such as donations to the Church, pilgrimages, or charity, indulgences were the quickest route to God's mercy. The living might even purchase indulgences for the dead, so God did not seem to require voluntary repentance.

Possibilities for shortcuts to sanctification without faith and spiritual dedication incensed Luther and his followers. They were deeply offended because the whole logic of indulgences implied that God could be swayed by bribes or flattering gifts. The Indulgence trade exploited people's sacred yearnings and diminished God's dignity in order to support venal ecclesiastical elites. This profane exchange minimized the consequences of sin and made holiness a new kind of commodity. The reformers believed that God's judgment of human frailty and sin was wise and unwavering, and it could never be altered by human blandishments.

American evangelicals viewed the devil as a creature of darkness who opposed God in every possible way. Satan was forever trying to lure people from their paths to sanctification and their relationships to Christ through a menu of temptations that included alcoholic drink, sloth, gluttony, envy, erotic dreams or activities, and other sinful pursuits. During the Great Awakenings' tumultuous revivals and camp meetings, participants tearfully confessed their own sins and publicly begged God to forgive them. After they acknowledged their sins, they could accept Christ into their hearts and establish a deep and lasting personal connection with Him. They had been reborn.

The antislavery virtuosi argued that the capitalism had created a new peril because direct or indirect gain that was rooted in enslavement represented America's sinful bargain with the devil that had to be confessed and repudiated for true spiritual rebirth to take place. Like Luther, most American evangelicals saw fighting against sin as an individual matter. Abolitionists like Theodore Weld and Angelina Grimké redefined spiritual virtuosity as both deeply personal and inherently collective. They forcefully argued that before people could become new and whole they had to confess their complicity with the great sin of slavery.

Evangelicals believed that constant spiritual engagement and dedication to personal holiness and purification defeated the devil. However, activist evangelical abolitionists like Grimké and Weld defined mobilization against slavery as an essential part of the struggle against evil, and they hoped that thousands of other virtuosi could join together to redeem America from the collective sin of slavery. Even after they withdrew from public struggle, the couple continued their battle against sin and injustice.

The evangelical revivals never created anything like the sixteenth-century Church's indulgence trade. However, the personal relationship between God and each sinner made it possible for individuals to develop exchange relationships that they hoped might influence His decisions.[18] They could bargain directly with Him and promise to do better. And more importantly, they could sin and then be saved and reborn in Christ again and again.

Camp meetings and revivals also offered people on the rural frontier intrinsic rewards of fellowship and human contact that had little to do with their sacred purposes. They provided entertainment and collective excitement that enriched social lives in areas where farms were many miles apart from one another. They also offered adolescents rare opportunities for sociability and contact with potential mates. When it began to grow dark at outdoor revivals, young people often paired off and sought privacy in the woods. Neighbors used the term "camp meeting baby" to describe children born less that nine months after their parents married.[19]

The crowded events generated religious enthusiasm across America and a commitment to lives of holiness. But to the bitter disappointment of the abolitionists, most evangelicals were content either to concentrate on their personal sanctification or to make a show of piety. American Christians were deeply moved by emotional antislavery speeches that they heard at outdoor gatherings and in their churches and by reading abolitionist literature. The great majority of them, however, did little actively to support the cause. Because the upstart sects emphasized personal spiritual transformation, it was easy for their adherents to be politically indifferent and offer the Antislavery Movement mere passive support. Worse yet, abolitionists like Weld and Grimké came to believe that, in acknowledging the sin and expressing indignation while doing nothing concrete to stop it, American Christians were compounding their sin through hypocrisy and falsely reassuring themselves of their private salvation.

The Human Potential Movement began during a period of extraordinary economic growth and political turmoil, as had the Antislavery Movement and the Reformation before it. It developed at the point when the United States was clearly the richest, most powerful nation in the world. Middle- and working-class people had a new sense of empowerment and optimism about their futures. In the early 1960s, however, the Civil Rights Movement and best sellers like *The Other America* alerted the people to injustice and inequality in a land of plenty.[20]

In 1960, membership in established faiths was at an all-time high. Close to 70 percent of the population belonged to a church or religious organization. But by the late 1960s, liberal denominations were stagnant and many began to shrink. In the face of a rapidly changing culture, the old liberal churches like Episcopalians and Congregationalists dismissed the idea of a real devil, rarely mentioned sin, and embraced the Human Potential Movement's denial of absolutes.[21] The movement attracted liberal clergy and, to a lesser extent, their congregants, who still believed in a distant, if benevolent God, as well as groups that saw the divine as a diffuse force or possibly a charismatic guru like Bhagwan Shree Rajneesh. But the many groups shared the belief that a Higher Power lay both within them and outside and that they were somehow interconnected. In reaction to the new religious subjectivity that required few personal sacrifices, strict evangelical churches and new nondenominational Christian faiths surged by attracting worshippers from both the ranks of the old denominations and newcomers who had no previous religious affiliation.[22]

Since God or a divine spark lay within and outside of everyone, it was spiritually imperative to cultivate the self and the failure to work toward self-actualization and transcendence resembled a sin. Humanistic psychologist Abraham Maslow inadvertently provided the movement with the foundational doctrine that linked its diverse constituents' personal spirituality to social change. His motivational pyramid started with basic physiological needs, and he believed that it was necessary for everyone to be healthy, safe, and adequately housed. Self-actualization, the highest level of functioning, involved morality and lack of prejudice toward anyone or anything—precisely the values that Grimké and Weld hoped to implement.

The movement implicitly defined service and political advocacy as spiritual practices and its spiritual virtuosi sometimes advocated for causes like educational innovation, civil rights, prison reform, food security, and peace. Human Potential groups, however, never coalesced to confront structural issues such as racism or poverty.[23] Nevertheless, almost by chance, the movement made a major structural breakthrough by forever blurring the separation of the sacred and the secular and creating an ever-expanding market sector for goods and services to help everyone reach their full personal and spiritual potentials. Multinational corporations and small entrepreneurs all compete in the thriving commercial sector that monetizes spiritual virtuosity by offering new kinds of indulgences that almost anyone can afford.

Today's believers can actively pursue holiness and purification through innovative therapies for body and mind or by making pilgrimages to spiritual retreats that promise transcendent experiences. The many different experiences, services, and products that Oprah and her imitators offer reach consumer niches within every social class. Almost anyone can buy or borrow something from Oprah or another spiritual entrepreneur that extends their reach toward holiness.

Steve Jobs branded himself as a spiritual virtuoso and brilliantly marketed personal technology as means to pursue personal authenticity and sanctification. His persona and his products communicated Zen aesthetics that tapped into consumers'

Photo 7.2 A store window in Suffolk, England.

yearnings for some connection to holiness. People who had neither time nor money to pursue sanctification in the ways that Jobs did could purchase something associated with him that signified creativity and spiritual privilege.

Particularly at the upper end of the discretionary market, contemporary consumption is freighted with meaning. Jobs brilliantly exploited his rivalry with Microsoft's Bill Gates to define Apple users as cool and spiritual compared to mundane and boring PC people.[24] When Jobs died in 2011, crowds gathered outside of Apple stores to mourn his passing and remember him as a spiritual mentor. The Human Potential Movement provided new rationales to make almost anyone seem holy and almost anything become an amulet—even a computer.

Until the mid-twentieth century, dedicated spiritual virtuosi sought purification and holiness through asceticism, ethical heroism, or activist spirituality. Now, however, the purchases of iPads, organic produce, or electric vehicles can be used to signify sanctification. Lifestyles of Health and Sustainability (LOHAS), a major marketing group for purveyors of the new indulgences, serves hundreds of human potential businesses. In 2014, the group forecast that over that year alone, Americans would spend over $290 billion for products and services promising personal transformation.[25] In the contemporary spiritual marketplace, new indulgences appear daily and the money and time that people spend on them is one of the Human Potential Movement's lasting legacies. At the same time, in contrast to the 1960s when prosperity was

Photo 7.3 An improvised shrine honoring Steve Jobs.

spreading down into the working class, even small indulgences are becoming almost out of reach for increasing numbers of Americans.

Economic Decline, Spiritual Empowerment, and Social Transformation

All three virtuoso-led movements that we have described occurred during times of extraordinary economic expansion and social dislocation. Spiritual virtuosi sparked dramatic social and religious transformations that affirmed the importance of personal agency and human rights, while making possibilities for sanctification available to many more people. Luther broke the Church's grip on sanctification, the Antislavery Movement affirmed the full humanity and spiritual privilege of all Christians, and the Human Potential Movement opened up personal and spiritual expansion to people of every faith.

Luther first spread possibilities for spiritual virtuosity when he successfully attacked the Church's monopoly on sanctification. His forceful proclamations of everyone's right to pursue holiness without intercession empowered later spiritual virtuosi to step to the front of nineteenth- and twentieth-century social movements that mobilized collective concerns about the moral and emotional costs of economic expansion.

Successful virtuosi-inspired movements for greater equality and human rights are as rare as the periods of extraordinary economic growth where they flourish. The past four decades of fiscal stagnation and rising economic inequality in the West have constrained possibilities for spiritual virtuosi to marshal widespread support for social and spiritual equality. Since the 1970s, the average growth rates of mature capitalist economies have fallen and extraordinary technological innovations have not produced widely shared prosperity.[26] The incomes of the rich have increased sharply, while those of the many have stagnated or even declined.

Opportunities to pursue sanctification may become more limited and virtuosi-led movements for social and spiritual equality could all but disappear in the face of economic deprivation and political suppression. Americans' growing material distress has fueled support for conservative evangelicals who preach a prosperity gospel that informs believers that God wants them to be rich. It is a doctrine of individualism and resentment about anything or anyone that may be standing in the way of their good fortune. Rob Bell, once a rising star in those circles, was expelled from his church and ostracized by many other pastors when he attacked self-serving individualism and began to preach about tolerance, compassion, and activist virtuosity.[27]

In the midst of economic downturns, people who feel that someone or something has destroyed the best of their old lives are often attracted to faiths that draw strict distinctions between those who will be saved and those who are lost to hell. Conservative evangelical leaders offer the recently displaced solace and hope for recognition and restoration of what they believe was rightfully theirs. They pledge to bring them back to an imagined promised land.[28] As old workplace communities and local houses of worship vanish, conservative evangelicals support an exclusive virtuoso ethic that limits possibilities for sanctification and defines strict institutional boundaries.

This conservative ethic fosters a new pessimism. It is the opposite of the activist virtuosi's commitment to spiritual equality for everyone. The activist spiritual virtuosi that we have described believed in extending possibilities for sanctification to wider circles, because they had faith that a fair and just God or Higher Power wants more people to be able to pursue holiness. The three consequential movements were fueled by confidence in human possibilities, although they were often confronted with virulent opposition or plagued by passive indifference to their goals.

If a consequential virtuoso-led movement for religious and social equality develops in the twenty-first century, it will probably be supported by a coalition of groups that come together under a canopy of faith that shelters both communities drawn from established denominations like Roman Catholics and sympathetic skeptics like members of the Sunday Assembly. Pivotal communities with histories of trust, cooperation, and commitment to equality will be at the center of the next movement. Virtuosi in progressive faiths may become models of spiritually informed activism. For example, in 2015, when a white supremacist slaughtered nine members studying the Bible in the sanctuary at Emanuel African Methodist Church in Charleston, the entire congregation and many other African American churches stood together as virtuosi activists to urge the wider community to forgive the wrongdoer as Jesus would have forgiven him. Subsequently, the South Carolina congregation was at the heart of a broad religious coalition that successfully supported a statute to remove the Confederate flag from all public buildings on the grounds that it symbolized racial oppression and had inspired terrorism.

During the nineteenth century, liberal denominations supported the Antislavery Movement and became sanctuaries for escaped and hunted African Americans. That tradition inspired the Sanctuary Movement in the 1980s when over 500 congregations housed or found safe homes for immigrants who had fled violence and persecution in El Salvador and Guatemala, but faced deportation because of restrictive immigration policies.[29] Because President Donald J. Trump's policies have produced invasive and sometimes illegal immigration enforcement, activist spiritual virtuosi have led organized resistance and close to 1,000 congregations in the United States are now part of a new Sanctuary Movement that includes Quakers, Unitarians, and Methodists, as well as Roman Catholics, Latter-day Saints, and Jews.

A United Church of Christ pastor observed:

There is, across Abrahamic faith traditions at least, this dictate to welcome the stranger, for you were once a stranger in the land of Egypt. What are faith communities, if not sanctuaries?[30]

Activists will continue to come together in communities of faith and work toward spiritual equality for everyone. The task for twenty-first-century spiritual virtuosi will be to find new ways to remain optimistic and link widespread spiritual longings to concrete and inclusive demands for institutional change.

Photo 7.4 Support for Charleston's Emanuel African Methodist Church after the 2015 attack.

Notes

Chapter 1

1. Max Weber, *The Sociology of Religion* (Boston: Beacon Press 1963 [1922]), 166–83.
2. Walter Isaacson, *Steve Jobs* (New York: Simon & Schuster, 2011), 49–52.
3. Steven Bruce, *God is Dead: Secularization in the West* (Oxford: Wiley-Blackwell, 2002).
4. Eckhart Tolle, *A New Earth: Awakening to Your Life's Purpose* (New York: Penguin Books 2005), 17.
5. Ibid., 18.
6. Michael P. Young, *Bearing Witness Against Sin: The Evangelical Birth of the American Social Movement* (Chicago: University of Chicago Press, 2006).
7. Richard Rabinowitz, *The Spiritual Self in Everyday Life: The Transformation of Personal Religious Experience in Nineteenth-Century New England* (Boston: Northeastern University Press, 1989).
8. Philip Slater, *The Pursuit of Loneliness: American Culture at the Breaking Point (Boson:* Beacon Press, 1970).
9. Jean Henri Merle Aubigne [tr by Henry Beveridge], *History of the Reformation of the 16th Century (*Whitefish, Montana: Kessinger Publishers [1846]), 540–41.
10. Lee Palmer Wandell, *The Eucharist in the Reformation* (New York: Cambridge University Press, 2006), 73–74.
11. Peter George Wallace, *The Long European Reformation: Religion, Political Conflict, and the Search for Conformity, 1350–1750* (London: Palgrave: Macmillan, 2012*)*, 94.
12. Charlie Reid and Craig Reid [The Proclaimers] *I'm Gonna Be (500 Miles), 1987).*
13. Roger Scruton, *Our Church: A Personal History of the Church of England* (London: Atlantic Books, 2014).
14. Fenggang Yang, "2015 SSSR Presidential Address: Exceptionalism or Chinamerica?: Measuring Religious Change in the Globalizing World Today." *Journal of the Scientific Study of Religion* 55/1 (2016): 7–22.
15. James Beckford, "SSSR Presidential Address: Public Religions and the Postsecular: Critical Reflections." *Journal for the Scientific Study of Religion* 51 (1) March 2012: 1–19.
16. See Grace Davie, *Religion in Britain since 1945: Believing Without Belonging* (London: Wiley, 1994). Also see David Voas, "The Rise and Fall of Fuzzy Fidelity in Europe," *European Sociological Review* (2009) 25: 155–88; and Alisdair Crockett and David Voas, "Generations of decline: religious change in Twentieth-century Britain." *Journal for the Scientific Study of Religion*, 45 (2006), 567–84.

17. Pew Research Center, May 12, 2015, "America's Changing Religious Landscape." http://www.pewforum.org/2015/05/12/americas-changing-religious-landscape/. Accessed March 4, 2017.

18. Ronald Dworkin, *Religion without God* (Cambridge, MA: Harvard University Press, 2013).

19. Walter Isaacson, *Einstein: His Life and Universe* (New York: Simon and Schuster, 2007), 388–89.

20. "Atheist Church Split: Sunday Assembly And Godless Revival's 'Denominational Chasm,'" Huffington Post, January 6, 2014. *http://www.huffingtonpost.com/2014/01/06/atheist-church-split_n_4550456.html*. Accessed May 21, 2015.

21. Rodney Stark and William Sims Bainbridge, *The Future of Religion: Secularization, Revival and Cult Formation* (Berkeley, CA: University of California Press, 1985), 114–15.

22. Charles Taylor, *A Secular Age* (Cambridge, MA: The Belknap Press of Harvard University Press, 2007).

23. Stark and Bainbridge, *The Future of Religion*, 1–16.

24. Nancy Tatom Ammerman, "Spiritual but Not Religious? Beyond Binary Choices in the Study of Religion." *Journal for the Scientific Study of Religion* 52 (2) 2013, 258–59.

25. Meredith McGuire, *Lived Religion: Faith and Practice in Everyday Life*, (New York: Oxford University Press, 2008), 6–17.

26. Ammerman, "Spiritual But Not Religious," 258–78.

27. Dick Houtman and Stef Aupers, "The Spiritual Turn and the Decline of Tradition: The Spread of Post-Christian Spirituality in 14 Western Countries, 1981–2000*," Journal for the Scientific Study of Religion*, 52 (3) 2007, 306.

28. Sylvia Boorstein, *That's Funny, You Don't Look Buddhist: On Being a Faithful Jew and a Passionate Buddhist* (San Francisco: HarperCollins, 1998).

29. McGuire, *Lived Religion*, 3–16.

30. Sir James George Frazer, *The Golden Bough: A Study in Magic and Religion* (New York: Macmillan, 1922 [1890]).

31. Rodney Stark, *One True God: Historical Consequences of Monotheism* (Princeton: Princeton University Press, 2001), 31–66.

32. Paul Froese and Christopher Bader, *America's Four Gods: What We Say About God and What That Says About Us* (New York: Oxford University Press, 2010).

33. Robert H. Abzug, *Passionate Liberator: Theodore Dwight Weld & the Dilemma of Reform* (New York: Oxford University Press, 1980).

34. Jonathan D. Sassi, *A Republic of Righteousness: The Public Christianity of the Post-Revolutionary New England Clergy* (New York: Oxford University Press, 2001), 199–201.

35. Abzug, *Passionate Liberator*.

36. Angelina Emily Grimké, *Appeal to Christian Women of the South* (New York: American Anti-Slavery Society, 1836), 44.

37. William G. McLoughlin, *Revivals, Awakenings, and Reform* (Chicago: University of Chicago Press, 1978).

38. Marion Goldman, *The American Soul Rush: Esalen and the Rise of Spiritual Privilege* (New York: New York University Press, 2012), 5–12.

39. Elaine Pagels, *The Gnostic Gospels* (New York: Vintage, 2009).

40. Thomas Merton, *The New Man* (New York: Farrar, Strauss and Giroux, 1961), 46, 144.

41. Weber, *The Sociology of Religion*, 151–183.

42. Isaacson, *Steve Jobs*, 143.

43. Weber, *The Sociology of Religion*, 166–7.

44. Isaacson, *Steve Jobs*, 143.

45. Ibid., 34–37.

46. Ibid., 41.

47. Shunryu Suzuki, *Zen Mind, Beginner's Mind* (Boston: Shambala Publications/Weatherhill, 1970).

48. Isaacson, *Steve Jobs*, 45–48.

49. David Downing, *Shoes Outside the Door: Desire, Devotion, and Excess at the San Francisco Zen Center*, (Washington, DC: Counterpoint Press, 2001).

50. Isaacson, *Steve Jobs*, 49–50.

51. Ibid.,105–6; Baba Ram Dass, *Remember Be Here Now* (Santa Fe, NM: Hanuman Foundation, 1971).

52. Isaacson, *Steve Jobs,* 453–54.

53. "San Francisco Zen Center Facebook Page Memorial for Steve Jobs," October 6, 2011: https//www.facebook.com/zencenter/posts/123766057728034. Accessed May 30, 2016.

54. Max Weber, *The Protestant Ethic and the Spirit of Capitalism* (London: Routledge 2007 [1910]), 40–42.

55. Richard Wolin, "Steve Jobs and the 'Me' Generation," *The Chronicle of Higher Education Review*, December 4, 2015, B20.

56. Erving Goffman, *Stigma: Notes on the Management of Spoiled Identity* (Englewood Cliffs, NJ: Prentice Hall, 1963), 44.

Chapter 2

1. Max Weber, *The Sociology of Religion* (Boston: Beacon Press 1963) and Stephen Sharot, *A Comparative Sociology of World Religions: Virtuosos, Priests, and Popular Religions* (New York; New York University Press, 2001).

2. Roland Bainton, *Here I Stand: A Life of Martin Luther* (New York: Abinddon Press, 1950) and Heiko Oberman, *Luther, Man Between God and the Devil* (New Haven: Yale University Press, 1989.

3. Diarmaid MacCulloch, "The World Took Sides," *London Review of Books* 38/16 (2016): 25–27.

4. Weber, *The Sociology of Religion*, 162–65.

5. Marianne Weber, *Max Weber: A Biography* (New Brunswick, New Jersey: Transaction Publishers, 1988 [1926]), 324.

6. Max Weber, *From Max Weber: Essays in Sociology*, edited by Hans Gerth and C. Wright Mills (Oxford: Oxford University Press, 1958 [1946]), 4–6.

7. Wolfgang Schluchter, *The Rise of Western Rationalism: Max Weber's Developmental History* (Berkeley: University of California Press, 1981).

8. Lorne L. Dawson, Editor, *Cults and New Religious Movements: A Reader* (Oxford: Blackwell, 2002).

9. Barbara Newman, "Sybil of the Rhine: Hildegard's Life and Times," in *Hildegard of Bingen and Her World* (Berkeley: University of California Press, 1988), 1.

10. Bruce Holsinger, "The Flesh of the Voice: Embodiment and the Homoerotics of Devotion in the Music of Hildegard of Bingen," *Signs: A Journal of Women in Culture and Society* 19 (1993), 92–125.

11. Ibid. Von Bingen's attitude was not unusual. Monastic orders routinely required substantial donations in exchange for entry, excluding most commoners from becoming initiates.

12. Newman, "Hildegard's Life and Times," 20–21.

13. Oberman, *Luther*, 289–97 and Bainton, *Here I Stand.*

14. Weber, *The Sociology of Religion*, 166.

15. R. W. Southern, *Western Society and the Church in the Middle Ages* (New York: Pelican, 1970), and Patricia Wittberg, *The Rise and Decline of Catholic Religious Orders* (Albany: SUNY Press, 1994).

16. Ilana F. Silber *Virtuosity, Charisma, and Social Order* (Cambridge: Cambridge University Press, 1995), 214–5.

17. Robert B. Ekelund, Robert F. Herbert, Robert D. Tollison, Gary M. Anderson, and Audrey B. Davidson, *Sacred Trust: The Medieval Church as an Economic Firm* (New York: Oxford University Press, 1996).

18. Weber, *Sociology of Religion*, 104–05.

19. Ágnes Erdélyi, "Varieties of Moral Beliefs in the 'Sociology of Religion,'" *Max Weber Studies* 7/2 (2007): 163–84.

20. Malcolm Muggeridge, *Something Beautiful for God: The Classic Account of Mother Theresa's Journey into Compassion* (New York: HarperOne, 2003 [1971]).

21. Weber, *Sociology of Religion*, 46–59.

22. Terry Bisson, *Nat Turner: Slave Revolt Leader* (Philadelphia: Chelsea House, 2005).

23. David L. Chappell, *A Stone of Hope: Prophetic Religion and the Death of Jim Crow* (Chapel Hill, NC: University of North Carolina, 2005).

24. Dave Thompson, *Hearts of Darkness: James Taylor, Jackson Browne, Cat Stevens and the Unlikely Rise of the Singer Songwriter* (Montclair, NJ: Backbeat Books, 2012).

25. Yusef, *Why I Carry a Guitar: The Spiritual Journey of Cat Stevens to Yusef* (Abu Dhabi, Dubai: Motivate Publishing Company, 2014).

26. Dag Hammerskjöld, *Markings* (London: Faber and Faber, 1964), 23.

27. Rodney Stark, *One True God: Historical Consequences of Monotheism* (Princeton: Princeton University Press, 2001), 4–6; and Emile Durkheim, *The Elementary Forms of Religious Life* (New York: the Free Press, 1995 [1915]), xvii.

28. For instance, a distraught Mary Magdalene mistook the newly risen Christ for a gardener (John 20: 11–18).

29. Ann Taves, *Religious Experience Reconsidered: A Building-Block Approach to the Study of Religion and other Special Things* (Princeton: Princeton University Press, 2009).

30. Evelyn Underhill, *Mystics of the Church* (Harrisburg, Pennsylvania: Morehouse Publishing Company), 3–14.

31. Sabina Flanagan, *Hildegard of Bingen: A Visionary Life* (London: Routledge, 1998), 1–18.

32. Oliver Sacks, *Migraine* (New York: Vintage Books, 1992[1970]), 13–33.

33. Walter Isaacson, *Steve Jobs* (New York: Simon and Schuster, 2011), 14–15

34. Daniel Goleman, *The Meditative Mind: The Varieties of Meditative Experience* (New York: Jeremy Tarcher/Penguin, 1988); Jeff Wilson, *Mindful America: The Mutual Transformation of Buddhism and American Culture* (New York: Oxford University Press, 2014), 42–75.

35. Aldous Huxley, *The Doors of Perception* (London: Chato and Windus, 1954), 1–15.

36. Ibid., 36.

37. Martin Buber, *The Knowledge of Man: Selected Essays* (New York: Harper and Row, 1965).

38. Robert Charles Zaehner, *Mysticism Sacred and Profane an Inquiry into the Varieties of Preternatural Experience* (Oxford: Oxford University Press, 1961 [1957).

39. Huston Smith, *Cleansing the Doors of Perception: The Religious Significance of Etheogenic Plants and Chemicals* (New York: Tarcher/Putnam, 2000).

40. Scott M. Hendrix, *Recultivating the Vineyard: The Reformation Agendas of Christianization* (Louisville: KY: Westminster/John Knox, 2004).

41. Marion Goldman, *The American Soul Rush: Esalen and the Rise of Spiritual Privilege* (New York: New York University Press, 2012), 95–97.

42. Ibid., 95–99.

43. Peter Coyote, *Sleeping Where I Fall: A Chronicle* (Berkeley: Counterpoint, 1998), 75–83.

44. Steven Tipton, *Getting Saved From the Sixties: The Transformation of Moral Meaning in American Culture* (Berkeley: University of California Press, 1982).

45. Peter Berger, *The Sacred Canopy: Elements of a Sociological Theory of Religion* (Garden City, NY: Doubleday, 1967).

46. John Lofland and Rodney Stark, "Becoming a World Saver: A Theory of Conversion to a Deviant Perspective," *American Sociological Review* 40, No. 6 (1965): 863–74.

47. Rodney Stark, "Upper Class Asceticism: Social Origins of Ascetic Movements and Medieval Saints," *Review of Religious Research* 45, No. 1 (2003), 5–19.

48. Ibid., and Weber, *The Sociology of Religion*, 140.

49. See Ronald Burt, *Brokerage and Closure: An Introduction to Social Capital* (New York: Oxford University Press, 2005); and Bradford Verter, "Spiritual Capital: Theorizing Religion with Bourdieu Against Bourdieu," *Sociological Theory* 21, No. 2 (2003), 150–73.

50. Anita M. Caspary, *Witness to Integrity: The Crisis of the Immaculate Heart Community of California* (Collegeville, MN: The Liturgical Press, 2003), 183–222.

51. Nan Deane Cano, *Take Heart: Growing a Faith Community* (New York: Paulist Press 2016), 46–51.

52. Pierre Bourdieu, *The Social Structures of the Economy* (New York: Polity Press, 2005).

53. Manisha Sinha, *The Slave's Cause: A History of Abolition* (New Haven: Yale University Press, 2016); Michael P. Young, *Bearing Witness against Sin: The Evangelical Birth of the American Social Movement* (Chicago: University of Chicago Press, 2006).

54. Goldman, *The American Soul Rush*, 25–48.

55. Lee Gilmore, *Theater in a Crowded Fire: Ritual and Spirituality at Burning Man* (Berkeley: University of California Press, 2010).

56. Claude Levi-Strauss, *The Savage Mind: The Nature of Human Society* (Chicago: University of Chicago Press, 1966).

57. Rodney Stark, *The Rise of Christianity: A Sociologist Reconsiders History* (Princeton: Princeton University Press, 1996), 191–201.

58. Edward Muir, *Ritual in Early Modern Europe* (Cambridge: Cambridge University Press, 1997).

59. Rodney Stark, *One True God*, 72–75.

60. Fenggang Yang, "Exceptionalism or Chinamerica: Measuring Religious Change in the Globalizing World Today," *Journal for the Scientific Study of Religion* 55/1 (2016), 12–13.

61. Ibid., 19–21 and Laurence Iannaccone, "Risk, Rationality and Religious Portfolios," *Economic Inquiry* 32 (1995): 285–95.

Chapter 3

1. David Sloan Wilson, *Does Altruism Exist?: Culture, Genes, and the Welfare of Others* (New Haven, CN: Yale University Press, 2015), 9–18.

2. Ibid., 75–92.

3. Larry Ceplair, Editor, *The Public Years of Sarah and Angelina Grimke, 1835–1839* (New York: Columbia University Press, 1989), 20.

4. Max Weber, *The Protestant Ethic and the Spirit of Capitalism* (New York: Scribner, 1930), 182.

5. Max Weber, *The Sociology of Religion* (Boston: Beacon Press, 1963), 175.

6. Richard Rabinowitz, *The Spiritual Self in Everyday Life: The Transformation of Personal Religious Experience in Nineteenth-Century New England* (Boston: Northeastern University Press, 1999), xviii.

7. The crucial role played by slavery in the rise of modern capitalism has been a focus of recent global history. See Sven Beckert, *Empire of Cotton: A Global History* (New York: Vintage, 2014); Edward E. Baptist, *The Half Has Never Been Told: Slavery and the Making of American Capitalism* (New York: Basic, 2014); and Sven Beckert and Seth Rockman, Editors, *Slavery's Capitalism: A New History of American Economic Development* (Philadelphia: University of Pennsylvania Press, 2016).

8. Wendy Warren, *New England Bound: Slavery and Colonization in Early America* (New York: W.W. Norton, 2016).

9. Marion Goldman, *The American Soul Rush: Esalen and the Rise of Spiritual Privilege* (New York: NYU Press, 2012), 37–38.

10. Linda Sargent Wood, "Contact, Encounter, and Exchange at Esalen." *Pacific Historical Review* 77/2 (2003): 453–87.

11. The agrarian revolution had radical consequences. See, for example, Daniel Chirot, *How Societies Change*, 2nd edition (Los Angeles: Sage, 2012); Michael Mann, *The Sources*

of Social Power, Volume I (New York: Cambridge University Press, 1986); and Douglass C. North, Structure and Change in Economic History (New York: Norton, 1981).

12. Eric R. Wolf, Peasants (Englewood Cliffs, NJ: Prentice Hall, 1965).

13. Weber, The Sociology of Religion, 140. On the universal quest for God, see Rodney Stark, Discovering God: The Origins of the Great Religions and the Evolution of Belief (New York: HarperOne 2007).

14. See Weber, Sociology of Religion; and Sharot, A Comparative Sociology of World Religions; Schluchter, The Rise of Western Rationalism; and Wittberg, The Rise and Decline of Catholic Religious Orders.

15. Paul Tillich, A History of Christian Thought (New York: Simon and Schuster, 1967), 234.

16. Steven Ozment, The Age of Reform, 1250–1550: An Intellectual and Religious History of Late Medieval and Reformation Europe (New Haven, CT: Yale University Press, 1980), 182–222.

17. Randall Collins, Weberian Sociological Theory (Cambridge: Cambridge University Press, 1986), 47–55.

18. Peter Blickle, The Revolution of 1525: The German Peasants War from a New Perspective (Baltimore: Johns Hopkins University Press, 1981).

19. See Rodney Stark, One True God: Historical Consequences of Monotheism (Princeton, NJ: Princeton University Press, 2001).

20. On the causes and cultural consequences of the modern transformation, see Daniel Chirot, "The Rise of the West," American Sociological Review 52/2 (1985): 181–95; Brad Gregory, The Unintended Reformation: How a Religious Revolution Secularized Society (Cambridge, MA: Harvard University Press, 2012); and Deidre N. McCloskey, Bourgeois Dignity: Why Economics Can't Explain the World (Chicago: University of Chicago Press, 2010).

21. Christopher Dawson, Religion and the Rise of Western Culture (New York: Doubleday Image Books, 1957), 63.

22. Peter Stamatov, The Origins of Global Humanitarianism: Religion, Empires, and Advocacy (New York: Cambridge University Press, 2013).

23. Rodney Stark, The Rise of Christianity: A Sociologist Reconsiders History (Princeton: Princeton University Press, 1996), 55.

24. Rodney Stark, The Victory of Reason: How Christianity led to Freedom, Capitalism, and Western Success (New York: Random House, 2005), 13–15.

25. Stark, Rise of Christianity, 209–11.

26. Stark, "Upper Class Asceticism" and Weber, The Sociology of Religion, 140–41

27. See Weber, Sociology of Religion; for an ecological-comparative perspective on the origins and function of religion in agrarian societies, see Patrick Nolan and Gerhard Lenski, Human Societies: An Introduction to Macrosociology (Boulder: Paradigm, 2009).

28. On the evolution of the concept of the soul and of salvation, see Weber, Sociology of Religion. On the broakder implictions of the retreat of existential threat, see Pippa Norris and Ronald Inglehart Sacred and Secular: Religion and Politics Worldwide (New York: Cambridge University Press, 2004).

29. Rodney Stark, The Rise of Christianity, 29–48 and 212–15.

30. Ibid., 156–58.

31. Roger Finke and Rodney Stark, *The Churching of America, 1776–1990: Winners and Losers in Our Religious Economy* (Berkeley: University of California Press, 1992), 55–86.

32. For applications of the religious economies model in understanding the pressure for religious change, see Ekelund et al. *The Marketplace of Christianity*, 113; Laurence Iannaccone, "The Consequences of Religious Market Structures," *Rationality and Society* 3/2 (1991): 156–77; and Rodney Stark and William Sims Bainbridge, *The Future of Religion: Secularization, Revival and Cult Formation* (Berkeley and Los Angeles: University of California Press, 1985).

33. On the formation of religious orders in response to economic expansion and secularization, see Michael Hill, *The Religious Order;* Ilana Silber, *Virtuosity, Charisma and Social Order;* and Patricia Wittberg, *The Rise and Decline of Catholic Religious Orders* (Albany: SUNY Press, 1994).

34. See Weber, *Sociology of Religion;* and expansion of this theme in Sharot, *Comparative Sociology of World Religions.*

35. Andrew Pettegree, *Brand Luther: How an Unheralded Monk Turned His Small Town into a Center for Publishing, Made, Himself the most Famous Man in Europe — and Started the Protestant Reformation* (New York: Penguin Publishing, 2015).

36. Heather Havemann, *Magazines and the Making of America: Modernization, Community, and Print Culture, 1741–1860* (Princeton: Princeton University Press, 2015).

37. See Richard Rabinowitz, *The Spiritual Self in Everyday Life: The Transformation of Personal Religious Experience in Nineteenth-Century New England* (Boston: Northeastern University Press, 1989); Jonathan A. Sassi, *A Republic of Righteousness: The Public Christianity of the Post-Revolutionary New England Clergy* (New York: Oxford University Press, 2001); and Michael P. Young, *Bearing Witness against Sin: The Evangelical Birth of the American Social Movement* (Chicago: Chicago University Press, 2006).

38. On the consequences of religious deregulation in the United States in the 1960s, see Laurence Iannaccone, Roger Finke and Rodney Stark, "Deregulating Religion: The Economics of Church and State," *Economic Inquiry* 35/2 (1997): 350–64.

39. Tracy Daugherty, *The Last Love Song: A Biography of Joan Didion* (New York: St. Martin's Press, 1025), 164.

40. George Leonard, "Where the California Game is Taking Us," *Look Magazine*, 1966 (December 28), 108–16.

41. See Doug McAdam, John D. McCarthy and Meyer Zald, editors, *Comparative Perspectives on Social Movements* (New York: Cambridge University Press, 1996); and Sidney Tarrow, *Power in Movement: Social Movements, Collective Action and Politics* (New York: Cambridge University Press, 1994); and Charles Tilly, *From Mobilization to Revolution* (New York: McGraw Hill, 1978).

42. Goldman, *The American Soul Rush*, 86–87 and 147.

43. Doug McAdam and Ronnelle Paulsen, "Specifying the Relationship between Social Ties and Activism." *American Journal of Sociology* 99/3 (1993); and Mario Diani and Doug McAdam, *Social Movements and Networks: Relational Approaches to Collective Action* (New York: Oxford University Press, 2003).

44. Rebecca Kolins Givan, Kenneth M. Roberts and Sarah A. Soule, editors, *The Diffusion of Social Movements: Actors, Mechanisms and Political Effects* (New York: Cambridge University Press, 2010).

45. Thomas R. Rochon, *Culture Moves: Ideas, Activism and Changing Values* (Princeton: Princeton University Press, 1998).

46. Robert Wuthnow, *Communities of Discourse: Ideology and Social Structure in the Reformation, the Enlightenment, and European Socialism* (Cambridge, MA: Harvard University Press, 1989).

47. Ronald Burt, *Brokerage and Closure: An Introduction to Social Capital* (New York: Oxford University Press, 2005).

48. On bridging activism in the US Civil Rights Movement, see Aldon Morris, *The Origins of the Civil Rights Movement: Black Communitie Organizing for Change* (New York: Free Press, 1984); Belinda Robnett, *How Long? How Long? African-American Women in the Struggle for Civil Rights* (New York: Oxford University Press, 2000); and Larry Isaac, "Movement of Movements: Culture Moves in the Long Civil Rights Struggle," *Social Forces* 87/1 (2008): 33–63.

49. See Katherine Stovel and Lynette Shaw, "Brokerage," *Annual Review of Sociology 38* (2012): 139–58; and Katherine Stovel, Benjamin Golub and Eva M. Meyersson Milgrom, "Stabilizing Brokerage," *Proceedings of the National Academy of Sciences* 108/4 (2011): 21326–32.

50. Sassi, *A Republic of Righteousness*.

51. See Lorne Dawson, editor, *Cults and New Religious Movements* (Malden, MA: Blackwell, 2003).

52. Rodney Stark, *The Rise of Christianity: A Sociologist Reconsiders History* (Princeton: Princeton University Press, 1996).

53. Nathan O. Hatch, *The Democratization of American Christianity* (New Haven, Yale University Press, 1989).

54. Weber, *The Sociology of Religion*, 28–29.

55. Lorne L. Dawson, *Comprehending Cults: The Sociology of New Religious Movements*, 2nd edition (Don Mills, Canada: Oxford University Press, 2006),152–560.

56. Weber, *The Sociology of Religion*, 244–45.

57. Weber, *Economy and Society*, 245.

58. Benton Johnson, "On Founders and Followers: Some Factors in the Development of New Religious Movements," *Sociological Analysis* 53 (1992): 1–13.

59. Eric Lincoln and Lawrence H. Manya, *The Black Church in the African American Experience* (Durham, NC: Duke University Press, 1990).

60. Johnson, "On Founders and Followers," 9–11.

61. David J. Garrow, *Bearing the Cross: Martin Luther King Jr. and the Southern Christian Leadership Conference* (New York: William Morrow, 1986), 11–83.

62. John Lewis with Michael D'Orso, *Walking With the Wind: A Memoir of the Movement* (New York: Harcourt Brace and Company, 1998), 45–46.

63. Gershom Scholem, *Sabbatai Zevi: The Mystical Messiah* (Princeton, NJ: Princeton University Press, 1973).

64. Lis Harris, *Holy Days: The World of a Hasidic Family* (New York: Macmillan Publishing Company, 1985), 47–53.

65. Ibid., 50–52.

66. Jeff Goodwin and James M. Jasper, *The Social Movements Reader: Cases and Concepts* (New York: Wiley, 2009), 4.

67. Young, *Bearing Witness against Sin*, 3.

68. For discussions of the "post-materialist values" and their implications for social movements, see, for example, Jürgen Habermas, "New Social Movements," *Telos* 49 (1981): 33–37; Ronald Inglehart, *Culture Shift in Advanced Industrial Society* (Princeton: Princeton University Press, 1990); and Alberto Melucci, "The New Social Movements: A Theoretical Approach," *Social Science Information* 19/2 (1981): 199–226.

69. Craig Calhoun, "'New Social Movements' of the Early Nineteenth Century," *Social Science History* 17/3 (1993), 388.

70. James Davison Hunter, *Culture Wars: The Struggle to Define America* (New York: Basic Books, 1991); and James Davison Hunter and Alan Wolfe, *Is There a Culture War? A Dialogue on Values and American Life* (Washington, DC: Brookings Institution Press, 2006).

71. Sean Chabot, *Transnational Roots of the Civil Rights Movement: African American Expansions of the Gandhian Repertoire* (Lexington Books, 2011).

Chapter 4

1. Heiko Oberman, *Luther: Man Between God and the Devil* (New Haven: Yale University Press, 1989), 125.

2. We focus not on Lutheranism but on Luther, his thought, and its enduring influence on spiritual virtuosity. On Lutheranism see Eric W. Gritsch, *A History of Lutheranism* (Minneapolis: Fortress Press, 2002); and Robert A. Kolb and Timothy J. Wengert, editors., *The Book of Concord, the Confessions of the Evangelical Lutheran Church* (Minneapolis: Fortress Press, 2000).

3. Roland Bainton, *Here I Stand: A Life of Martin Luther* (Nashville: Abingdon, 1950); Martin Marty, *Martin Luther* (New York: Penguin, 2004); Oberman, *Luther;* Scott H. Hendrix, *Recultivating the Vineyard: The Reformation Agendas of Christianization* (Louisville, KY: Westminster John Knox, 2004); and Paul Tillich, *A History of Christian Thought* (New York: Simon and Schuster, 1967).

4. Hendrix, *Recultivating the Vineyard;* Hans J. Hillberbrand, *The Division of Christendom: Christianity in the Sixteenth Century* (Louisville, KY: Westminster John Knox, 2007; and "Review essay" by Ronald K. Rittgers in *Church History* 80/4 (2011): 863–75.

5. Max Weber, *The Sociology of Religion* (Boston: Beacon, 1963), 166.

6. See Alfred Kohler, *Das Reich im Kampf um die Hegemonie in Europa, 1521–1648* (Munich: Oldenbourg, 1990); Helmut Neuhaus, *Das Reich in der Frühen Neuzeit* (Munich: Oldenbourg, 1997); Daniel H. Nexon, *The Struggle for Power in Early Modern Europe* (Princeton: Princeton University Press, 2009); and Ernst Schubert, *Fürstliche Herrschaft und Territorium im späten Mittelalter* (Munich: Oldenbourg, 1996).

7. R. H. Tawney, *Religion and the Rise of Capitalism* (New York: Harcourt, Brace and Jovanovich 1954), 64–65.

8. See Thomas A. Brady, *German Histories in the Age of Reformations, 1400–1650* (New York: Cambridge University, 2009); Arthur G. Dickens, *The Age of Humanism and Reformation* (New York: Prentice Hall, 1972); Alister McGrath, *The Intellectual Origins of the European Reformation* (Oxford: Blackwells, 1987); Bernd Moeller, *Deutschland im Zeitalter der Reformation* (Gottingen: Vandenhoek and Ruprecht, 1977); Tom Scott, *Society and Economy in Germany, 1300–1600* (New York: Palgrave, 2002); Robert W. Scribner (ed.), *Germany: A New Social and Economic History, 1450–1630* (London and New York: Arnold, 1996); and Heinz Schilling, *Aufbruch und Krise: Deutschland, 1517–1648* (Berlin: Siedler, 1988).

9. On printing and the Reformation, see Mark U. Edwards, *Printing, Propaganda, and Martin Luther* (Berkeley: University of California Press, 1994); Elizabeth L. Eisenstein, *The Printing Press as an Agent of Change* (New York: Cambridge University Press, 1980); Jean-François Gilmont, editor, *The Reformation and the Book* (Aldershot: Ashgate, 1998); Louise W. Holborn, "Printing and the Growth of a Protestant Movement in Germany from 1517 to 1524," *Church History* 11/2 (1942): 123–37; and Jared Rubin, "Printing and Protestants: an empirical test of the role of printing in the Reformation," *Review of Economics and Statistics* 96/2 (2014): 270–86.

10. William J. Courtenay and Jürgen Miethke, editors, *Universities and Schooling in Medieval Society* (Leiden: Brill, 2000); Walter Rüegg, *A History of the University in Europe, Volume II* (New York: Cambridge University Press, 2003).

11. See Euan Cameron, *The European Reformation,* 2nd Edition (New York: Oxford University Press 2012); Eamon Duffy, *The Stripping of the Altars: Traditional Religion in England, 1400–1580.* 2nd Edition (New Haven: Yale University Press, 2005); Bridget Heal, *The Cult of the Virgin Mary in Early Modern Germany: Protestant and Catholic Piety, 1500–1654* (New York: Cambridge University Press, 2007); Robert W. Scribner, *Religion and Culture in Germany, 1400–1800* (Boston: Brill, 2001); and Donald Weinstein and Rudolf M. Bell, *Saints and Society: The Two Worlds of Western Christendom, 1100–1700* (Chicago: University of Chicago Press, 1982).

12. Brad S. Gregory, *The Unintended Reformation: How a Religious Revolution Secularized Society* (Cambridge, MA: Harvard University Press, 2012).

13. Ekelund, *Sacred Trust*, 152–68.

14. See Robert W. Scribner, "Practice and Principle in the German Towns," in Peter Brooks, editor, *Reformation in Principle and Practice* (London: Scholar, 1980); and Larissa Taylor, *Soldiers of Christ: Preaching in Late Medieval and Reformation France.* Toronto: University of Toronto Press, 2002).

15. "At the beginning of the sixteenth century everyone that mattered in the Western Church was crying out for reformation," Owen Chadwick, *The Reformation* (New York. Penguin, 1990) 11. See Johann Huizinga, *The Waning of the Middle Ages* (New York: Edward Arnold, 1924); Josef Lortz *The Reformation in Germany* (New York: Herder & Herder, 1968); and Steven E. Ozment, *The Age of Reform, 1250–1550* (Yale University Press, 1980). For more recent views, see Thomas A. Brady, *German Histories in the*

Age of Reformations; Euan Cameron, *The European Reformation*, 2nd Edition, (New York: Oxford, 2012); Hans J. Hillerbrand, *The Division of Christendom: Christianity in the Sixteenth Century* (Louisville, KY: Westminster John Knox, 2007); and Diarmaid MacCulloch, *The Reformation* (New York: Penguin, 2005).

16. The papacy was "the greatest financial institution of the Middle Ages," Tawney, *Religion and the Rise of Capitalism*, 33. Also see Ekelund et al. *Sacred Trust* and Robert B. Ekelund, Robert F. Hébert, and Robert D. Tollison, *The Marketplace of Christianity* (Cambridge, MA: MIT Press, 2006).

17. See Sascha O. Becker, Steven Pfaff and Jared Rubin, "Causes and Consequences of the Protestant Reformation," *Explorations in Economic History* 62 (2016): 1–25; and Steven Pfaff and Katie E. Corcoran, "Piety, Power, and the Purse: Religious Economies Theory and Urban Reform in the Holy Roman Empire," *Journal for the Scientific Study of Religion* 51/4 (2012): 757–76.

18. Tawney, *Religion and the Rise of Capitalism*, 80.

19. See Huizinga, *Waning of the Middle Ages;* Ozment, *Age of Reform;* and Keith Thomas, *Religion and the Decline of Magic* (Oxford: Oxford University Press, 1971).

20. Oberman, *Luther,* 124–5.

21. Tillich, *History of Christian Thought*, p. 234.

22. Bainton, *Here I Stand*, 45.

23. Oberman *Luther*, 313–24.

24. Eric W. Gritsch, *Martin Luther: Faith in Christ and the Gospel* (New York: New City Press, 1996), 144–5.

25. Oberman, *Luther,* 149.

26. Bainton, *Here I Stand*, 50.

27. On "the fool in Rome"; see Oberman, *Luther*, 146–50.

28. Oberman, *Luther*, 139.

29. Marty, *Martin Luther*, 20.

30. Gritsch, *Faith in Christ and the Gospel*, 13.

31. Ernest F. Winter, editor, *Discourse on Free Will: Desiderius Erasmus and Martin Luther* (London: Bloomsbury, 2013).

32. Luther, "The Freedom of a Christian," in Gritsch, *Faith in Christ and the Gospel,* 102.

33. Gregory, *Unintended Reformation*, 180–234; Oberman, *Luther*, 154.

34. Hillerbrand, *The Division of Christendom*, 2.

35. See Susan C. Karant-Nunn, "Preaching the Word in Early Modern Germany" in Larissa Taylor, Editor, *Preachers and People in the Reformation and Early Modern Period* (Leiden: Brill 2001); and Joon-Chul Park, "Philip Melanchthon's Reform of German Universities and its Significance: A Study of Relationship between Renaissance Humanism and the Reformation" (Ph.D. dissertation, Department of History, Ohio State University, 1995).

36. Paul F. Grendler, "The Universities of the Renaissance and Reformation," *Renaissance Quarterly* 57/1 (2004), 18.

37. The term "evangelical" derives from the Greek and Latin terms for the "good news," or Gospel. The movement later became known as "Protestant" after the Diet of Speyer in

1529. For simplicity's sake, we refer to Luther and his followers, along with the Zwinglians and the Reformed wing of the Reformation, as Protestants.

38. Rodney Stark, *For the Glory of God* (Princeton, NJ: Princeton University Press, 2003), 16.

39. Oberman, *Luther*, 188.

40. Ibid., 74–77; 190–91.

41. Ibid., 191.

42. Bainton, *Here I Stand*, 295.

43. Andrew Pettegree, *Brand Luther: How an Unheralded Monk Turned His Small Town into a Center of Publishing, Made Himself the Most Famous Man in Europe—and Started the Protestant Reformation* (New York: Penguin, 2015), 334.

44. About 80 percent of Lutheran editions were published in German versus about half of Catholic treatises. See Edwards, *Print, Propaganda and Martin Luther;* and David N. Bagchi, *Luther's Earliest Opponents: Catholic Controversialists, 1518–1525* (Minneapolis: Augsburg Fortress, 2007).

45. "'How-to' Introduction to the 'Twitter Storm'" at the website Global Revolution, http://globalrevolution.tv/blog/547. Accessed on August 15, 2016.

46. Gritsch, *Faith in Christ and the Gospel,* 95.

47. Robert W. Scribner, *The German Reformation* (London: Macmillan, 1986).

48. Hillerbrand, *Division of Christendom*, 87.

49. Bagchi, *Luther's Earliest Opponents*, 228–29; and Oliver K. Olson, *Matthias Flacius and the Survival of Luther's Reform* (Minneapolis: The Lutheran Press, 2011).

50. Oberman, *Luther*, 195–97.

51. Bainton, *Here I Stand*, 117.

52. James D. Tracy, *Europe's Reformations, 1450–1650* (New York: Rowman & Littlefield, 1995), 55.

53. Bainton, *Here I Stand*, 185.

54. Oberman, *Luther*, 29–30; Nexon, *The Struggle for Power in Early Modern Europe.*

55. Gritzsch, *Faith in Christ and the Gospel,* 9.

56. Ibid., *Faith in Christ and the Gospel*, 155.

57. Tillich, *History of Christian Thought*, 253.

58. On Luther's ecclesiology, see Ibid., 251–6; and Oberman, *Luther,* 178–9.

59. Tillich, *History of Christian Thought,* 244–5.

60. Stephan Füssel, *The Luther Bible of 1534: A Cultural-Historical Introduction* (Cologne: Taschen 2003), 34.

61. Philip Schaff, *History of the Christian Church, Vol. VI* (New York: Scribner 1910), 93.

62. Bainton, *Here I Stand*, 349.

63. Luther's penitential hymn of 1524, "From Depths of Woe I Cry to Thee," captures the insufficiency of human works and spiritual suffering. Bach wrote a church cantata based on the hymn (BWV 38) which brilliantly captures spiritual distress. See *Lutheran Service Book*, No. 607 (St. Louis: Concordia, 2006); and Julian Mincham, *The Cantatas of Johann Sebastian Bach* (2010). Available athttp://www.jsbachcantatas.com/documents. Retrieved 8/9/16.

64. "Secular Authority: To What Extent It Should Be Obeyed," in John Dillenberger, Editor, *Martin Luther: Selections from His Writings* (New York: Doubleday, 1962).

65. C. Scott Dixon "Princely Reformation in Germany" in Andrew Pettegree, Editors, *The Reformation World* (London: Routledge, 2000); and James D. Tracy, Editor, *Luther and the Modern State in Germany* (Kirksville, MO: Sixteenth Century Society, 1989).

66. Hyojoung Kim and Steven Pfaff, "Structure and Dynamics of a Religious Insurgency: Students and the Spread of the Reformation," *American Sociological Review* 77/2 (2012): 188–215.

67. Kim and Pfaff analyzed the biographies of 232 activists born between 1450 and 1505 from detailed entries found in Klaus Ganzer, and Bruno Steiner, *Lexikon der Reformationszeit* (Freiburg: Herder, 2002) and Robert Stupperich, *Reformatorenlexikon* (Gutersloh: Gerd Mohn, 1984).

68. Robert W. Scribner, "Practice and Principle in the German Towns: Preachers and the People" in Peter Brooks, Editors, *Reformation in Principle and Practice* (London: Scholar, 1980).

69. Jack A. Goldstone, *Revolution and Rebellion in the Early Modern World* (Berkeley: University of California Press, 1991) and *Revolutions: A Very Short Introduction* (New York: Oxford, 2014).

70. Schilling, *Aufbruch und Krise: Deutschland, 1517–1648,* 104; Schwiebert, *The Reformation as a University Movement,* 471.

71. Lortz, *The Reformation in Germany*, 399.

72. Lyndal Roper, *Martin Luther: Renegade and Prophet* (London: Bodley Head, 2016).

73. Bernd Moeller, "What was preached in German towns in the early Reformation?" in C. Scott Dixon, Editor, *The German Reformation* (Oxford: Blackwell, 1999).

74. McGrath, *Intellectual Origins of the European Reformation*, 49.

75. See Ulrich Gäbler, *Huldrych Zwingli: His Life and Work* (Philadelphia: Fortress Press, 1986); and G. R. Potter, *Ulrich Zwingli* (London: Historical Association Press, 1977).

76. Tracy, *Europe's Reformations,* 241.

77. See David Nicholas, *Urban Europe, 1100–1700* (London: Palgrave Macmillan, 2003), especially 92–93; and Max Weber, *The City* (New York: Collier, 1962).

78. See Thomas J. Brady, "The Reformation of the Common Man, 1521–1524," in C. Scott Dixon, Editor, *The German Reformation* (London: Blackwell, 1999); Bernd Moeller, *Imperial Cities and the Reformation* (Philadelphia: Fortress, 1972); Mörke, *Reformation;* and John Witte, *Law and Protestantism: The Legal Teachings of the Lutheran Reformation* (New York: Cambridge University Press, 2002).

79. On the Protestant-Catholic struggle, see Scribner, *The German Reformation;* and Wayne te Brake, *Shaping History: Ordinary People in European Politics, 1500–1700* (Berkeley: University of California Pres, 1998).

80. C. Scott Dixon, "The Princely Reformation in Germany."

81. Gerald Strauss, *Nuremberg in the Sixteenth Century* (New York: Wiley, 1966).

82. See Joy Kammerlin, "Andreas Osiander's Sermons on the Jews," *Lutheran Quarterly* 15/1 (2001): 59–84; and Anselm Schubert, "Andreas Osiander als Kabbalist," *Archiv für Reformationsgeschichte* 105 (2014): 30–54.

83. "Osiander only believed in the absolute truth in the realm of revelation, and he asserted that science was based only on testable propositions," Steinmetz, *Reformers in the Wings* (New York: Oxford, 2001), 66; see also Gunter Zimmermann, "Die Publikation von 'De Revolutionibis Orbium Coelestium,'" *Zeitschrift für Kirchengeschichte* 96/3(1985): 320–43.

84. See Steinmetz, *Reformers in the* Wings; and Ronald K. Rittgers, "Luther on Private Confession," *The Lutheran Quarterly* 19/3 (2005): 312–31.

85. Olson, *The Survival of Luther's Reform*, 284.

86. Justo González, *A History of Christian Thought, Volume III* (Nashville: Abingdon Press, 1975), 103–105; and Steinmetz, *Reformers in the Wings*, 64–68.

87. See Timothy Wengert, *Defending Faith: Lutheran Responses to Andreas Osiander's Doctrine of Justification* (Tubingen: Mohr Siebeck, 2012) and Olson, *The Survival of Luther's Reform*, 284–301.

88. Michael J. Halvorson, *Heinrich Hesshusius and Confessional Polemics in early Lutheran Orthodoxy* (Farnham: Ashgate, 2010).

89. Karin Dovring, "Quantitative Semantics in the 18th Century," *Public Opinion Quarterly* 18/4 (1954–55): 389–94.

90. Dietrich Bonhoeffer, *The Cost of Discipleship* (New York: Macmillan, 1959).

91. Mark A. Noll, *The Rise of Evangelicalism: The Age of Edwards, Whitefield and the Wesleys* (Downers Grove, IL: InterVarsity Press, 2003), 60–5.

92. Mark A. Noll, *America's God: From Jonathan Edwards to Abraham Lincoln* (New York: Oxford University Press, 2002), 383.

Chapter 5

1. Robert K. Nelson, "'The Forgetfulness of Sex': Devotion and Desire in the Courtship Letters of Angelina Grimké and Theodore Dwight Weld," *Journal of Social History* 37/3 (2004): 663–76.

2. Michael Young, *Bearing Witness against Sin: The Evangelical Birth of the American Social Movement* (Chicago: University of Chicago Press, 2007), 131.

3. See Angela Lahr, "'Bound in the Dust': Guilt and Conscience in the Life of Angelina Grimké Weld," *The Historian* (2015): 1–25; and Stephen H. Browne, *Angelina Grimké: Rhetoric, Identity, and the Radical Imagination* (East Lansing: Michigan State University Press, 1999).

4. See Manisha Singh, *The Slave's Cause: A History of Abolition* (New Haven: Yale University Press, 2016); Owen B. Muelder, *Theodore Dwight Weld and the American Anti-Slavery Society* (Jefferson, NC: McFarland and Company, 2011); Robert H. Abzug, *Passionate Liberator: Theodore Dwight Weld and the Dilemma of Reform* (New York: Oxford University Press, 1980); Benjamin Thomas, *Theodore Weld: Crusader for Freedom* (New Brunswick, NJ: Rutgers University Press, 1950); Henry Mayer, *All on Fire: William Lloyd Garrison and the Abolition of Slavery* (New York: St. Martin's Press, 1998); and James Brewer Stewart, *Holy Warriors: The Abolitionists and American Slavery* (New York: Hill and Wang, 1976).

5. Susan Juster, *Disorderly Women: Sexual Politics and Evangelicalism in Revolutionary New England* (Ithaca: Cornell University Press, 1994).

6. Richard Rabinowitz, *The Spiritual Self in Everyday Life: The Transformation of Personal Religious Experience in Nineteenth-Century New England* (Boston: Northeastern University Press, 1989).

7. Jon Grinspan, *The Virgin Vote: How Young Americans Made Democracy Social, Politics Personal, and Voting Popular in the Nineteenth Century* (Chapel Hill: University of North Carolina Press, 2016).

8. Mark A. Noll, *The Rise of Evangelicalism: The Age of Edwards, Whitefield and the Wesleys* (Downers Grove, IL: InterVarsity Press, 2003); Nathan O. Hatch, *The Democratization of American Christianity* (New Haven: Yale University Press, 1989); Jonathan Sassi, *A Republic of Righteousness: The Public Christianity of the Post-Revolutionary New England Clergy* (New York: Oxford University Press, 2001); and Douglas M. Strong, *Perfectionist Politics: Abolitionism and the Religious Tensions of American Democracy* (Syracuse: Syracuse University Press, 1999).

9. "On Money" in David McLellan, Editor, *Karl Marx: Selected Writings* (Oxford: Oxford University Press, 1977), 109–111.

10. Peter Stamatov, *The Origins of Global Humanitarianism: Religion, Empires, and Advocacy* (New York: Cambridge University Press, 2013).

11. Eric Williams, *Capitalism and Slavery* (Chapel Hill: University of North Carolina Press, 1994 [1944]).

12. Sven Beckert, *Empire of Cotton: A Global History* (New York: Vintage, 2014); Edward A. Baptiste, *The Half Has Never Been Told: Slavery and the Making of American Capitalism* (New York: Basic Books, 2014); and "Cotton" in Martin A. Klein, *Historical Dictionary of Slavery and Abolition* (Lanham, MA: Rowan & Littlefield, 2014).

13. Sven Beckert and Seth Rockman, Editors, *Slavery's Capitalism: A New History of American Economic Development* (Philadelphia, University of Pennsylvania Press, 2016), 2–15.

14. Robert W. Vogel, *Without Contract or Consent: The Rise and Fall of American Slavery* (New York: Norton, 1991).

15. Sassi, *Republic of Righteousness*, 186–94.

16. Ann Hagedorn, *Beyond the River: The Untold Story of the Heroes of the Underground Railroad* (New York: Simon & Schuster, 2002), 203.

17. Angelina Grimké in *American Slavery as It Is: Testimony of a Thousand Witnesses* (New York: American Anti-Slavery Society, 1839), 52.

18. Gerda Lerner, *The Grimké Sisters from South Carolina: Pioneers for Woman's Rights and Abolition* (New York: Schocken, 1971).

19. Singh, *Slave's Cause*, 461–99.

20. Noll, *Rise of Evangelicalism*, 41.

21. Roger Finke and Rodney Stark, *The Churching of America, 1776-1990: Winners and Losers in our Religious Economy* (New Brunswick: Rutgers University Press, 1992).

22. Noll, *Rise of Evangelicalism*, 126.

23. Frank Lambert, *"Pedlar in Divinity": George Whitefield and the Transatlantic Revivals, 1737-1770* (Princeton: Princeton University Press, 1994).

24. Noll, *Rise of Evangelicalism*, 105–108; Finke and Stark, *Churching of America*, 55–56.

25. Sassi, *Republic of Righteousness*; Young, *Bearing Witness*.

26. Rabinowitz, *Spiritual Self,* especially 147–85.

27. Finke and Stark, *Churching of America*, 85.

28. Singh, *Slave's Cause*, 217.

29. Sassi, *Republic of Righteousness*, 172–86.

30. Michael O. Emerson and Christian Smith, *Divided by Faith: Evangelical Religion and the Problem of Race in America* (New York: Oxford University Press, 2000), 29–30.

31. Susan Jacoby, *Freethinkers: A History of American Secularism* (New York: Henry Holt, 2004), 69–82.

32. Muelder, *Theodore Dwight Weld*.

33. Young, *Bearing Witness,* 181.

34. Thomas, *Theodore Weld.*

35. Abzug, *Passionate* Liberator, 42–65.

36. Mayer, *All on Fire.*

37. See, for example, Numbers 11: 16–17; and Luke 10: 1–24.

38. Muelder, *Theodore Dwight Weld*, 68–97.

39. Thomas, *Theodore Weld*; Young, *Bearing Witness*, 4.

40. Stamatov, *Origins of Global Humanitarianism*, 163–73.

41. Lerner, *Grimké Sisters*, 122–3.

42. See Singh, *Slave's Cause*, 228–39; and Leonard L. Richards, *"Gentlemen of Property and Standing": Anti-Abolition Mobs in Jacksonian America* (New York: Oxford University Press, 1970).

43. See the biographies of American abolitionists collected in Klein, *Historical Dictionary of Slavery and Abolition*.

44. Lerner, *Grimké Sisters*, 123.

45. Bernd Moeller, "Stadt und Buch," in Wolfgang Mommsen, Editors, *Stadtbürgertum und Adel in der Reformation* (Stuttgart: Ernst Klett, 1979), 30.

46. Noll, *Rise of Evangelicalism*, 115–19; Lambert, *Pedlar in Divinity*; and Stamatov, *Origins of Global Humanitarianism.*

47. Heather Havemann, *Magazines and the Making of America: Modernization, Community and Print Culture, 1741–1860* (Princeton, NJ: Princeton University Press, 2015).

48. See Finke and Stark, *Churching of America*; and Lee Soltow and Edward Stevens, *The Rise of Literacy and the Common Schools in the United States: A Socioeconomic Analysis to 1870* (Chicago: University of Chicago Press, 1981).

49. Lerner, *Grimké Sisters*, 243.

50. Emerson and Smith, *Divided by Faith*, 34–37.

51. On slavery in American religious thought, see Noll, *America's God*, 386–401; Hatch, *Democratization,* 93; and Molly Oschatz, *Slavery and Sin: The Fight Against Slavery and the Rise of Liberal Protestantism* (New York, Oxford University Pres, 2012), 61–65.

52. Singh, *Slave's Cause*, 217–23.

53. *American Slavery*, 7.

54. Harriet Beecher Stowe, *Uncle Tom's Cabin: A Tale of Life among the Lowly* (London: Routledge, 1852).

55. Browne, *Angelina Grimké*.

56. Lerner, *Grimke Sisters*, 5–10.

57. Singh, *Slave's Cause*, 279.

58. Noll, *Rise of Evangelicalism*, 265.

59. See Jennifer McKinney, "Sects and Gender: Reaction and Resistance to Cultural Change," *Priscilla Papers* 29/4 (2015), 16–17; and Susan Juster, *Disorderly Women* 145–79.

60. Noll, *Rise of Evangelicalism*, 108; and *America's God,* 402–21.

61. Emerson and Smith, *Divided by Faith,* 34–37.

62. Singh, *Slave's Cause*, 277–83.

63. Ibid., 281.

64. Emerson and Smith, *Divided by Faith*, 32–34.

65. Abzug, *Passionate Liberator*, 239–49.

66. Singh, *Slave's Cause,* 284–88.

67. Lerner, *Grimké Sisters*, 314.

68. Abzug, *Passionate Liberator*, ix.

Chapter 6

1. Anita M. Caspary, *Witness to Integrity: The Crisis of the Immaculate Heart Community of California* (Collegeville, MN: The Liturgical Press, 2003), 38.

2. Bernard Galm (interviewer), "Los Angeles Art Community: Group Portrait, Corita Kent" (University of California at Los Angeles Oral History Program, unpublished manuscript, 1977), 33.

3. Kenneth Woodward, *Getting Religion: Faith, Culture, and Policies from the Age of Eisenhower to the Era of Obama* (New York: Convergent Books, 2016), 78–80.

4. Walter Truett Anderson, *The Upstart Spring: Esalen and the American Awakening* (Reading, MA: Addison Wesley, 1983), 148–49.

5. Ibid., 150.

6. Ibid.

7. Ibid.

8. Caspary, *Witness to Integrity*, 23–24; Melissa J. Wilde, *Vatican II: A Sociological Analysis of Religious Change* (Princeton: Princeton University Press, 2007), 51–56.

9. Abraham Maslow, *The Farther Reaches of Human Nature* (New York/Viking Esalen, 1971).

10. Jacqueline Doyle, editor, *Interaction: Readings in Human Potential* (Lexington, MA; DC Heath, 1973).

11. Charlotte Selver, *A Taste of Sensory Awareness* (Mill Valley, CA: Sensory Awareness Foundation, 1979).

12. Jane Kramer, *Allen Ginsberg in America* (New York: Fromm International Publishing, [1969] 1997), 23.

13. Jeffrey J. Kripal, *Esalen: America and the Religion of No Religion* (Chicago: University of Chicago Press, 2007), 202–21.

14. Robert D. Putnam and David E. Campbell, "Religiosity in America: Shocks and Two Countershocks," in *American Grace: How Religion Unites and Divides Us* (New York: Simon & Schuster, 2010), 91–133.

15. Kevin Star, *California: A History* (New York: Modern Library, 2007).

16. Wade Clark Roof, *Spiritual Marketplace: Babyboomers and the Remaking of American Religion* (Princeton: Princeton University Press, 1999).

17. Dean M. Kelley, *Why Conservative Churches Are Growing* (New York; Harper and Row, 1972).

18. Roger Finke and Rodney Stark, *The Churching of America, 1776-1990: Winners and Losers in Our Religious Economy* (New Brunswick: Rutgers University Press, 1992), 129–34.

19. John W. O'Malley, *The Jesuits: A History from Ignatius to the Present* (London: Rowman and Littlefield, 2014).

20. Galm, "Los Angeles Art Community: Group Portrait," 15.

21. Margaret Thompson, "Discovering Foremothers: Sisters, Society, and the American Catholic Experience," *U.S. Catholic Historian* 5 (1986), 273–90.

22. Rodney Stark and Roger Finke, *Acts of Faith: Explaining the Human Side of Religion* (Berkeley: University of California Press, 2000), 194–77.

23. Ian Berry and Michael Duncan, editors, *Someday Is Now: The Art of Corita Kent* (New York: Prestel Publishing, 2013), 82–83.

24. Ibid., 41.

25. Mark Massa *The American Catholic Revolution: How the Sixties Changed the Church Forever* (New York: Oxford University Press, 2010).

26. Nan Dean Cano, *Take Heart: Growing A Faith Community* (New York: Paulist Press), 40.

27. Wilde, *Vatican II*, 1–10.

28. Caspary, *Witness to Integrity*, 85–108.

29. Ibid., 49–50

30. Ibid., 51–52.

31. Steven M. Tipton, *Getting Saved from The Sixties: The Transformation of Moral meaning in American Culture* (Berkeley: University of California Press, 1982).

32. Marion Goldman, *The American Soul Rush: Esalen and the Rise of Spiritual Privilege* (New York: New York University Press, 2012), 34–38.

33. Kripal, *Esalen*, 202.

34. George Leonard, *Mastery: The Keys to Success and Longterm Fulfillment* (New York: Penguin/Plume, 1993).

35. Anderson, *Upstart Spring*, 160–65.

36. Goldman, *American Soul Rush*, 45–47.

37. George Leonard, "The Turned on People," *Look Magazine* (June 28, 1966), 30–33.

38. Galm, "Corita Kent," 4–5.

39. Ibid., 33.

40. Ibid., 18.

41. Ibid., 41–43

42. Ruth Wallace, "Transformation from Sacred to Secular," 99–112 in *Gender and the Academic Experience: Berkeley Women Sociologists* edited by Kathryn P. Meadow-Orlans and Ruth A. Wallace (Lincoln: University of Nebraska Press, 1994).

43. Roof, *Spiritual Marketplace*.

44. Don Lattin, *Following Our Bliss: How the Spiritual Ideals of the Sixties Shape Our Lives Today* (San Francisco: Harper San Francisco, 2003).

45. Goldman, *American Soul Rush*, 139–40.

46. Ibid, 142–47.

47. Berry and Duncan, *Someday is Now*, 36.

48. Ibid., 36.

49. Galm, "Corita Kent," 7–13.

50. Ibid., 11.

51. Ibid., 37–40.

52. Berry and Duncan, *Someday Is Now*, 42.

53. Ibid., 72–73.

54. Galm, "Corita Kent," 72.

55. Berry and Duncan, *Someday Is Now*, 77.

56. Wilde, *Vatican II*, 126–28.

57. Berry and Duncan, *Someday is Now*, 80.

58. Caspary, *Witness to Integrity*, 88

59. Berry and Duncan, *Someday Is Now*, 80–81.

60. Ibid., 81.

61. Ibid., 83.

62. Ibid., 167.

63. Francine du Plessix Gray, *Adam & Eve and the City: Selected Nonfiction (New York: Simon and Schuster, 1987)*, 36–39.

64. Berry and Duncan, *Someday is Now*, 169.

65. Ibid., 71 and 162.

66. Ibid., 132.

67. Wilde, *Vatican* II, 29–56.

68. Ibid., 68–81 and Cano, *Take Heart*, 63–65.

69. Cano, *Take Heart*, 65.

70. Ibid., 45–46.

71. Helen Rose Fuchs Ebaugh, *Women in the Vanishing Cloister* (New Brunswick, NJ: Rutgers University Press, 1993), 72–77.

72. Caspary, *Witness to Integrity*, 192–93.

73. William Coulson, "We Overcame their Traditions, We Overcame Their Faith," *The Latin Mass* 3 (January–February 1994), 12–17.

74. Robert Kugelmann, "An Encounter between Psychology and Religion: Humanistic Psychology and the Immaculate Heart of Mary Nuns." *Journal of the History of the Behavioral Sciences* 41 (September 2005): 347–65.

75. Tom Wolfe, "The Me Decade and the Third Great Awakening," *New York Magazine* 23 (August 1976): 236–40.

76. Peter Kreeft, *How to Win the Culture War: A Christian Battle Plan for a Society in Crisis* (Downers Grove, IL: InterVarsity Press, 2002).

77. Flo Conway and Jim Siegelman, *Snapping: America's Epidemic of Sudden Personality Change* (Philadelphia: J.B. Lippincott, 1979).

78. Don Lattin, *The Harvard Psychedelic Club* (New York: HarperCollins, 2010).

Chapter 7

1. Thomas A. Brady Jr., *German History in the Age of Reformations* (Cambridge: Cambridge University Press, 2009), 3.

2. Gregory, *The Unintended Reformation: How a Religious Revolution Secularized Society* (Cambridge, MA: Harvard University Press, 2102). Also see C. B. Macpherson, *The Political Theory of Possessive Individualism* (Oxford: Clarendon Press, 1962).

3. Rodney Stark, *The Triumph of Christianity: How the Jesus Movement Became the World's Largest Religion* (New York: HarperCollins, 2011), 375–76; Meredith McGuire, *Lived Religion: Faith and Practice in Everyday Life* (New York: Oxford University Press, 2008)25–28; more generally, Keith Thomas, *Religion and the Decline of Magic* (New York: Scribner's, 1971), 151–76, 253–82.

4. Darren E. Sherkat, *Changing Faith: The Dynamics and Consequences of Americans' Shifting Religious Identities* (New York: New York University Press, 2014), 90–114.

5. James K. Wellman, Katie E. Corcoran, and Kate Stockly-Meyerdirk, "God is Like Drug . . .: Explaining Interaction Ritual Chains in American Megachurches." *Sociological Forum* 29/3 (2014): 650–72.

6. Philip S. Gorski, David Kuyman Kim, John Torpey, and Jonathan Van Antwerpen, eds., *The Post-Secular in Question: Religion in Contemporary Society* (New York: New York University Press, 2012).

7. Paul Froese, *On Purpose: How We Create the Meaning of Life* (New York: Oxford University Press, 2016).

8. William G. McLoughlin, *Revival, Awakening, and Reform: An Essay on Religion and Social Change in America, 1607 to 1977* (Chicago: University of Chicago Press, 1980).

9. On the "Americanization" of Calvinism, see Mark Noll, *America's God: From Jonathan Edwards to Abraham Lincoln* (New York: Oxford University Press, 2012), 293–329.

10. Paul Froese and Christopher Bader, *America's Four Gods: What We Say about God and What That Says about Us* (New York: Oxford University Press, 2015).

11. Marion Goldman, *The American Soul Rush: Esalen and the Rise of Spiritual Privilege* (New York; New York University Press, 2012), 45–47.

12. George Leonard, *Walking on the Edge of the World: A Memoire of the Sixties and Beyond* (Boston: Houghton Mifflin, 1980), 108.

13. Froese, *On Purpose,* 5; Joseph E. Baker and Buster G. Smith, *American Secularism: Cultural Contours of Nonreligious Belief Systems* (New York: New York University Press,

2015); and Christel Manning, *Losing Our Religion: How Unaffiliated Parents are Raising their Children* (New York: New York University Press, 2015).

14. Katheryne Lofton, *Oprah: The Gospel of an Icon* (Berkeley: University of California Press, 2011), 51–82.

15. Sherkat, *Changing Faith,* 90–114.

16. Patricia S. Churchland, *Braintrust: What Neuroscience Tells Us about Morality* (Princeton: Princeton University Press, 2011); Jonathan Haidt, *The Righteous Mind: Why Good People are Divided by Politics and Religion* (New York: Vintage, 2013).

17. Robert Kolb, *Bound Choice, Election, and Wittenberg Theological Method from Martin Luther to the Formula of Concord* (Grand Rapids, MI: Eerdmans, 2005).

18. Rodney Stark, *One True God: The Historical Consequences of Monotheism* (Princeton: Princeton University Press, 2010), 175–84.

19. Lee Sandlin, *Wicked River: The Mississippi When It Ran Wild* (Pantheon Books, New York, 2010), 95–96; on young people in antebellum America also see Jon Grinspan, *The Virgin Vote: How Young Americans Made Democracy Social, Politics Personal, and Voting Popular in the Nineteenth Century* (Chapel Hill, NC: University of North Carolina Press, 2016).

20. Michael Harrington, *The Other America: Poverty in the United States* (New York: Macmillan, 1962).

21. Robert Ellwood, *The Sixties Spiritual Awakening* (New Brunswick, NJ: Rutgers University Press, 1994).

22. Roger Finke and Rodney Stark, *The Churching of America, 1776-1990: Winners and Losers in our Religious Economy* (New Brunswick, NJ: Rutgers University Press), 245–55.

23. Goldman, *The American Soul Rush*, 45–47.

24. Walter Isaacson, *Steve Jobs* (New York: Simon and Schuster, 2011).

25. Unpublished at LOHAS Business Conference, Los Angeles, California, October 30, 2014.

26. Thomas Piketty, *Capital in the Twenty-first Century* (Cambridge, MA: Harvard University Press, 2014).

27. James K. Wellman, *Rob Bell and a New American Christianity* (Nashville, TN: Abington Press, 2012).

28. Tony Judt, *Reappraisals: Reflections on the Forgotten Twentieth Century* (New York, Penguin, 2008), 411–32.

29. Miriam Davidson, *Convictions of the Heart: Jim Corbett and the American Sanctuary Movement* (Tucson, AZ: University of Arizona Press, 1988).

30. Dwyer Grimm, "The Sanctuary Movement: How Religious Groups Are Sheltering the undocumented, *The Guardian*: Us Edition, February 7,2019. https://www.theguardian.com/us-news/2017/feb/08/sanctuary-movement-undocumented-immigrants-america-trump-obama#img-1

Bibliography

Abzug, Robert H. *Passionate Liberator: Theodore Dwight Weld and the Dilemma of Reform.* New York: Oxford University Press, 1980.

Ammerman, Nancy T. "Spiritual But Not Religious? Beyond Binary Choices in the Study of Religion." *Journal for the Scientific Study of Religion* 52/2 (2013): 258–78.

Anderson, Walter Truett. *The Upstart Spring: Esalen and the American Awakening.* Reading, MA: Addison Wesley, 1983.

Aubigne, Jean Henri Merle. *History of the Reformation of the 16th Century.* Whitefish, Montana: Kessinger Publishers, 1846.

Baker, Joseph E. and Buster G. Smith. *American Secularism: Cultural Contours of Nonreligious Belief Systems.* New York: New York University Press, 2015.

Bagchi, David N. *Luther's Earliest Opponents: Catholic Controversialists, 1518-1525.* Minneapolis: Augsburg Fortress, 2007.

Bainton, Roland. *Here I Stand: A Life of Martin Luther.* New York: Abingdon Press, 1950.

Baptiste, Edward A. *The Half Has Never Been Told: Slavery and the Making of American Capitalism.* New York: Basic Books, 2014.

Becker, Sascha O., Steven Pfaff and Jared Rubin. "Causes and Consequences of the Protestant Reformation." *Explorations in Economic History* 62 (2016): 1–25.

Beckert, Sven. *Empire of Cotton: A Global History.* New York: Vintage, 2014.

Beckert, Sven and Seth Rockman, eds. *Slavery's Capitalism: A New History of American Economic Development.* Philadelphia, University of Pennsylvania Press, 2016.

Beckford, James. "Public Religions and the Postsecular: Critical Reflections." *Journal for the Scientific Study of Religion* 51/1 (2012): 1–19.

Berger, Peter. *The Sacred Canopy: Elements of a Sociological Theory of Religion.* Garden City, NY: Doubleday, 1967.

Berry, Ian and Michael Duncan, eds. *Someday Is Now: The Art of Corita Kent.* New York: Prestel Publishing, 2013.

Bisson, Terry. *Nat Turner: Slave Revolt Leader.* Philadelphia: Chelsea House, 2005.

Blickle, Peter. *The Revolution of 1525: The German Peasants War from a New Perspective.* Baltimore: Johns Hopkins University Press, 1981.

Bonhoeffer, Dietrich. *The Cost of Discipleship.* New York: Macmillan, 1959.

Boorstein, Sylvia. *That's Funny, You Don't Look Buddhist: On Being a Faithful Jew and a Passionate Buddhist.* San Francisco: HarperCollins, 1998.

Bourdieu, Pierre. *The Social Structures of the Economy.* New York: Polity Press, 2005.

Brady, Thomas J. "The Reformation of the Common Man, 1521-1524." In C. Scott Dixon (ed.), *The German Reformation.* London: Blackwell, 1999.

Brady, Thomas A. *German Histories in the Age of Reformations, 1400-1650.* New York: Cambridge University, 2009.

Browne, Stephen H. *Angelina Grimké: Rhetoric, Identity, and the Radical Imagination.* East Lansing: Michigan State University Press, 1999.

Bruce, Steven. *God is Dead: Secularization in the West.* Oxford: Wiley-Blackwell, 2002.

Buber, Martin. *The Knowledge of Man: Selected Essays.* New York: Harper and Row, 1965.

Burt, Ronald. *Brokerage and Closure: An Introduction to Social Capital.* New York: Oxford University Press, 2005.

Calhoun, Craig. "'New Social Movements' of the Early Nineteenth Century." *Social Science History* 17/3 (1993): 385–427.

Cameron, Euan. *The European Reformation*, 2nd edn. New York: Oxford University Press 2012.

Cano, Nan Deane. *Take Heart: Growing a Faith Community.* New York: Paulist Press, 2016.

Caspary, Anita M. *Witness to Integrity: The Crisis of the Immaculate Heart Community of California.* Collegeville, MN: The Liturgical Press, 2003.

Ceplair, Larry, ed. *The Public Years of Sarah and Angelina Grimke, 1835-1839.* New York: Columbia University Press, 1989.

Chabot, Sean. *Transnational Roots of the Civil Rights Movement: African-American Expansions of the Gandhian Repertoire.* Lanham, MD: Lexington Books, 2011.

Chadwick, Owen. *The Reformation.* New York: Penguin, 1990.

Chappell, David L. *A Stone of Hope: Prophetic Religion and the Death of Jim Crow.* Chapel Hill, NC: University of North Carolina, 2005.

Chirot, Daniel. "The Rise of the West." *American Sociological Review* 52/2 (1985): 181–95.

Chirot, Daniel. *How Societies Change*, 2nd edn. Los Angeles: Sage, 2012.

Churchland, Patricia S. *Braintrust: What Neuroscience Tells Us about Morality.* Princeton: Princeton University Press, 2011.

Collins, Randall. *Weberian Sociological Theory.* Cambridge: Cambridge University Press, 1986.

Conway, Flo and Jim Siegelman. *Snapping: America's Epidemic of Sudden Personality Change.* Philadelphia: J.B. Lippincott, 1979.

Coulson, William. "We Overcame their Traditions, We Overcame Their Faith."*The Latin Mass* 3 (January–February 1994): 12–17.

Courtenay, William J. and Jürgen Miethke, eds. *Universities and Schooling in Medieval Society.* Leiden: Brill, 2000.

Coyote, Peter. *Sleeping Where I Fall: A Chronicle.* Berkeley: Counterpoint, 1998.

Crockett, Alisdair and David Voas. "Generations of decline: religious change in Twentieth-century Britain." *Journal for the Scientific Study of Religion*, 45 (2006): 567–84.

Daugherty, Tracy. *The Last Love Song: A Biography of Joan Dideon.* New York: St. Martin's Press, 2015.

Dass, Ram. *Remember Be Here Now.* Santa Fe, NM: Hanuman Foundation, 1971.

Davidson, Miriam. *Convictions of the Heart: Jim Corbett and the American Sanctuary Movement.* Tucson, AZ: University of Arizona Press, 1988.

Davie, Grace. *Religion in Britain since 1945: Believing Without Belonging.* London: Wiley, 1994.

Dawson, Christopher. *Religion and the Rise of Western Culture.* New York: Doubleday Image Books, 1957.

Dawson, Lorne L., ed. *Cults and New Religious Movements.* Malden, MA: Blackwell, 2003.

Dawson, Lorne L. *Comprehending Cults: The Sociology of New Religious Movements*, 2nd edn. New York: Oxford University Press, 2006.

Diani, Mario and Doug McAdam, eds. *Social Movements and Networks: Relational Approaches to Collective Action.* New York: Oxford University Press, 2003.

Dickens, Arthur G. *The Age of Humanism and Reformation.* New York: Prentice Hall, 1972.

Dillenberger, John, ed. *Martin Luther: Selections from His Writings.* New York: Doubleday, 1962.

Dixon, C. Scott. "Princely Reformation in Germany." In Andrew Pettegree (ed.), *The Reformation World.* London: Routledge, 2000.

Dovring, Karin. "Quantitative Semantics in the 18th Century", *Public Opinion Quarterly* 18/4 (1954-55): 389–94.

Downing, David. *Shoes outside the Door: Desire, Devotion, and Excess at the San Francisco Zen Center.* Washington, DC: Counterpoint Press, 2001.

Doyle, Jacqueline, ed. *Interaction: Readings in Human Potential.* Lexington, MA; DC Heath, 1973.

Duffy, Eamon. *The Stripping of the Altars: Traditional Religion in England, 1400-1580*, 2nd edn. New Haven: Yale University Press, 2005.

Dworkin, Ronald. *Religion Without God* Cambridge, MA: Harvard University Press, 2013.

Durheim, Emile. *The Elementary Forms of Religious Life.* New York: the Free Press, 1995 [1915].

Ebaugh, Helen Rose Fuchs. *Women in the Vanishing Cloister.* New Brunswick, NJ: Rutgers University Press, 1993.

Ekelund, Robert B., Robert F. Herbert, Robert D. Tollison, Gary M. Anderson, and Audrey B. Davidson. *Sacred Trust: The Medieval Church as an Economic Firm*. New York: Oxford University Press, 1996.

Ekelund, Robert B., Robert F. Hébert, and Robert D. Tollison. *The Marketplace of Christianity* Cambridge, MA: MIT Press, 2006.

Edwards, Mark U. *Printing, Propaganda, and Martin Luther.* Berkeley: University of California Press, 1994.

Eisenstein, Elizabeth L. *The Printing Press as an Agent of Change.* New York: Cambridge University Press, 1980.

Ellwood, Robert. *The Sixties Spiritual Awakening.* New Brunswick, NJ: Rutgers University Press, 1994.

Emerson, Michael O. and Christian Smith. *Divided by Faith: Evangelical Religion and the Problem of Race in America.* New York: Oxford University Press, 2000.

Erdélyi, Ágnes. "Varieties of Moral Beliefs in the 'Sociology of Religion.'" *Max Weber Studies* 7/2 (2007): 163–84.

Finke, Roger Finke and Rodney Stark. *The Churching of America, 1776-1990: Winners and Losers in our Religious Economy.* New Brunswick, NJ: Rutgers University Press, 1992.

Flanagan, Sabina. *Hildegard of Bingen: A Visionary Life*. London: Routledge, 1998.

Frazer, James George. *The Golden Bough: A Study in Magic and Religion.* New York: Macmillan, 1922.

Froese, Paul. *On Purpose: How We Create the Meaning of Life.* New York: Oxford University Press, 2016.

Froese, Paul and Christopher Bader. *America's Four Gods: What We Say about God and What That Says About Us*. New York: Oxford University Press, 2010.

Füssel, Stephan. *The Luther Bible of 1534: A Cultural-Historical Introduction.* Cologne: Taschen, 2003.

Gäbler, Ulrich. *Huldrych Zwingli: His Life and Work.* Philadelphia: Fortress Press, 1986.

Galm, Bernard. "Los Angeles Art Community: Group Portrait, Corita Kent." University of California at Los Angeles Oral History Program, unpublished manuscript, 1977.

Ganzer, Klaus Ganzer, and Bruno Steiner, eds. *Lexikon der Reformationszeit.* Freiburg: Herder, 2002.

Garrow, David J. *Bearing the Cross: Martin Luther King Jr. and the Southern Christian Leadership Conference.* New York: William Morrow, 1986.

Gilmont, Jean-Franscois, ed. *The Reformation and the Book.* Aldershot: Ashgate, 1998.

Gilmore, Lee. *Theater in a Crowded Fire: Ritual and Spirituality at Burning Man.* Berkeley: University of California Press, 2010.

Givan, Rebecca Kolins, Kenneth M. Roberts and Sarah A. Soule, eds. *The Diffusion of Social Movements: Actors, Mechanisms and Political Effects*. New York: Cambridge University Press, 2010.

Goffman, Erving. *Stigma: Notes on the Management of Spoiled Identity.* Englewood Cliffs, NJ: Prentice Hall, 1963.

Goldstone, Jack A. *Revolution and Rebellion in the Early Modern World.* Berkeley: University of California Press, 1991.

Goldstone Jack A., *Revolutions: A Very Short Introduction.* New York: Oxford, 2014.

Goodwin, Jeff and James M. Jasper, eds. *The Social Movements Reader: Cases and Concepts*. New York: Wiley, 2009.

Gray, Francine du Plessix. *Adam & Eve and the City: Selected Nonfiction.* New York: Simon and Schuster, 1987.

Gregory, Brad S. *The Unintended Reformation: How a Religious Revolution Secularized Society.* Cambridge, MA: Harvard University Press, 2012.

Grendler, Paul F. "The Universities of the Renaissance and Reformation." *Renaissance Quarterly* 57/1 (2004): 1–42.

Grimm, Dyer. "The Sanctuary Movement: How Religious Groups Are Sheltering the undocumented, The Guardian: Us Edition, February 7, 2019. https://www.theguardian.com/us-news/2017/feb/08/sanctuary-movement-undocumented-immigrants-america-trump-obama#img-1

Grinspan, Jon. *The Virgin Vote: How Young Americans Made Democracy Social, Politics Personal, and Voting Popular in the Nineteenth Century.* Chapel Hill: University of North Carolina Press, 2016.

Gritsch, Eric W., ed. *Martin Luther: Faith in Christ and the Gospel.* New York: New City Press, 1996.

Gritsch, Eric W. *A History of Lutheranism.* Minneapolis: Fortress Press, 2002.

Goldman, Marion. *The American Soul Rush: Esalen and the Rise of Spiritual Privilege.* New York: NYU Press, 2012.

Goleman, Daniel. *The Meditative Mind: The Varieties of Meditative Experience.* New York: Jeremy Tarcher/Penguin, 1988.

González, Justo. *A History of Christian Thought, Volume* III. Nashville: Abingdon Press, 1975.

Gorski, Philip S., David Kuyman Kim, John Torpey, and Jonathan VanAntwerpen, eds. *The Post-Secular in Question: Religion in Contemporary Society.* New York: New York University Press, 2012.

Grimké, Angelina Emily. *Appeal to Christian Women of the South.* New York: American Anti-Slavery Society, 1836.

Habermas, Jürgen. "New Social Movements." *Telos* 49 (1981): 33–37.

Hagedorn, Ann. *Beyond the River: The Untold Story of the Heroes of the Underground Railroad.* New York: Simon & Schuster, 2002.

Haidt, Jonathan. *The Righteous Mind: Why Good People are Divided by Politics and Religion.* New York: Vintage, 2013.

Halvorson, Michael J. *Heinrich Hesshusius and Confessional Polemics in early Lutheran Orthodoxy.* Farnham: Ashgate, 2010.

Hammerskjöld, Dag. *Markings.* London: Faber and Faber, 1964.

Harrington, Michael. *The Other America: Poverty in the United States.* New York: Macmillan, 1962.

Harris, Lis. *Holy Days: The World of a Hasidic Family.* New York: Macmillan Publishing Company, 1985.

Hatch, Nathan O. *The Democratization of American Christianity.* New Haven: Yale University Press, 1989.

Havemann, Heather. *Magazines and the Making of America: Modernization, Community and Print Culture, 1741-1860.* Princeton, NJ: Princeton University Press, 2015.

Heal, Bridget. *The Cult of the Virgin Mary in Early Modern Germany: Protestant and Catholic Piety, 1500-1654.* New York: Cambridge University Press, 2007.

Hendrix, Scott H. *Recultivating the Vineyard: The Reformation Agendas of Christianization.* Louisville, KY: Westminster John Knox, 2004.

Hillerbrand, Hans J. *The Division of Christendom: Christianity in the Sixteenth Century.* Louisville, KY: Westminster John Knox, 2007.

Holborn, Louise W. "Printing and the Growth of a Protestant Movement in Germany from 1517 to 1524." *Church History* 11/2 (1942): 123–37.

Holsinger, Bruce. "The Flesh of the Voice: Embodiment and the Homoerotics of Devotion in the Music of Hildegard of Bingen." *Signs: A Journal of Women in Culture and Society* 19 (1993): 92–125.

Huizinga, Johann. *The Waning of the Middle Ages.* New York: Edward Arnold, 1924.

Houtman, Dick and Stef Aupers. "The Spiritual Turn and the Decline of Tradition: The

Spread of Post-Christian Spirituality in 14 Western Countries, 1981–2000." *Journal for the Scientific Study of Religion*, 52/(2007): 305–20.

Hunger, James Davison. *Culture Wars: The Struggle to Define America*. New York: Basic Books, 1991.

Hunger, James Davison and Alan Wolfe. *Is There a Culture War? A Dialogue on Values and American Life*. Washington, DC: Brookings Institution Press, 2006.

Huxley, Aldous. *The Doors of Perception*. London: Chato and Windus, 1954.

Iannaccone, Laurence. "The Consequences of Religious Market Structures." *Rationality and Society 3/2* (1991): 156–77.

Iannaccone, Laurence. "Risk, Rationality and Religious Portfolios." *Economic Inquiry* 32 (1995): 285–95.

Iannaccone, Larry, Roger Finke and Rodney Stark. "Deregulating Religion: The Economics of Church and State." *Economic Inquiry* 35/2 (1997): 350–64.

Inglehart, Ronald. *Culture Shift in Advanced Industrial Society*. Princeton: Princeton University Press, 1990.

Isaac, Larry. "Movement of Movements: Culture Moves in the Long Civil Rights Struggle." *Social Forces* 87/1 (2008): 33–63.

Isaacson, Walter. *Einstein: His Life and Universe*. New York: Simon and Schuster, 2007.

Isaacson, Walter. *Steve Jobs*. New York: Simon and Schuster, 2011.

Jacoby, Susan. *Freethinkers: A History of American Secularism*. New York: Henry Holt, 2004.

Johnson, Benton. "On Founders and Followers: Some Factors in the Development of New Religious Movements." *Sociological Analysis* 53 (1992): 1–13.

Judt, Tony. *Reappraisals: Reflections on the Forgotten Twentieth Century*. New York: Penguin, 2008.

Juster, Susan. *Disorderly Women: Sexual Politics and Evangelicalism in Revolutionary New England*. Ithaca: Cornell University Press, 1994.

Kammerlin, Joy. "Andreas Osiander's Sermons on the Jews." *Lutheran Quarterly* 15/1 (2001): 59–84.

Karant-Nunn, Susan C. "Preaching the Word in Early Modern Germany." In Larissa Taylor (ed.), *Preachers and People in the Reformation and Early Modern Period*. Leiden: Brill, 2001.

Kelley, Dean M., *Why Conservative Churches Are Growing*. New York: Harper and Row, 1972.

Kim, Hyojoung Kim and Steven Pfaff. "Structure and Dynamics of a Religious Insurgency: Students and the Spread of the Reformation." *American Sociological Review* 77/2 (2012): 188–215.

Klein, Martin A., ed. *Historical Dictionary of Slavery and Abolition*. Lanham, MA: Rowan & Littlefield, 2014.

Kohler, Alfred. *Das Reich im Kampf um die Hegemonie in Europa, 1521-1648*. Munich: Oldenbourg, 1990.

Kolb, Robert A. *Bound Choice, Election, and the Wittenberg Theological Method from Martin Luther to the Formula of Concord*. Grand Rapids, MI: Eerdmans, 2005.

Kolb, Robert A. and Timothy J. Wengert, eds. *The Book of Concord, the Confessions of the Evangelical Lutheran Church*. Minneapolis: Fortress Press, 2000.

Kramer, Jane. *Allen Ginsberg in America*. New York: Fromm International Publishing, 1997.

Kripal, Jeffery J. *Esalen: America and the Religion of No Religion*. Chicago: University of Chicago Press, 2007.

Kreeft, Peter. *How to Win the Culture War: A Christian Battle Plan for a Society in Crisis*. Downers Grove, IL: InterVarsity Press, 2002.

Kugelmann, Robert. "An Encounter between Psychology and Religion: Humanistic Psychology and the Immaculate Heart of Mary Nuns." *Journal of the History of the Behavioral Sciences* 41 (2005): 347–65.

Lahr, Angela. "'Bound in the Dust': Guilt and Conscience in the Life of Angelina Grimké Weld." *The Historian* (2015): 1–25.

Lambert, Frank. *"Pedlar in Divinity": George Whitefield and the Transatlantic Revivals, 1737-1771.* Princeton: Princeton University Press, 1994.

Lattin, Don. *The Harvard Psychedelic Club.* New York: HarperCollins, 2010.

Lattin, Don. *Following Our Bliss: How the Spiritual Ideals of the Sixties Shape Our Lives Today.* San Francisco: Harper San Francisco, 2003.

Leonard, George. "Where the California Game is Taking Us." *Look Magazine*, December 28, 1966: 108–16.

Leonard, George. "The Turned on People." *Look Magazine*, (June 28, 1966): 30–33.

Leonard, George. *Walking on the Edge of the World: A Memoire of the Sixties and Beyond.* Boston: Houghton Mifflin, 1980.

Leonard, George. *Mastery: The Keys to Success and Longterm Fulfillment.* New York: Penguin/Plume, 1993.

Lerner, Gerda. *The Grimké Sisters from South Carolina: Pioneers for Woman's Rights and Abolition.* New York: Schocken, 1971.

Levi-Strauss, Claude. *The Savage Mind: The Nature of Human Society.* Chicago: University of Chicago Press, 1966.

Lewis, John with Michael D'Orso. *Walking With the Wind: A Memoir of the Movement.* New York: Harcourt Brace and Company, 1998.

Lincoln, Eric and Lawrence H. Manya. *The Black Church in the African American Experience.* Durham, NC: Duke University Press, 1990.

Lofland, John and Rodney Stark, "Becoming a World Saver: A Theory of Conversion to a Deviant Perspective." *American Sociological Review* 40/6 (1965): 863–74.

Lofton, Katheryne. *Oprah: The Gospel of an Icon.* Berkeley: University of California Press, 2011.

Lortz, Josef. *The Reformation in Germany.* New York: Herder & Herder, 1968.

Mann, Michael. *The Sources of Social Power, Volume* I. New York: Cambridge University Press, 1986).

Manning, Christel. *Losing Our Religion: How Unaffiliated Parents are Raising their Children* (New York: New York University Press, 2015).

Marty, Martin. *Martin Luther.* New York: Penguin, 2004.

Maslow, Abraham. *The Farther Reaches of Human Nature.* New York: Viking/Esalen, 1971.

Massa, Mark. *The American Catholic Revolution: How the Sixties Changed the Church Forever.* New York: Oxford University Press, 2010.

Mayers, Henry. *All on Fire: William Lloyd Garrison and the Abolition of Slavery.* New York: St. Martin's Press, 1998.

MacCulloch, Diarmaid. *The Reformation.* New York: Penguin, 2005.

MacCulloch, Diarmaid. "The World Took Sides." *London Review of Books* 38/16 (2016): 25–27.

Macpherson, C. B. *The Political Theory of Possessive Individualism.* Oxford: Clarendon Press, 1962.

McAdam, Doug, John D. McCarthy and Meyer Zald, eds. *Comparative Perspectives on Social Movements.* New York: Cambridge University Press, 1996.

McAdam, Doug and Ronnelle Paulsen. "Specifying the Relationship Between Social Ties and Activism." *American Journal of Sociology* 99/3 (1993): 640–67.

McCloskey, Deidre N. *Bourgeois Dignity: Why Economics Can't Explain the World.* Chicago: University of Chicago Press, 2010.

McGrath, Allister. *The Intellectual Origins of the European Reformation.* Oxford: Blackwells, 1987.

McGuire, Meredith. *Lived Religion: Faith and Practice in Everyday Life.* New York: Oxford University Press, 2008.

McGurie, Meredith. *Lived Religion: Faith and Practice in Everyday Life.* New York: Oxford University Press, 2008.

McKinney, Jennifer. "Sects and Gender: Reaction and Resistance to Cultural Change." *Priscilla Papers* 29/4 (2015): 15–25.

McLellan, David. *Karl Marx: Selected Writings*. Oxford: Oxford University Press, 1977.

McLoughlin, William G. *Revival, Awakening, and Reform: An Essay on Religion and Social Change in America, 1607 to 1977*. Chicago: University of Chicago Press, 1980.

Melucci, Alberto. "The New Social Movements: A Theoretical Approach." *Social Science Information* 19/2 (1981): 199–226.

Merton, Thomas. *The New Man*. New York: Farrar, Strauss and Giroux, 1961.

Moeller, Bernd. *Imperial Cities and the Reformation*. Philadelphia: Fortress, 1972.

Moeller, Bernd. *Deutschland im Zeitalter der Reformation*. Gottingen: Vandenhoek and Ruprecht, 1977.

Moeller, Bernd. "Stadt und Buch." In Wolfgang Mommsen (ed.), *Stadtbürgertum und Adel in der Reformation*. Stuttgart: Ernst Klett, 1979.

Moeller, Bernd. "What was preached in German towns in the early Reformation?" In C. Scott Dixon (ed.), *The German Reformation*. Oxford: Blackwell, 1999.

Morris, Aldon. *The Origins of the Civil Rights Movement: Black Communities Organizing for Change*. New York: Free Press, 1984.

Muelder, Owen B. *Theodore Dwight Weld and the American Anti-Slavery Society.* Jefferson, NC: McFarland and Company, 2011.

Muir, Edward. *Ritual in Early Modern Europe*. Cambridge: Cambridge University Press, 1997.

Muggeridge, Malcolm. *Something Beautiful for God: The Classic Account of Mother Theresa's Journey into Compassion*. New York: HarperOne, 2003 [1971].

Nelson, Robert K. "'The Forgetfulness of Sex': Devotion and Desire in the Courtship Letters of Angelina Grimké and Theodore Dwight Weld." *Journal of Social History* 37/3 (2004): 663–76.

Neuhas, Helmut. *Das Reich in der Frühen Neuzeit.* Munich: Oldenbourg, 1997.

Newman, Barbara, editor. *Hildegard of Bingen and Her World*. Berkeley: University of California Press, 1988.

Nexon, Daniel H. *The Struggle for Power in Early Modern Europe.* Princeton: Princeton University Press, 2009.

Nicholas, David. *Urban Europe, 1100-1700*. London: Palgrave Macmillan, 2003.

Noland, Patrick and Gerhard Lenski, *Human Societies: An Introduction to Macrosociology.* 11th edn. Boulder: Paradigm, 2009.

Noll, Mark A. *America's God: From Jonathan Edwards to Abraham Lincoln.* New York: Oxford University Press, 2002.

Noll, Mark A. *The Rise of Evangelicalism: The Age of Edwards, Whitefield and the Wesleys.* Downers Grove, IL: InterVarsity Press, 2003.

Norris, Pippa Norris and Ronald Inglehart. *Sacred and Secular: Religion and Politics Worldwide.* New York: Cambridge University Press, 2004.

North, Douglass C. *Structure and Change in Economic History* (New York: Norton, 1981).

Oberman, Heiko. *Luther, Man between God and the Devil.* New Haven: Yale University Press, 1989.

Olson, Oliver K. *Matthias Flacius and the Survival of Luther's Reform.* Minneapolis: The Lutheran Press, 2011.

O'Malley, John W. *The Jesuits: A History from Ignatius to the Present.* London: Rowman and Littlefield, 2014.

Oschatz, Molly. *Slavery and Sin: The Fight Against Slavery and the Rise of Liberal Protestantism.* New York: Oxford University Pres, 2012.

Ozment, Steven. *The Age of Reform, 1250-1550; An Intellectual and Religious History of Late Medieval and Reformation Europe.* New Haven, CT: Yale University Press, 1980.

Pagels, Elaine. *The Gnostic Gospels.* New York: Vintage, 2009.

Park, Joon-Chul. "Philip Melanchthon's Reform of German Universities and its Significance: A Study of Relationship between Renaissance Humanism and the Reformation." PhD dissertation, Ohio State University, 1995.

Pettegree, Andrew. *Brand Luther: How an Unheralded Monk Turned His Small Town into a Center of Publishing, Made Himself the Most Famous Man in Europe–and Started the Protestant Reformation.* New York: Penguin, 2015.

Pew Research Center, "America's Changing Religious Landscape." May 12, 2015.

Piketty, Thomas. *Capital in the Twenty-first Century.* Cambridge, MA: Harvard University Press, 2014.

Pfaff, Steven and Katie E. Corcoran. "Piety, Power, and the Purse: Religious Economies Theory and Urban Reform in the Holy Roman Empire." *Journal for the Scientific Study of Religion* 51/4 (2012): 757–76.

Potter, G. R. *Ulrich Zwingli.* London: Historical Association Press, 1977.

Putnam, Robert D. and David E. Campbell. *American Grace: How Religion Unites and Divides Us.* New York: Simon & Schuster, 2010.

Rabinowitz, Richard. *The Spiritual Self in Everyday Life: The Transformation of Personal Religious Experience in Nineteenth-Century New England.* Boston: Northeastern University Press, 1989.

Richards, Leonard L. *"Gentlemen of Property and Standing": Anti-Abolition Mobs in Jacksonian America.* New York: Oxford University Press, 1970.

Rittgers, Ronald K. "Luther on Private Confession." *The Lutheran Quarterly* 19/3 (2005): 312–31.

Rittgers, Ronald K. "Review Essay." *Church History* 80/4 (2011): 863–75.

Robnett, Belinda. *How Long? How Long? African-American Women in the Struggle for Civil Rights.* New York: Oxford University Press, 2000.

Rochon, Thomas R. *Culture Moves: Ideas, Activism and Changing Values.* Princeton: Princeton University Press, 1998.

Roof, Wade Clark. *Spiritual Marketplace: Babyboomers and the Remaking of American Religion.* Princeton: Princeton University Press, 1999.

Roper, Lyndal. *Martin Luther: Renegade and Prophet.* London: Bodley Head, 2016.

Rubin, Jared. "Printing and Protestants: An empirical test of the role of printing in the Reformation." *Review of Economics and Statistics* 96/2 (2014): 270–86.

Rüegg, Walter, ed. *A History of the University in Europe, Volume II.* New York: Cambridge University Press, 2003.

Sacks, Oliver. *Migraine.* New York: Vintage Books, 1992[1970].

Sandlin, Lee. *Wicked River: The Mississippi When It Ran Wild.* New York: Pantheon Books, 2010.

Sassi, Jonathan. *A Republic of Righteousness: The Public Christianity of the Post-Revolutionary New England Clergy* (New York: Oxford University Press, 2001).

Schaff, Philip. *History of the Christian Church, Vol. VI.* (New York: Scribner 1910.

Schilling, Heinz. *Aufbruch und Krise: Deutschland, 1517-1648.* Berlin: Siedler, 1988.

Schluchter, Wolfgang. *The Rise of Western Rationalism: Max Weber's Developmental History.* Berkeley: University of California Press, 1981.

Scholem, Gershom. *Sabbatai Zevi: The Mystical Messiah.* Princeton, NJ: Princeton University Press, 1973.

Schubert, Ernst. *Fürstliche Herrschaft und Territorium im späten Mittelalter.* Munich: Oldenbourg, 1996.

Scott, Tom. *Society and Economy in Germany, 1300-1600.* New York: Palgrave, 2002.

Scribner, Robert W. "Practice and Principle in the German Towns." In Peter Brooks (ed.), *Reformation in Principle and Practice.* London: Scholar, 1980.

Scribner, Robert W. *The German Reformation.* London: Macmillan, 1986.

Scribner, Robert W., ed. *Germany: A New Social and Economic History, 1450-1630.* London and New York: Arnold, 1996.

Scribner, Robert W. *Religion and Culture in Germany, 1400-1800.* Boston: Brill, 2001.

Schubert, Anselm. "Andreas Osiander als Kabbalist." *Archiv für Reformationsgeschichte* 105 (2014): 30–54.

Scruton, Roger. *Our Church: A Personal History of the Church of England.* London: Atlantic Books, 2014.

Selver, Charlotte. *A Taste of Sensory Awareness.* Mill Valley, CA: Sensory Awareness Foundation, 1979.

Sharot, Stephen. *A Comparative Sociology of World Religions: Virtuosos, Priests, and Popular Religions.* New York: New York University Press, 2001.

Sherkat, Darren E. *Changing Faith: The Dynamics and Consequences of Americans' Shifting Religious Identities.* New York: New York University Press, 2014.

Silber, Ilana F. *Virtuosity, Charisma, and Social Order.* New York: Cambridge University Press, 1995.

Singh, Manisha. *The Slave's Cause: A History of Abolition.* New Haven: Yale University Press, 2016.

Slater, Philip. *The Pursuit of Loneliness: American Culture at the Breaking Point.* Boston: Beacon Press, 1970.

Smith, Huston. *Cleansing the Doors of Perception: The Religious Significance of Etheogenic Plants and Chemicals.* New York: Tarcher/Putnam, 2000.

Soltow, Lee and Edward Stevens. *The Rise of Literacy and the Common Schools in the United States: A Socioeconomic Analysis to 1870.* Chicago: University of Chicago Press, 1981.

Southern, R.W. *Western Society and the Church in the Middle Ages.* New York: Pelican, 1970.

Stamatov, Peter. *The Origins of Global Humanitarianism: Religion, Empires, and Advocacy.* New York: Cambridge University Press, 2013.

Star, Kevin. *California: A History.* New York: Modern Library, 2007.

Stewart, James Brewer. *Holy Warriors: The Abolitionists and American Slavery.* New York: Hill and Wang, 1976.

Stowe, Harriet Beecher. *Uncle Tom's Cabin: A Tale of Life among the Lowly.* London: Routledge, 1852.

Stark, Rodney. *The Rise of Christianity: A Sociologist Reconsiders History.* Princeton: Princeton University Press, 1996.

Stark, Rodney. A. *For the Glory of God.* Princeton, NJ: Princeton University Press, 2003.

Stark, Rodney. B. "Upper Class Asceticism: Social Origins of Ascetic Movements and Medieval Saints." *Review of Religious Research* 45/1 (2003): 5–19.

Stark, Rodney. *The Victory of Reason: How Christianity led to Freedom, Capitalism, and Western Success.* New York: Random House, 2005.

Stark, Rodney. *Discovering God: The Origins of the Great Religions and the Evolution of Belief.* New York: HarperOne, 2007.

Stark, Rodney. *One True God: The Historical Consequences of Monotheism.* Princeton: Princeton University Press, 2010.

Stark, Rodney. *The Triumph of Christianity: How the Jesus Movement Became the World's Largest Religion.* New York: HarperCollins, 2011.

Stark, Rodney and William Sims Bainbridge. *The Future of Religion: Secularization, Revival and Cult Formation.* Berkeley and Los Angeles: University of California Press, 1985.

Stark, Rodney and Roger Finke, *Acts of Faith: Explaining the Human Side of Religion.* Berkeley: University of California Press, 2000.

Steinmetz, David C. *Reformers in the Wings: From Geiler von Kaysersberg to Theodore Beza.* New York: Oxford University Press, 2001.

Strauss, Gerald. *Nuremberg in the Sixteenth Century.* New York: Wiley, 1966.

Strong, Douglas M. *Perfectionist Politics: Abolitionism and the Religious Tensions of American Democracy.* Syracuse: Syracuse University Press, 1999.

Stovel, Katherine, Benjamin Golub and Eva M. Meyersson Milgrom. "Stabilizing Brokerage." *Proceedings of the National Academy of Sciences* 108/4 (2011): 21326–32.

Stovel, Katherine and Lynette Shaw. "Brokerage." *Annual Review of Sociology* 38 (2012): 139–58.

Stupperich, Robert. *Reformatorenlexikon.* Gutersloh: Gerd Mohn, 1984.

Suzuki, Shunryu. *Zen Mind, Beginner's Mind.* Boston: Shambala Publications/Weatherhill, 1970.

Tawney, R.H. *Religion and the Rise of Capitalism.* New York: Harcourt, Brace and Jovanovich, 1954.

Tarrow, Sidney. *Power in Movement: Social Movements, Collective Action and Politics.* New York: Cambridge University Press, 1994.

Taves, Ann. *Religious Experience Reconsidered: A Building-Block Approach to the Study of Religion and other Special Thing.* Princeton: Princeton University Press, 2009.

Taylor, Charles. *A Secular Age.* Cambridge, MA: The Belknap Press of Harvard University Press, 2007.

Taylor, Larissa. *Soldiers of Christ: Preaching in Late Medieval and Reformation France.* Toronto: University of Toronto Press, 2002.

Te Brake, Wayne. *Shaping History: Ordinary People in European Politics, 1500–1700.* Berkeley: University of California Press, 1998.

Thomas, Benjamin. *Theodore Weld: Crusader for Freedom.* New Brunswick, NJ: Rutgers University Press, 1950.

Thomas, Keith. *Religion and the Decline of Magic.* Oxford: Oxford University Press, 1971.

Thompson, Dave. *Hearts of Darkness: James Taylor, Jackson Browne, Cat Stevens and the Unlikely Rise of the Singer Songwriter.* Montclair, NJ: Backbeat Books, 2012.

Thompson, Margaret. "Discovering Foremothers: Sisters, Society, and the American Catholic Experience." *U.S. Catholic Historian* 5 (1986): 273–90.

Tillich, Paul. *A History of Christian Thought.* New York: Simon and Schuster, 1967.

Tilly, Charles. *From Mobilization to Revolution.* New York: McGraw Hill, 1978.

Tipton, Steven. *Getting Saved From the Sixties: The Transformation of Moral Meaning in American Culture.* Berkeley: University of California Press, 1982.

Tolle, Eckhart. *A New Earth: Awakening to Your Life's Purpose.* New York: Penguin Books 2005.

Tracy, James D., ed. *Luther and the Modern State in Germany.* Kirksville, MO: Sixteenth Century Society, 1989.

Tracy, James D. *Europe's Reformations, 1450-1650.* New York: Rowman & Littlefield, 1995.

Underhill, Evelyn. *Mystics of the Church.* Harrisburg, Pennsylvania: Morehouse Publishing Company.

Verter, Bradford. "Spiritual Capital: Theorizing Religion with Bourdieu against Bourdieu." *Sociological Theory* 21/2 (2003), 150–73.

Voas, David. "The Rise and Fall of Fuzzy Fidelity in Europe." *European Sociological Review* 25 (2009): 155–88,

Vogel, Robert W. *Without Contract or Consent: The Rise and Fall of American Slavery.* New York: Norton, 1991.

Wallace, Peter George. *The Long European Reformation: Religion, Political Conflict, and the Search for Conformity, 1350-1750.* London: Palgrave Macmillan, 2012.

Wallace, Ruth. "Transformation from Sacred to Secular," in Kathryn P. Meadow-Orlans and Ruth A. Wallace (eds.), *Gender and the Academic Experience: Berkeley Women Sociologists.* 99–112, Lincoln: University of Nebraska Press, 1994.

Wandel, Lee Palmer. *The Eucharist in the Reformation.* New York: Cambridge University Press, 2006.

Warren, Wendy. *New England Bound: Slavery and Colonization in Early America.* New York: W.W. Norton, 2016.

Weber, Marianne. *Max Weber: A Biography.* New Brunswick: Transaction Publishers, 1988 [1926].

Weber, Max. *The Protestant Ethic and the Spirit of Capitalism.* New York: Scribner, 1930.

Weber, Max. *From Max Weber: Essays in Sociology*, edited by Hans Gerth and C. Wright Mills. Oxford: Oxford University Press, 1958 [1946].

Weber, Max. *The City.* New York: Collier, 1962.

Weber, Max. *The Sociology of Religion.* Boston: Beacon Press, 1963.

Weinsten, Donald and Rudolf M. Bell. *Saints and Society: The Two Worlds of Western Christendom, 1100-1700.* Chicago: University of Chicago Press, 1982.

Wellman, James K. *Rob Bell and a New American Christianity.* Nashville, TN: Abington Press, 2012.

Wellman, James K., Katie E. Corcoran, and Kate Stockly-Meyerdirk, "God is Like Drug…': Explaining Interaction Ritual Chains in American Megachurches." *Sociological Forum* 29/3 (2014): 650–72.

Weld, Theodore Dwight. *American Slavery as It Is: Testimony of a Thousand Witnesses.* New York: American Anti-Slavery Society, 1839.

Wengert, Timothy. *Defending Faith: Lutheran Responses to Andreas Osiander's Doctrine of Justification.* Tubingen: Mohr Siebeck, 2012.

Wilde, Melissa J. *Vatican II: A Sociological Analysis of Religious Change.* Princeton: Princeton University Press, 2007.

Williams, Eric. *Capitalism and Slavery.* 2nd edn. Chapel Hill: University of North Carolina Press, 1994.

Wilson, David Sloan. *Does Altruism Exist? Culture, Genes, and the Welfare of Others.* New Haven, CN: Yale University Press, 2015.

Wilson, Jeff. *Mindful America: The Mutual Transformation of Buddhism and American Culture.* New York: Oxford University Press, 2014.

Winter, Ernest F., ed. *Discourse on Free Will: Desiderius Erasmus and Martin Luther.* London: Bloomsbury, 2013.

Wittberg, Patricia. *The Rise and Decline of Catholic Religious Orders.* Albany, NY: SUNY Press, 1994.

Witte, John. *Law and Protestantism: The Legal Teachings of the Lutheran Reformation.* New York: Cambridge University Press, 2002.

Wolf, Eric R. *Peasants.* Englewood Cliffs, NJ: Prentice Hall, 1965.

Wolfe, Tom. "The Me Decade and the Third Great Awakening." *New York Magazine* 23 (August 1976): 236–40.

Wolin, Richard. "Steve Jobs and the 'Me' Generation." *The Chronicle of Higher Education Review*, December 4, 2015.

Wood, Linda Sargent. "Contact, Encounter, and Exchange at Esalen." *Pacific Historical Review* 77/2 (2003): 453–87.

Woodward, Kenneth. *Getting Religion: Faith, Culture, and Policies from the Age of Eisenhower to the Era of Obama* (New York: Convergent Books, 2016)

Wuthnow, Robert. *Communities of Discourse: Ideology and Social Structure in the Reformation, the Enlightenment, and European Socialism.* Cambridge, MA: Harvard University Press, 1989.

Yang, Fenggang. "Exceptionalism or Chinamerica: Measuring Religious Change in the Globalizing World Today." *Journal for the Scientific Study of Religion* 55/(2016), 7–22.

Young, Michael P. *Bearing Witness against Sin: The Evangelical Birth of the American Social Movement.* Chicago: Chicago University Press, 2006.

Yusef. *Why I Carry a Guitar: The Spiritual Journey of Cat Stevens to Yusef.* Abu Dhabi: Motivate Publishing Company, 2014.

Zaehner, Robert Charles. *Mysticism Sacred and Profane an Inquiry into the Varieties of Preternatural Experience.* Oxford: Oxford University Press, 1957.

Zimmermann, Gunter. "Die Publikation von 'De Revolutionibis Orbium Coelestium.'" *Zeitschrift für Kirchengeschichte* 96/3(1985): 320–43.

Index